CHESTERTON

IMAGE BOOKS

DOUBLEDAY

New York London Toronto

Sydney Auckland

CHESTERTON

Garry
Wills

AN IMAGE BOOK
PUBLISHED BY DOUBLEDAY
a division of Random House, Inc.
1540 Broadway, New York, New York 10036

IMAGE, DOUBLEDAY, and the portrayal of a deer
drinking from a stream are trademarks of Doubleday,
a division of Random House, Inc.

Chesterton was previously published by
Sheed & Ward, Inc., in 1961.

Book design by Dana Leigh Treglia

LIBRARY OF CONGRESS CATALOG CARD
NUMBER 61-7283

ISBN 978-0-385-50290-0

First Image Books Edition: October 2001

145038997

To Natalie

ACKNOWLEDGEMENTS

This book could not have been written but for the help of many people, many more than I can name. Dorothy Collins, once Chesterton's secretary, now his executrix, kindly let me study his papers and letters, at Beaconsfield, over a period of three months. Others who gave me their valuable assistance are Mr. Frank S. Meyer and Mr. Neil McCaffrey; and, above all the rest—both in England and America nursing the book through all its difficulties—typing and advising and criticizing, so that she is almost co-author, my wife.

Almost as helpful as those who gave personal advice to the project were those who have written the indispensable works on Chesterton. But for John Sullivan's thorough and scholarly book, *G. K. Chesterton, A Bibliography* (Barnes and Noble, 1959), my quest for Chesterton's wide-scattered articles and lesser-known works would, too often, have been baffled; and Mr. Sullivan's comments, even in the brief time I was able to spend with him, were as valuable and learned as his published work. Maisie Ward's biography, and Hugh Kenner's critical study, were useful to me at every turn; a service I may seem to repay in litigious vein, but for the fact that I could not advance my own interpretations had they not done the pioneer work, work obviously meant (like my own) to generate such constructive conflict of ideas. Unfortunately, Michael Mason's very perceptive treatment of Chesterton in *The Centre of Hilarity* (Sheed and Ward, 1960) arrived too late for me to use it as extensively as I should have wished.

Gratitude for permission to quote from the works of Chesterton and others must again go first to Dorothy Collins, who generously allowed quotation from Chesterton's notebooks and private manuscripts, as well as from material published in Maisie Ward's *Gilbert Keith Chesterton* and *Return to Chesterton,* from articles in *The Daily News* and *The Speaker,* from the letter to Msgr. Ronald Knox printed in Mr. Evelyn Waugh's biography of Knox, from the fragment "Ballad of Arthur" which appeared in *The Albany Review,* and from poems in the Ariel Poems Series published by Faber and Faber, Ltd. Selections from the following works by G. K. Chesterton reprinted by permission of Dodd, Mead, and Company: *The Man Who Was Thursday, Charles Dickens, A Critical Study, What I Saw in America, The New Jerusalem, The Everlasting Man,* and *The Outline of Sanity.* Selections from *The Collected Poems of G. K.*

CONTENTS

PART TWO (1900–1912): *Controversy*

PART THREE (1913–1921): *Vigil*

PART FOUR (1922–1936): *Incarnation*

. . . any public comments on my religious position seem like a wind on the other side of the world; as if they were about somebody else—as indeed they are. I am not troubled about a great fat man who appears on platforms and in caricatures; even when he enjoys controversies on what I believe to be the right side. I am concerned about what has become of a little boy whose father showed him a toy theatre, and a schoolboy whom nobody ever heard of, with his brooding on doubts and dirt and daydreams of crude conscientiousness so inconsistent as to be near to hypocrisy, and all the morbid life of the lonely mind. . . .

Letter from Gilbert Chesterton to Ronald Knox (1922)

INTRODUCTION TO

THE NEW EDITION

I hope other writers, looking back to their first book, have reason to wince, as I do looking back forty years to this first book of mine, written when I was in graduate school. Reading it now, I wince because it is a deeply personal statement trying to masquerade as an impersonal one. I was discharging a personal debt—one that made me break off my graduate work to spend a summer going through the private papers of Chesterton. I had been intrigued by notebook poems written during his days at the Slade School of Art, since quotations from them in the Maisie Ward biography had helped me through a crisis in my life. In 1952, when I was in a Jesuit seminary, I had succumbed to a nihilist mood that made me see no God or goodness in the world. A shrewd mentor, Father Joseph Fisher, pointed out to me how closely Chesterton seemed to be addressing my condition in his student notebooks, while he fought off the solipsism that had brought him close to suicide.

Chesterton worked himself free of his nihilism by recognizing what he called the "mystical minimum" of goodness in the fact that any single thing can *be* in the first place. He was not assured by some rational pattern in everything, but by mere existence in anything. That is such an inexplicable miracle that it sufficed to refute every contrary mood or argument that dogged him. With his help, I followed that thread out of my own labyrinth, the trapping of myself inside myself. Since the notebook passages I relied on were partial quotations, I took the first opportunity I could to look at the notebooks in their entirety. Given a small grant to travel to England in 1959, I spent three months going through all the private papers of Chesterton. It was the first time I had worked with original manuscripts, and it was unlike any later research I would do. When, later, I dealt with the manuscripts of Thomas Jefferson or James Wilson—or with the actors' union records of Ronald Reagan, or the studio records of John Wayne's movies—I was using archives kept and catalogued in public repositories. But Chesterton's papers were preserved, haphazardly, just as he had left them in his own home, which he had bequeathed to his devoted secretary, Dorothy Collins.

When I went out from London to Beaconsfield, I found the papers scattered around an attic. After some hurried sorting, in search of the notebooks, I asked Miss Collins how I could come back to take notes without disturbing her (in the quarters below). She told me, casually, to take anything I wanted back to London—she would lend me a suitcase for carrying it—and to return for a new supply when I had exhausted that. I had intended to write an essay on the importance of the notebooks to Chesterton's later work, but this invitation to dive into a rich untended trove—not only of Chesterton's own work, but of letters sent him by Bernard Shaw, H. G. Wells, T. S. Eliot, and others—made me think I should try for something more ambitious, a survey of all his writings. In the process, I lost some of the focus on the notebooks that I began with. I append to this edition a later essay I did on *The Man Who Was Thursday,* which adheres better to my initial program, trying to show how central were the notebooks to Chesterton's thought.

The book has the faults of my own obligation to the man, though I hope, now, that it conveys some of the enthusiasm I was trying to hide. I was not as strict as I should have been on his faults—his anti-Semitism, his glorification of war, his whitewashing of the Middle Ages. But for the big things in him I still feel a kind of awe—for his lightning insights into the mysteries of the Christian faith (creation, the Trinity, the Incarnation). He is the best exponent of the ethos of democracy that I know. He presented this over and over in images that reveal the whole secret at a glance—as when he said that democracy is like blowing one's nose (one may not do it well, but one should do it oneself); that we do not cry out that a man with a high IQ is drowning, but that a *man* is drowning; that the essence of the jury system is a belief that every human is responsible for every other human being. He is the only one I know who has the gift of Samuel Johnson (a great hero of his)—that one wants to hear what he has to say on any subject. Even when he is wrong, he comes at a topic from such an individual viewpoint as to light up new scenery all around the topic. Yet this individuality is not, with either man, mere idiosyncrasy. The shock of the new comes from seeing how uncommon is real common sense. It is a shock that has never worn off for me, and I hope some of it comes through this halting first effort to share it with others.

INTRODUCTION

Though he is supposed to have indulged beyond discretion in paradox, Gilbert Chesterton is normally described in the same few platitudes. Those who admire him assume, with no apparent difficulty, that he possessed some preternatural goodness which kept him from trial, error, and the heartbreaking irrelevancies that frustrate human endeavor. Hints of this legend haunt the principal work on Chesterton, Maisie Ward's, which suggests at times the older style of hagiography. And there are many entirely uncritical encomia, books with titles like *The Evangel of G. K. Chesterton, The Wild Knight of Battersea, The Laughing Prophet: The Seven Virtues of G. K. Chesterton, The Innocence of G. K. Chesterton*.

Those who dismiss Chesterton as a negligible figure do it, frequently, for the same reasons that attract his admirers. They, too, feel that he was unaware of contradiction and complexity, that his life was somehow unclouded by doubt, that his facility and optimism were made possible by a kind of stupid serenity. We must grant at least some evidence for this kind of argument. Chesterton said he thought of life as a toy theater; he was tempted to substitute cardboard heroes for the more awe-inspiring vision of man as a divided being. His style seems, at times, to run and glitter because it encounters no obstacles and is stilled near no depths. He did not, apparently, have any development in wisdom; almost everyone agrees that he merely repeated the first words he gave the public. His optimism seems monochromatic, ignorant of death, evil, sex, and the serious problems that defeat man or call forth greatness. The man who played Johnson and Tony Weller in popular masquerades, who appears as "Immenso Chapernoon" in Shaw's *Domesticity of Franklyn Barnabas*, who is annually re-created as Dr. Gideon Fell in the mystery novels of John Dickson Carr, who lives in a thousand caricatures, becomes elusive by his very omnipresence in so many roles; as if he had no real life, but lived only in the thin world which a cartoonist sketches with his pencil.

So much there is of apparent evidence. But no man can live in the idiot serenity attributed to Chesterton. Such a man is either the figment of the critics' imagination, or a poseur equipped with a uniformly smiling mask to go with his theatrical cloak and hat. To a few, indeed, this *persona* has seemed deliberately artificial; they suspect something hidden and sinister which had to be cloaked in such giant pantomime. Very early his own sister-in-law claimed, in a full-length book, that he had been hen-pecked out of contact with reality by a frigid wife.[1] Others have thought that his flourishing of sword-stick and pistol, his cries for rebellion and the barricades, his glorification of wine, were means of achieving a spurious virility. In this view, Chesterton can be used as a symbol—a Puck or Pickwick—because he is only two-dimensional, not fully human.

Once this kind of analysis is set in motion in today's critical circles, an implicit challenge is issued, and Elizabeth Sewell answered the call, marking off Chesterton's place on the critical measure for all modern works—homosexuality. In "G. K. Chesterton: the Giant Upside Down"[2] she argued that Chesterton was a decadent, afraid of his inner similarity to Oscar Wilde, forever trying to talk away his infirmities in a protective nonsense. This thesis, however ill argued, has more to support it than the idiosyncrasies of its author. Chesterton did feel, as Miss Sewell observes, that Oscar Wilde was a personal threat. One of the first monographs devoted to him, that written by Julius West in 1915, treated him as a product of the decadent 1890's.[3] Miss Sewell merely carries this early interpretation to an unpleasant extreme:

> He wants both God and himself in the safe Nonsense world where the writer's mind is in control of what happens, where protection is afforded by the intellect against the offering of the self to God, and worse still, His acceptance of the offer, against all the other areas of life, love, people, sex, dreams, and imagination, where submission is, in part at least, the order. Nonsense is the safest place in the world for those who want to protect themselves from God, from life and from themselves.[4]

Another exposé of Chesterton, Margaret Clarke's "Chesterton the Classicist,"[5] described him as fundamentally pagan, one who

3

used Christian values for a "gnostic" improvement of earthly life. The principal evidence for this view is the largely pragmatic basis for the argument in *Orthodoxy*. Like Elizabeth Sewell, Miss Clarke feels that Chesterton avoided the serious content of his faith, using his religion for the spinning of pleasant fancies:

> Automatically Catholics supply what is missing. They imagine that G. K. is as persuasive to the Non-Catholic as he is useful to themselves in providing them with arguments they would never have thought of. . . . While it [the Chestertonian apologetic] has prepared the conversion (through other agencies) of many, it has alienated through its lack of intellectual and spiritual distinction the best and leading minds, and has to that extent undone the work of Newman.[6]

A third such interpretation, based on the feeling that Chesterton was posing, always, and covering something, is that of Herbert Palmer,[7] who feels that Chesterton was a crypto-Puritan, disguising his early heresy beneath a winebibbing that was curiously divorced from drunkenness and eroticism. Others note the lack of realistic sexual themes in his work, and make the same judgment of the man's suspiciously angelic materialism.

The common denominator of these interpretations which "unmask" Chesterton is a suspicion that his optimism, large gestures, and childish joys cannot have been real, nor explicable in their own terms. Many, even, who admire Chesterton's intellect and would scoff at the charges mentioned, feel there is an unsolved problem in the exaggeration that was everywhere his trademark. Even Hilaire Belloc was made uncomfortable by his style, and expressed surprise at his reception into the Church of Rome: he thought his friend's enthusiasm for the Catholic faith was simply a romantic mood.[8]

THE FAILURE OF
SIMPLE EXPLANATIONS

One short but excellent book of analysis was devoted to Chesterton by the acute literary critic Mr. Hugh Kenner, whose first book was *Paradox in Chesterton*. To Kenner, Chesterton was a philosopher, one who had grasped the Thomistic doctrine of analogy and expressed this insight without the advantages, or the corresponding burdens, of a systematic terminology and discipline. This is a view which is perhaps endorsed by Etienne Gilson's reference to Chesterton's book on Aquinas,[9] and by many who have suspected, but could not state as convincingly as Mr. Kenner, that Chesterton's real value is as a philosopher. Mr. Kenner argues his point well, but he can advance it only by refusing to deal with many aspects of Chesterton's work. He ignores his political writings. He not only ignores Chesterton's poetry; he denies that he was a literary artist of any sort. For him, the famous "paradox," when it is not a simple trick played for fun, is a mode of thought, not a stylistic vehicle—the Thomistic mode of thought-by-analogy.

Thus Kenner establishes a paradox of his own, but one which involves more of anomaly, I fear, than of analogy. Chesterton is praised as a non-systematic philosopher; yet the only way Kenner can lay bare his thought, behind the irrelevant rhetoric, is by using a system, by equating Chesterton's misleading words with the precise definitions of St. Thomas. Certainly, if Chesterton is solely valuable as a philosopher, he is operating under a disadvantage that entirely blunts his efforts. Most men do not realize that he is a philosopher (nor did he), and only those who are learned in Thomistic lore seem able to isolate it, to unearth it from Chesterton's mountain of verse and essays. The natural question is: why

5

not read Aquinas and forget about Chesterton? I have singled out Mr. Kenner's book for preliminary comment because it represents a tempting approach to the difficulties which Chesterton's work presents. Mr. Kenner *did* see through the Chesterton legend. But, unless I am deceived, he was trying to "save" Chesterton by admitting that his poetry and rhetoric lack sincerity and depth; asserting, as a counterbalance, the keenness of his intellect and trying to isolate this intellectual activity as some kind of "philosophy." From this sophisticated point of vantage, he can ignore Chesterton's claims as journalist, political thinker, Catholic apologist, literary critic, and poet. He seems relieved—and even relishes the task—when he can dismiss all attempts to deal with Chesterton's work *aesthetically:*

> The vision came so easily, with so little struggle, and inspired so great a confidence, that he could realize no real personal conflict centering on it. . . . Chesterton never achieves a great poem because his poems are compilations of statements not intensely felt but only intensely meant.[10]

In the introduction to Kenner's book, the social critic Marshall McLuhan is even more emphatic:

> it is always embarrassing to encounter the Chesterton fan who is keen about *The Ballad of the White Horse* or the hyperbolical descriptive parts of Chesterton's prose.

This view is simply a variant of that which seems to determine every approach to Chesterton, the belief that he was somehow spared the firsthand knowledge of life's grimmer aspects. Of course, the Kenner-McLuhan reading offers advantages for the salvaging of Chesterton: according to this interpretation, his quick perception was the result of emotional detachment, not of partisan pleading. It was this detachment and clarity which made it possible for him to formulate an entire philosophy of life in his youth which, according to Kenner, needed no major revision in later years.[11] But, ultimately, "saving" Chesterton by sophistication is as hopeless an effort as using him with naïveté.

Even a brief glance at significant opinions of this sort makes nonsense of the assumption that Chesterton was a simple hero or a mere journalistic hack. Consider the views that are expressed. Not only do they conflict with each other, they have internal contradictions that are basic. If Chesterton was the laughing prophet and saint, why did his religious quest mark time between his entrance into the Anglican communion and his transfer of allegiance to Catholicism? How could he ignore the practice of his Anglican faith, and all but the minimal action of a "practicing Catholic"? How could asceticism and vocation be so absent from his life?

If he was an apologist for orthodoxy, how could he ignore sin and the need for penance? Did he know what original sin really is, or was an ignorance of it at the root of his optimism, his glorification of the common man, his utopian politics?

If he was a philosopher, why did he never speak except in symbols and highly colored language? If he lacked emotional depth, why did he use the heightened rhetoric of passion? Are his poems and prose not merely aesthetically negligible, but empty bombast incapable of any justification at all? In short, if he is a philosopher, he chants his meditation to rather hysterical rhythms.

Why did he channel most of his professional efforts, against the wishes and advice of those nearest him, into political commentary?

Was he a monster of innocence and insight, or a neurotic with a defensive smile and desperate gaiety? Did his gaiety surmount evil, or simply ignore it?

These questions have puzzled many, I am sure, but they have rarely been discussed in print. Men seem more intent on using, or saving, or dismissing Chesterton's writings than on reading them. They approach him, too often, to defend or attack, rather than to learn. I intend at least to pose the questions; and then to investigate Chesterton's texts, published and unpublished, as far as possible in their entirety, searching for answers. I intend simply to read the man's own words with something of that "virgin vision" which he recommended. In order to do this, I must use a bit more care in the dating and documentation of those words than most critics have felt necessary in the study of Chesterton. There is an objection to this method: Chesterton's own defiance of dates, of footnotes, and even of facts, makes careful treatment of his texts look somewhat ridiculous, and disposes one to suspect a lack of sympathy between the author and his plodding commentator; but there may be an incidental advantage in the approach which necessity forces me to adopt.

Chesterton described his style as the representation of familiar things from unsuspected angles, under new lights of the imagination, that we might see them with the innocence of surprise. He even practiced this method on himself and his own life, giving us, in the *Autobiography* and in his frequent humorous references to himself, a series of symbols rather than a prosaic account of fact. But these descriptions, so often repeated, have themselves become a convention, veiling instead of revealing mystery. A glance at the critics will show that men are now willing to accept the most fantastic readings of Gilbert Chesterton's life, without strain on their credulity or reason. Those who reject Chesterton's other exaggerations calmly accept his wildest caricature, which was self-caricature. That is why I may, by accident, be using Chesterton's own method. To consider Chesterton prosaically may be the way to achieve the inversion, the "upside-down view," which brings a shock of surprised recognition.

PART ONE (1874–1899)

Isolation

1.

THE CRYSTAL PALACE

Chesterton was born in London; at the time of his birth, the largest city in the world. He praised small and self-contained communities, yet lived in the world's most cosmopolitan hub of empire. He claimed, later, that Jews were not real Englishmen; but his circle of boyhood friends in London was predominantly Jewish. He became, in the eyes of many, a champion of Christendom and of Europe's past; but he thought, throughout his youth, that all good things had come to Europe on the wind of the French Revolution.

Chesterton came from the stable middle class of Victorian England. He was brought up in a home where vulgarity, dropped h's, familiarity with servants, and unnecessary expenses (especially the hiring of cabs) were severely discouraged.[1] Very early the son of this home became slangy, familiar, and a spendthrift, famous for never moving an inch up or down Fleet Street except in a hansom. He entered the fringes of the art world (what Shaw called "that anarchic refuge of the art-struck, the Slade School"[2]), then drifted into the circle of radical political journalism. He seemed to do these things almost by accident or aimlessness, moving with the most freely drifting elements of a large and incoherent city.

Yet this was the man who became the image of rooted and English earthiness, of sunny common sense, of a peasant sanity. Bernard Shaw, who understood Chesterton better than any other of his friends, knew that he was not a typical Englishman, with a mind vaguely poetic; but swift, sharp, and precariously balanced; that he had more of the Gallic wit in him, the rapid and logical satire of France, than his ally Hilaire Belloc. "France did not break the mould in which she formed Rabelais. It got to Camden Hill in the year 1874; and it never turned out a more complete Frenchman than it did then."[3]

Chesterton showed this edge, this need for precise balance, in the most unlikely surroundings, in the haze of Victorian middle-class domesticity. He was brought up as the artist of the family, at a time when middle-class burghers were certain that a Keats or Browning would be born under their roof. Chesterton's father, Edward, was certain that his own hopes were fulfilled in his beautiful first child, a boy with long golden curls, lustrous eyes, and a pen which traced cloudy shapes over every available inch of paper. One can still look at these precocious drawings, carefully labeled;

the flowing curls were preserved in a portrait, and a lock of them put among the treasures of Edward Chesterton.

Chesterton went to St. Paul's, the school founded by Colet and illumined by Milton. Always last or near the last in his "form" there, Chesterton is not considered one of the lights in that school's constellation. Murphy's bust of him, still displayed in a Beaconsfield pub, gathers dust in a cupboard at St. Paul's. He could not even reach the highest form on his own merits; when he was two years behind his fellows he was given the privileges of the highest form, though he still did not belong to it. Meanwhile, since he could not join the higher form's debating association, he founded the Junior Debating Club and served as its president.

His academic failure did not seem to bother Chesterton; he was barely conscious of it, as of many things that surrounded him. Nor were his parents disturbed. After all, this was as it should be with the young genius and artist. Gilbert's friends—his sharp-witted juniors, a bit precocious themselves, and with the talent of their race—accepted him as the poet of their circle, by rights their leader when they formed a literary society. The authorities were probably less certain that genius lurked in the absent-minded student; they wryly conceded that "He ought to be in a studio not at school."[4]

He was a quiet and retiring boy, backward in as many ways as he was precocious, and he spent most of his time alone with books. As Rilke said of Rodin, this immersion in books is most often, in a young man, the means of being alone with oneself, of sifting early impressions and weighing their significance. The habit grew upon Chesterton and became dangerous until, at a crisis, he deliberately fostered that outward thrust of the mind toward things which is the theme of his later writings. His written memories of school are usually accounts of the "J.D.C." (Junior Debating Club) as a mystical fellowship. But the emphasis he put on this friendship was the result of his loneliness. E. C. Bentley, the popular schoolboy who became his friend toward the end of his school days and drew the other "debaters" around Chesterton, is the hero of most of the tales written in early notebooks, and he is described in terms that a Copperfield would hesitate to use of Steerforth. Chesterton continued to live in that first protective circle of friends long after it had been dispersed. When the other debaters had gone to Oxford or Cambridge, and Chesterton was left in London at the art school, he wrote of them all in his notebooks as if they were still present with him every day. Among his descriptions of meetings with the club and arguments with his younger brother Cecil, there are some lines that go farther back into his childhood and deeper into his mind:

> For the first half of his time at school he was very solitary and futile. He never regretted the time, for it gave him two things, complete mental self-sufficiency and a comprehension of the psychology of outcasts.[5]

The best evidence we have of these "lazy and silent"[6] years, of youth's shadowy pursuit of itself, is given us in the fairy tales he wrote while at St. Paul's. Two of them are included in *The Coloured Lands*,[7] but there are notebooks full of such dreams, where children yearn through misty quests and seek impossible things, in stories which resemble Ruskin's *King of the Golden River*. These prose fantasies remind us that Maeterlinck and Whistler are the expression of a vast atmosphere that hung over this period. They have a quality which is reflected in the boy's hazily limned illustrations— scenes of ragged mist peopled with insubstantial figures. When Chesterton finally came before the public, his style, both of drawing and of writing, was one of sharp thrusts, but these first dreams show the opening in him of an entirely different poetry. This poetry expressed itself, after the fairy tales, in historical romances based on the poems of Scott and Macaulay, tales in which the past is a symbol of one's half-forgotten self.

A FRENCH LIBERAL IN ENGLAND

The other force at work on Chesterton's youth was the mystique of nineteenth-century Liberalism, a spirit which bustled in this world instead of palely loitering with Keats. This different spirit received a different expression—in the prose and poetry he wrote for *The Debater,* the journal of the J.D.C. This was sonorous stuff, the prose modeled on Ruskin's, the poetry a blend of Swinburne's rhetoric and Browning's doctrine. The best writing he did in the journal was his contribution to a correspondence between fictitious but apt characters assumed by the three leaders of the club. Since there was to be consonance of initials as well as of mentality, he became "Guy Crawford, an artist of strong socialistic tendencies."[8] In this character he finally escaped the J.D.C.'s ban on the discussion of politics and waged a crusade for the true faith of Liberals. He is repelled by the oppression and anti-Semitism of the Russian government, so he sets out for Moscow "to see if I can't examine the Nihilists or help the Hebrews, or get knocked in the head, or do something else that will be for the good of humanity."[9]

The dreamy English artist can be over-stressed in accounts of Chesterton's youth. That was the side of him, described in the *Autobiography,* which, though very real and important, was later baffled and left abortive; whereas the analytic and critical mind, driven by a French passion for discussion and reform, became increasingly important in his life. It was first nurtured by the serious air of Liberalism in Chesterton's family, an air which had replaced religion and subsumed all of politics and science. It was this secular orthodoxy and moral purpose which made the aesthetic movement of the nineties repel Chesterton, precipitating a crisis of opposition between his artistic and his critical instincts, so that he surrendered the career in art which had been mapped out for him.

By Liberalism Chesterton meant the movement for reform and progress, to be achieved through free thought and the rejection of dogma (what Newman called "the anti-dogmatic principle"). He was not content with the English version of this creed, which made belief in inevitable progress an endorsement of the developing order of things. The materialistic, Benthamite form of Liberalism did not appeal to Chesterton, who turned instinctively to France and the great democratic revolutionaries—to Rousseau, Danton, Robespierre. He believed that the French Revolution broke up the descent over Europe of a spiritual ice age; that the rights of man had been preached for the first time by Danton and Robespierre; that enlightened religious sentiment had appeared only with the final destruction of rigid dogma. All his first enthusiasms clustered around this single nucleus: Whitman was the modern Rousseau. Christ was one of their forerunners, preaching the brotherhood of men.

In this spirit, Chesterton defended Liberalism even when he had to transgress the rules against political discussion in that organization whose chairmanship he took very seriously. He protested when the French Revolution was called a failure,[10] he championed the republican theory;[11] he wrote a series of poetic monologues by great rebels.[12] He advocated equal and universal education,[13] and endorsed his friend Bentley's resolution that scientific studies should replace the classics at the heart of the modern curriculum.[14] Even more surprising, in the light of things later to be written, was his ardent feminism; the movement for women's rights he considered a clear sign of the progress of humanity in the nineteenth century.[15]

Religion was, for Chesterton, merely an aspect of this humanitarian Liberalism. His parents were vaguely reverent, pantheistic "Christians," who took him to hear Stopford Brooke's variations on the theme of Christianity and gave him George Macdonald's books of humanistic theology. Browning taught Chesterton to look for "aspects of truth" in every creed, religious and secular, and Chesterton's historical monologues soon yielded, in *The Debater,* to what he called "ethical poems."[16] The general purport of these is that the pretensions of jealous priests and exclusive dogmas are finally destroyed, supplanted by the universal revelation of Rousseau:

> Though the fetish that towers be a fetish, the man that kneels
> is a man.[17]

No more will human history be stained by the antics of those who "struggle for a name and slaughter for a sign."[18] From this height of toleration Chesterton can write a poem about the patroness of Papists, because she is only a symbol of Woman, and Woman is adored along with Man by good humanitarians.

> We love who have done with the churches, we worship who
> may not believe.

> For all faiths are as symbols, as human, and man is divine.[19]

Even in the dark ages pioneer spirits escaped the narrow measure wherewith pontiffs measured, spirits like that of St. Francis, who

> Did not claim a ruthless knowledge of the bounds
> of grace eternal,
> Did not cry "Thus far, not further, God has set the
> hopes of life."

> Aye, though far and faint the story, his the tale of
> mercy's triumph.
> Through the dimmest convent casements men have seen
> the stars above;

Dark the age and stern the dogma, yet the kind hearts are
   not cruel,
Still the true souls rise resistless to a larger world of love.[20]

When Chesterton turned to politics his comments on priests
and dogma grew more shrill, as in the poem on labor which appeared in *The Speaker* while he was still at St. Paul's:

God has struck all into chaos, princes and priests down-hurled,
But he leaves the place of the toiler, the old estate of the world.
When the old Priest fades to a phantom, when the old King
   nods on his throne,
The old, old hand of labour is mighty and holdeth its own.[21]

These were not incidental ideas, entertained in his youth but easily dismissed as Chesterton grew older. He had already the ardor
and the intellect which made his later commitments so absolute.
But to his acute dismay, these first "absolutes" could not stand before real challenge, and they were one by one destroyed.

YOUNG SOLEMNITY

The false picture of Chesterton's youth, of the happy giant "writ
small," will not stand investigation. One touch is enough to turn
the scale—that which Cecil Chesterton gives us when he notices
that his brother's early writings have in them no humor.[22] They are
deadly serious, and (as Cecil was hinting in his anonymous study,
which avoided personal comment as far as possible) so was Gilbert.
The records of the J.D.C. read like the posthumous papers of a more
famous but hardly more pompous club. It is true that one faction
was guilty of levity, but Chesterton resolutely opposed it, both at

the time and in his later record of events, and he temporarily expelled its leader. When the club's motto was under discussion, this group scored a triumph, winning official recognition for "Hence loathed Melancholy." But a sustained campaign finally altered this to the more becoming motto, suggested from the chair, "Conference maketh a ready man." With Pickwick's own innocence of irony, the chairman declared "his pride at the success of the Club, and his belief in the good effect such a literary institution might have as a protest against the lower and unworthy phases of school life."[23]

These lower phases invaded, at times, the sanctum of the club, and Chesterton had to "bestow upon them rebuke."[24] Bentley often sided with the lightsome brigade, and in the pseudonymous correspondence in volume three of *The Debater* he regrets a lack of humor in "Guy."[25] But Oldershaw, third party in the triple correspondence, defends Crawford, who taught his fellows how to be serious.[26] He admired what he called Chesterton's puritanism.[27] An argument that appears in the notebooks about this time, and is repeated in early publications,[28] reflects the crises among factions in the club: Chesterton argues that only the serious can truly enjoy life. We can almost hear him speaking it from the chair; and we know why Shaw called him French.

There is little of this prim solemnity in Chesterton's own account of his childhood; he calls up in the first chapters of his *Autobiography* a happy bewilderment and haze of beautiful memories, what Maisie Ward calls "one of the best childhoods in literature."[29] The book opens with a defence of his family's class and code; he satirizes the biographies which subtly or crudely trace one's failings to a tyrannical father or a pale, drug-poisoned mother. Yet all of this is argument and satire; there is no remembrance of incident for itself, no detail of portraiture, no vividly recaptured moment. Chesterton's parents are described by reference to characters out of Dickens and Thackeray.[30] Even a book whose accuracy, whose very motive is suspect—that by Cecil's wife—gives a picture of the Chesterton home more intimately remembered in its physical circumstances.

The one feature of Chesterton's boyhood which is recalled at length is the symbol around which the whole book is organized, the toy theater. As Chesterton says, one's sharp memories are not those which have endured, which have undergone the attrition of the changing years, but things recalled suddenly, for some reason, from across an abyss. The toy theater became, at a crucial time in Chesterton's life, a resurrection of this type; then it remained with him as a fixed symbol, and in this form it reaches us in the first chapters of Chesterton's last book. It takes its place there, along with discerning comments on children, memory, toys, and fairy tales; but this is not a particular childhood summoned up and re-lived. We have not seen the water tower on Camden Hill in one pointed moment, sharing a secret mood that disappeared yet has been revived and transmitted; as we can gaze with Ruskin into the swirling Tay, or watch the puppet show of Baring's memory. Whatever the content of these chapters, their manner tells us what became of the kindly dunce humorously described in them. The description comes to us in quick and analytic flashes, shaped into a rapid language of hieroglyphs; the past is brilliantly reflected through the mirrors of an almost painfully agile brain.

Chesterton's loyalty explains the defence he makes in the *Autobiography* of things he had often attacked—a narrowing "latitudinarianism," the religion of decorum, the prison of class-consciousness. Cecil had predicted that his brother would never attack his own roots directly.[31] Gilbert was already, in 1909, hiding from himself a growing disagreement with Liberal politics and Modernist theology, but allegiance to his first attachments had so far kept him from following Cecil's movement toward "Tory Fabianism." Loyalty is an instinct whose strength can hardly be exaggerated in Chesterton's life. It made him cling to certain concepts even when he was forced to give them meanings so altered as to seem perverse. He praised the "patriotism of the house" which made his father keep the family business going,[32] and he imitated this when he had to keep a family newspaper in existence, against disheartening odds. The same loyalty was put to its severest test by his developing certitude with regard to the Catholic Church. Whence the pause and suspense of a full decade when he longed for Rome but would not travel there.

This need for dedication is also the key to the next episode in his life. Those who see in him only a slowly awakening talent and a confusedly good-natured cheerfulness are bound to mistake the tragicomic turmoil of Chesterton's years at the Slade School. He had imbibed, during his youth, the ideals of his parents' era. But a reaction to this shallow idealism had already occurred in the world outside his home, taking the form of a fashionable cynicism—the reverse decorum of "decadents" with their *Yellow Book* and their green carnations. Whistler and Beardsley and Wilde had their brief moment of an almost magic influence during the nineties; and when Chesterton went to art school in 1892, he went from one point of high concentration direct to its opposite pole, passing from Victorian content to the *fin-de-siècle* gloom, each in its most exaggerated form. It was his devotion to the first set of ideals that caused his sad bewilderment among the aesthetes. His entire world was shattered, like a toy theater trampled into splinters. And the clash of these two shallow things drove Chesterton into depths.

2.

NOCTURNE

Like the white lock of Whistler that lit our aimless gloom
Men showed their own white feather as proudly as a plume.[1]

Chesterton's passage through art school proves with finality how
little English he was: from behind every picture, every paragraph
of criticism, there leaped out at him startling theories about the
universe. He was besieged by theoretical doubts about cognition
and certitude. He not only knew what theory is; he scented it
everywhere and harried it out of the most unlikely hiding places.
There was enough of England in him to send him reeling into

something perilously like madness. He turned the shy guilt and fear of adolescence into a suspicion of the intellect's processes. Adolescents are often given pause, as their childhood is withdrawn from them, by a feeling that the thing which follows on childhood is somehow tainted. But Chesterton was also losing a highly articulated set of concepts, a complete intellectual system; and he felt that the intellect itself was somehow unstrung by the doubts he encountered.

This was the solipsist threat, the "critical problem" which haunts the post-Kantian world; but it came to Chesterton embodied in a set of symbols—decadent art's relativism carried to an ultimate denial, Impressionism's subjectivity carried to a logically complete and paralyzing subjectivism. Chesterton had lost the friends with whom he debated (they had gone to the universities), and he formed no new ties in these three years of hesitation. But he had not lost the habit of arguing, and he wandered through this new world of shadows and challenge waging a cold argument with himself instead of the merry arguments he had conducted with his friends. This was the worst possible thing for one who had begun to doubt the whole discursive process. He ignored all work and purpose in life, caught up in a single and endless quarrel.

Art supported argument to hem in Chesterton's lonely intellect: the current school of English Impressionism suggested to Chesterton that things are only what they seem, that seeming is the only activity of "real" things. This explains the almost hysterical attitude Chesterton occasionally manifested toward Impressionism; making it, in *The Flying Inn,* a symbol of Lord Ivywood's desire to break the boundaries of reality, and sending it as the "last and worst" horror upon his hero "Thursday."[2] The *Autobiography* explains this violent and symbolic use of an art style that seems harmless enough to us now: the Impressionist vision drove his already toiling mind toward the philosophy of illusion.[3] This view was not merely a private fancy called up in

Chesterton by his own morbid time of transition. Impressionism was preached as a mystique of rebellion by Arthur Symons and the *Yellow Book* circle.[4] Chesterton, with a Gallic passion for the absolute statement of an idea, took this mystique to its logical extreme:

> I had thought my way back to thought itself. It is a very dreadful thing to do; for it may lead to thinking that there is nothing but thought. . . . I was simply carrying the scepticism of my time as far as it would go. And I soon found it would go a great deal further than most of the sceptics went. While dull atheists came and explained that there was nothing but matter, I listened with a sort of calm horror of detachment, suspecting that there was nothing but mind.[5]

The "detachment" mentioned here was the cause of the crisis. We have already noticed, in the account of his childhood, that Chesterton's loyal commitment was combined with a highly ideated approach to his own past: passion is there, but it is of a clear and intellectualized sort, like the ardent precision of the French. Such detached intellects *are* the sort which can literally detach themselves from reality, in a deracinated and circular logic.

To escape this circular pursuit of arguments, Chesterton looked for an outlet into the world of colors and sunlight and fact. But the sunlight itself, and the changing colors, were opponents. The ideas he feared were given compelling expression in the brilliant Impressionist mist. He looked for a counter-symbol which might purge his mind of the dissolving colors in which a philosophy of dissolution clothed itself. He found it in the hard lines and hues of Stevenson's tales: "his images stand out in very sharp outline; and are, as it were, all edges."[6] Stevenson, too, had left a sheltered home for an art school; he, too, pitted the aesthetics of a toy theater against the complicated chromaticism of French "decadents."

These and many other similarities are heavily underscored in Chesterton's book on Stevenson, written in 1926, a book whose organization and binding symbols resemble the structure and images of his own *Autobiography*. These resemblances, and Dorothy Collins' testimony to the fact that Chesterton wrote the early part of his *Autobiography* ten years before taking it up again in 1936, indicate that Chesterton analyzed his own formative years while writing on Stevenson, then exorcised this autobiographical mood by writing, immediately afterwards, a first-person analysis of his art-school crisis.

The symbolism of line and color worked itself deep into Chesterton's mind during his beleaguered years. The contrast between Impressionism's blurred palette and the burning hues of expressed fact runs through all his later thought. He would use this interplay to discuss creeds and literary style as well as paintings.[7] He thought in colors, and made the hero of one notebook story construct a language solely of altering, eloquent colors.[8] And everywhere this symbolism points to the conflict of the Slade period, between reality and illusion. For on these lines the conflict was joined. Some ignore his explicit statements to this effect, and consider his morbidities the normal throes of adolescence, intensified in Chesterton's case by his slow physical maturation and the loss of his friends. Yet Chesterton repeatedly said that it was the nineteenth century's evening twilight, not the morning twilight of his youth, which bred these fears. And though he frankly confesses the more sensual and imaginative temptations of youth,[9] he describes how these were dwarfed by the metaphysical issues into which they were subsumed. We shall see the marks of this period on everything he wrote and find that the influence is of the sort he describes, involving an intellectual struggle between realism and solipsism. Only in this context can we understand his later comments on Impressionism, Whitman, Stevenson, lunacy, childhood, and many other things.

THE TESTIMONY OF ORTHODOXY

More particularly, our understanding of this period will affect the interpretation of *Orthodoxy*—a book normally treated as an essay in Christian apologetics, though Chesterton wrote over its opening these words:

> This is not an ecclesiastical treatise but a sort of slovenly autobiography.[10]

All sorts of mistakes have been made because that sentence is ignored. Some protest that "democracy" and politics are too prominent; but Chesterton presents the republican enthusiasm as a "positive bias" present in him when he began his religious quest.[11] Others complain that the argument is pragmatic: Christianity is presented as the way to avoid madness. But this is not a catechumen's guide, advocating a journey through lunacy for all who would pursue the Grail. Chesterton is describing the way he extricated his intellect from its own toils. If anyone objects that *Orthodoxy* does not seem like mere case history or autobiography, the answer to this objection is simple: the mind that sees these issues naked in its own past is the kind of intellect which would encounter this danger. Besides, we who live after the appearance of Chesterton's *Autobiography* know how little that book resembles the memoirs of a man merely recollecting events. His intellect always turns events into issues, facts into symbols.

Orthodoxy is a record of the protection a man must erect against a devouring mind of this sort. It begins with a chapter called "The Maniac," which corresponds to the chapter in the *Autobiography* called "How To Be a Lunatic." Both books examine the peril of a voracious intellect, a peril which is, in its final stage, solipsism (to which Chesterton devotes the next chapter in *Orthodoxy,* "The Suicide of Thought"). Childhood and the toy theater, presented in the *Autobiography* as the path by which Chesterton returned to simple perception and realism, are considered in *Orthodoxy* under "The Ethics of Elfland." The next period in Chesterton's life was that of the Boer War and his early political contacts. The development of his thought in this period is described in the early book as "The Flag of the World" and in the last one as "Nationalism and Notting Hill." Thus Chesterton made the same analysis, in 1908 and in 1926, of his art-school years, of their dangers and of their significance.

We can well believe the danger was present, in Chesterton's lonely youth, of his "using mental activity so as to reach mental helplessness."[12] But how did he recover from this precarious imbalance? He tells us that he went back to fairy tales and the toy theater—to childhood. This will be called "escapism" today; but the important thing is that Chesterton *did* escape, along this route, from a real danger. And, as he analyzed in *Orthodoxy* the cure for lunacy, Chesterton came to see why such "poetry" is the only safeguard of man's sanity. The poet and the child grasp fact and are outgoing. They do not manipulate fact and twist it back upon itself in the purely internal processes of logic. But this analysis was to come later; Chesterton's immediate reaction was both more confused and more profound.

In order to escape the complications of self-involved logic, Chesterton returned to the simplest kind of perception, to the rapt, outward attention of the child. This simplicity of perception led to purity of insight; and Chesterton noticed first what Aquinas claims we *do* first perceive, though the fresh apprehension is dulled and covered over by the intellect's operation on this raw material. Chesterton saw the "first act" of things—their being—almost more vividly than he saw the things themselves.

This mode of insight led to an exact reversal of his former

quest for reality. He had asked what depth any real thing had of actuality and separate value. But now, looking at things under this new light of simplicity, he was led to wonder what thing, however slight and trivial, was not fathomless by reason of its existential act. He had felt men were empty dreams; but now he looked at the dreams and found them full of reality. The toy theater was a refutation of the Impressionists:

> If living dolls were so dull and dead, why in the world were dead dolls so very much alive? And if being a puppet is so depressing, how is it that the puppet of a puppet can be so enthralling?[13]

So was adumbrated what Chesterton called his concept of a "mystical minimum."[14] If a thing is nothing else that is good, it *is;* and *that* is good:

> existence, reduced to its most primary limits, was extraordinary enough to be exciting. Even if the very daylight were a dream, it was a day-dream; it was not a nightmare.[15]

With the mental quickness that had almost undone him, Chesterton reacted from the shuffling of concepts and essential forms, from the manufacture of symbols and mental constructs, to a metaphysical insight into "existence reduced to its primary limits"—and saw that in itself existence is *un*limited. He began to express in many poetic ways what the existential philosopher puts technically—the real distinction between essence and existence, between what a thing is (the static and defining form) and *that* a thing is (the extra-formal act not to be captured by a defining concept). He wrote tales in which a man relived, in a conscious flash, his own creation and emergence out of nothingness.[16] In one of these, the hero, who has undergone a symbolic re-entrance into reality, is so conscious of each thing's existential act that essential forms are totally forgotten:

> At one time I seemed to come to the end of the earth; to a place where it fell into space. A little beyond, the land re-commenced, but between the two I looked down into the sky. As I bent over, I saw another bending over under me, hanging head downwards in those fallen heavens, a little child with round eyes. It was some strange mercy of God assuredly that the child did not fall far into hopeless eternity.[17]

The interlocutor in this tale tries to form the word "pool" as this is recounted to him, but somehow cannot; he feels it would falsify what the speaker saw.

Over and over, in the crucial notebooks, Chesterton claims that things are equal on the existential level:

> If I set the sun beside the moon,
> And if I set the land beside the sea,
> And if I set the tower beside the country,
> And if I set the man beside the woman,
> I suppose some fool would talk about one being better.[18]

He soon extended these comparisons to ugly and trivial things, acquiring his taste for grotesque art, by which the vitality and beauty of being are thrown into relief by the imperfection of the essential form. Act and not form is what ennobles the gargoyles of nature and of art. This was the critical basis of Chesterton's work on Browning and Dickens.

Thus, in his criticism as well as his poetry, Chesterton sensed that *what* a thing is must be immeasurably different from the fact *that* it is. For one thing, we can write "the *fact that*" a thing is, but we cannot say "the fact what." Existence is a fact, an act. Essence, on the other hand, is a form, not a fact. It was a sense of this distinction which lifted Chesterton's "minimal" optimism above the pantheism of Whitman and the mere fighting mood of Stevenson.[19] Chesterton's quick mind found something solid even in crumbling supports: Stevenson and Whitman were symbolic props, not teachers. They gave Chesterton a color and rhetoric in which to clothe his own darting and still half-captured vision. For he was determined not to let this insight become a mere idea or theory and lead him back into the maze of void intellection. He expressed the purity of being in all its impure receptacles by calling up an energy that makes things glow with unmixed color.

THE TESTIMONY OF THE WILD KNIGHT

Fortunately, there is an accurate gauge of the Slade School's effect on Chesterton: we have the detailed record of a discussion that occurred then, and the poem that was fashioned out of this experience. The event is described in a *Daily News* article, reprinted in *Tremendous Trifles* as "The Diabolist." The poem gave its title to his first serious book, *The Wild Knight*.

Chesterton's childhood came back to him in the form of timeless symbols, as do most of the memories in the *Autobiography*. But "The Diabolist" captures a real moment, in detail neither altered nor heightened. Its significance lies entirely in what Chesterton actually felt at the time. He realized this unique quality in the article and emphasized that it was a simple narrative of event:

> What I have now to relate really happened. . . . It was simply
> a quiet conversation which I had with another man. . . . It
> happened so long ago that I cannot be certain of the exact
> words of the dialogue, but only of its main questions and an-

swers; but there is one sentence in it for which I can answer absolutely and word for word.

After thus forswearing rhetoric, he appends to this sober account the remark that this was "the most terrible thing that ever happened to me." Cecil, who must have known from his brother's emphasis on this how deeply it was meant, accepts the statement and repeats it in his book;[20] furthermore, he reprints almost all of the article when discussing Gilbert's early development.

The conversation Chesterton describes took place on a large flight of stone steps—probably those of the central building at London University, running down to the quadrangle in front of the Slade School. It took place on a wintry evening of the year 1893 (for he says here that he was at the breaking point, and in the next long vacation he wrote to Bentley that he would not break).[21] He was arguing with an art student prominent among those who were conducting personal experiments in evil. This fellow asked Chesterton why he had stiffened into a further conventionality, in the time since his entrance into the school, when all those around him were relaxing into a broader bohemianism. Then Chesterton trained on him all the arguments he had invented for exorcising his own morbidity. He protested that loose morals loosen the fabric of the world, suggesting as they do an intellectual relativism which dissolves reality. Pointing to the sparks that flew by from a bonfire on the lawn, he said that each spark was the apex of an intellectual pyramid, of piled arguments which "justify" its presence and identify its nature. Seduce a girl and you quench that star, Chesterton boldly preached to his comrade.

This line of argument shows what straits Chesterton was in. He had come to a shocking awareness of evil, and this had pushed his solipsism to its most terrible stage. If the world was his own illusion, all evil had its source in him, along with all "reality." That is why he identifies moral restrictions and the intellectual bounds of reality—

virgins seduced and stars dissolved. The "pyramid" is really a swaying tower for him, and the slightest relaxation or "relativism" will topple it. Chesterton was "creating" the star with arguments; the spark's foundation is a huge pyramid of symbolism hung in empty air.

The art student shattered the entire fabric of Chesterton's argument by admitting the indictment: he *wanted* to quench stars. Here was a desire not touched by the "justifying" arguments, the mutually supporting but mutually enclosed ideas of Chesterton's discourse. It entered that scheme of things like a destructive blast from another world. "What you call evil I call good," the Diabolist said, inverting the entire cosmos in Chesterton's mind. As the student went down the stairs to meet his friends, he left a stunned and defeated enemy behind him. But as Chesterton followed him down the stairs, he half heard whispered plans of some proposed innovation in evil, to which the Diabolist replied, in the words which Chesterton remembers with a compelled accuracy, "If I do that, I shan't know the difference between right and wrong."

> I rushed out without daring to pause, and as I passed the fire
> I did not know whether it was hell or the furious love of God.

Twice had a pure assertion, to do and not to do something, cut across all arguments in this episode; and on this assertion from outside the intellect Chesterton pondered for years. In *The Wild Knight,* the conversation merely recorded in his article is given its proper significance in symbol. "Orm," the poem's evil genius, is the Diabolist. He plans to seduce the poem's heroine, not through lust, but to experience the scope of one who creates and destroys. Both Orm and the Diabolist speak with an inhuman rationality; both admit reason and virtuous instincts, but only to oppose them. Both men completely disarm their opponents by refusing to argue with them, and both are told that they should be burnt for this attitude. They even use the same words.[22] In the case of both, their crucial self-revelation is connected with a symbolically ambivalent but physically actual fire.

The most horrifying thing about Orm is his impartiality.[23] He is not even human enough to rebel against law or to hate good. He seems simply to stand above all these distinctions, unbounded, "infinite." Orm's kindness is more shattering than Nero's cruelty. He condescends to the cosmos. Whistler and Wilde said that man should fashion of real things a poem, making every lie or murder an artifact. So does Orm use Redfeather and Olive as characters in a quaint drama. He is the supreme decadent; a dandy with the universe for his box of trinkets, the stars his stickpins, the world his watch fob, and real men's loves and hates his theater or library.

Against Orm stands Redfeather, "rake and poet." He cannot boast Cyrano's white plume; but even a gaudy and ragged feather can be the flag of a certain honor—a refusal to fly "the white lock of Whistler." He is the common man, who feels his community with earth and all real things:

> I have drunk to all that I know of,
> To every leaf on the tree,
> To the highest bird of the heavens,
> To the lowest fish in the sea.
> What toast, what toast remaineth,
> Drunk down in the same good wine
> By the tippler's cup in the tavern
> And the priest's cup at the shrine?

When the heroine enters, Redfeather rather feels his brotherhood with the slime. Yet the Devil, who knows all tricks, cannot make a man, not even Orm, and Redfeather boasts, "I will never curse a man, Even in a mirror."

In the toast and that scrap of dialogue we get the first hint of that paradox on which the play revolves. Man may be the Devil's plaything, but not his product—not even Orm. So, when the Wild Knight rushes in, ecstatic with recognition of the surroundings he had beheld in his dream, Olive muses in these lines on the mystery of anyone's seeking God in Orm's house:

> Yes—you are right—God is within that house.
> But he is all too beautiful
> For us who only know of stars and flowers.
> The thing within is all too pure and fair,
> Too awful in its ancient innocence,
> For men to look upon it and not die;
> Ourselves would fade into those still white fires
> Of peace and mercy.

She sees, deeper even than Redfeather had in his toast, the common quality uniting all thing: *existence,* in its separate reality, its "ancient innocence." This remains itself, and somehow pure, no matter what use it is put to. As Redfeather puts it, in his farthest reach of realization:

> This hour
> I see with mortal eye as in one flash
> The whole divine democracy of things,
> And dare the stars to scorn a scavenge heap.
> Olive, I tell you every soul is great.
> Weave we green crowns—how noble and how high,
> Fling we white flowers—how radiant and how pure
> Is he, whoe'er he be, who next shall cross
> This scrap of grass.
> [Enter Orm.]

It is left for the Wild Knight to see with finality that Orm's deepest foundation and ultimate fuel are pure, however ignoble the use this basis and energy are put to. Just as Orm is imitating God by ignoring Him, becoming (in his own eyes) the world's playwright, he burns the disputed title deed. The Wild Knight sees in this act the awful energy of Being. As it was promised, he sees God—the roaring "devil of the heavens," as Redfeather calls him, whose fires rage in the colors of wine and grass.

The Knight has destroyed Orm's hellish placidity. He has given him the one insult he could not stand, believing him God—not the new and anarchic artist, but the ancient Father, giver of good things, the Creator. Only this supremely mad compliment could insult the man who did not create the raw material of his free thought and lawless art; making him respond with that instant, involuntary acknowledgement of outside reality and solid norms which had stunned Chesterton in the Diabolist's hasty sentence. Orm, with the wit of the decadent, had referred to the myth of God,

> The horror of that ancient Eavesdropper
> Behind the starry arras of the skies.

The Knight makes him shudder when he says that God is not a distant spy, but the very fire in his hand and in his brain. The law of combat, which Orm had ignored when challenged by Redfeather, he now recognizes; and stabs the Knight. And when the mystic has betrayed Orm's real and involuntary divinity, the common man cuts him down.

There is no denial of evil in this poem, as Cecil claimed. Redfeather and Olive shudder at Orm, and the drunkard kills him without mercy. But there is a vision of the separate purity of existence in all the component things which are evil.[24] This is not a doctrinaire position, but a direct intuition shaped by confrontation with evil. It shows that Chesterton's own contact with decadents and doubters and diabolists had preyed upon him and worked toward a solution in his mind.

We shall give some attention later to the merits of *The Wild Knight* as a poem; but as a testimony to Chesterton's own mental history its value is clear. Taken in conjunction with the story told in "The Diabolist," it proves that the urgency and emphasis given to the Slade period in Chesterton's *Autobiography* and in *Orthodoxy* are not the product of afterthought or exaggeration. We can see, in the poem, turmoil giving birth to insight. The insight is metaphysical, as was the problem, and arises from the mind's encounter with evil. Thus *The Wild Knight* completely invalidates the assumption that Chesterton's "dark years" were simply a time of physical and moral "growing pains," and it invalidates the logical inference to be drawn from such a reading of his history—drawn with effect by Kenner and others—that Chesterton was a person jolly and contented by nature, who never had to struggle or know evil. Evil precipitated, at a time of stress, the very metaphysical insight which Kenner praises in Chesterton. It is true that Chesterton felt evil as a final puzzle and blank for the brain, as well as a tugging at the will; but this only made its negations more absolute and terrifying. An almost suicidal mental rapidity made him turn people and events into ideas, ideas which could be annihilated with an argument. A metaphysical insight rescued him at this stage, checking the intellect's headlong course; but this could not change the general tendency of his mind. He still felt an idea like a blow and saw the significance of real things with painful clarity. This, and not the subhuman complacency often attributed to him, is the reason Chesterton's mind works rapidly into depth, probing and rebounding and debating.

This also explains the pitch of tension sustained in the many note-books dating from this period. Their *sententiae* have a roaring rever-ence and fierce optimism which are not derived from mere jollity. Their insistence on one theme, fresh no matter how often reiter-ated, shows a sharpened preoccupation with a single problem. Whitman's sprawling rhetoric was neurotic, all of it a *self*-assertion. Chesterton's aphorisms, though modeled on Whitman's to some extent, have a far greater simplicity and balance; they follow a sin-gle thread of praise which is an escape from the self-immurement of intellect into the receptive world of childhood. There is gravity, economy, and innocence shining through all the rhetoric:

> It will be very interesting to go to heaven.
> It is quite wonderful to think of.
> For there will be things there better
> than a woman who is pure in heart.

A GLIMPSE

> A lady sat down to the piano
> And I lit two candles, one on each side of her.
> The angel of creation felt so
> When he stretched forth his hands and lit the
> evening and morning stars.[25]

At times Chesterton remembers the isolation from reality which threatened him, as in this troubled ripple of words:

> I am a wandering wind that kisses all things
> And cannot be kissed again.[26]

But most of the notebooks resolutely ignore the statement of that which was all too present in his mind. These books were meant to destroy the threat of solipsism by simple assertion and reception of reality. This is particularly true of the notebook quoted by Maisie Ward, in which the best maxims were collected to form a storehouse of ammunition. The foe against which such weapons were used is that accelerated intellection which Chesterton described so well in *Orthodoxy*. In the notebook he concentrates on things like

> The fact *unshakeable by doubts or theories*
> That I love a human being.[27]

Solipsism does appear in the prose narratives, as a dream of never meeting anyone, or of meeting oneself everywhere one turns.[28] "Impressionism" is represented in the characters of decadent artists who stroll languidly through his stories, forerunners of the aesthete in *The Napoleon of Notting Hill,* Auberon Quin. Another of these cynics, "Eric Peterson," undergoes a profound spiritual reversal and starts off on what became, by a later process of elaboration, the adventures of Innocent Smith in *Manalive*.

The major literary influence in the notebooks is scriptural; he had "discovered" the prophets in his period of despondency. Maisie Ward speaks of his fresh approach to the Gospels at this time,[29] but it was the Old Testament which fed his imagination in its deepest recesses, coloring his mind ever after with the rhetoric of Isaias and Job. There are several poems on Isaias in the notebooks, and several imitations of Job's speeches (imitations which led, as we shall see, to *The Man Who Was Thursday*). St. Paul hardly ever appeared in his writings; and, even in the Gospels, it was Christ's apocalyptic and prophetic style which first appealed to Chesterton's imagination. For this whole period, his own style is not paradoxical but prophetic, resembling Isaias' more than Oscar Wilde's. He worked very hard to construct poems from his *sententiae,* refashioning several of them for years, but their first form has a concentration and simplicity he could not match when he tried to expand them. He abandoned the unwieldy seven-foot line of his "ethical" poems in *The Debater;* the pointed nature of his intuitions made him gravitate toward a mantic abruptness. Furthermore, these aphorisms were, like all prophecy, national and popular, so he continued experimenting with the ballad stanza.

One of the subjects treated in his most seriously prophetic style, in the notebooks, is Laughter, which is described as if it were a private discovery of his own, a new revelation. Chided, earlier, for his solemnity, he had realized by this time that laughter can have a medicinal, even a metaphysical, effect—shattering thin arguments, opening great rifts in them to reveal the landscape of fact.[30] For a while he took laughter very seriously (as the French mind always does). He was already re-writing, often to prodigious length, the poem which eventually appeared as "The Fish":

> For I saw that finny goblin
> Hidden in the abyss untrod;
> And I knew there could be laughter
> On the secret face of God.

He wrote a long essay on the humor of the Bible, concentrating especially on the multiple ironies of situation and language in the Book of Job. The early draft of *The Napoleon of Notting Hill* which appears in the notebooks describes the crucifixion as humorous, a description retained in the final version of the novel.[31] In fact, that novel is concerned throughout with the place of humor in life— the place, that is, of Auberon Quin. Quin does not really enjoy life as much as the serious crusader Adam Wayne, but his fancy and humor alone make possible the other's war against monotony; his glancing imagination balances the splendid fanaticism of Notting

Hill's "Napoleon." Chesterton describes these two men as the two lobes of a single brain; they are certainly the two contending spirits in his Slade School notebooks, where "prophecy" towers up almost to the height of fanaticism, only to fall back in a shower of laughter.

3.

PARADOX AND NIGHTMARE

The Wild Knight is the most obvious sort of melodrama—threat of foreclosure, evicting villain, heroine asked to sell herself. Yet melodrama here becomes theophany: the villain shines with divinity, the hero must be saved by the idiot, the heroine is stronger in spirit than the hero. These reversals are not the result of sensationalism but of that oxymoron which overarches the entire drama—the Knight's vision attained in Orm. This paradox is a structural motif repeated in every stage of the action. Olive's description of the fires within, Redfeather's strange "democracy of things," are analogues of the central mystery. Even a stray contradiction like that contained in the Knight's opening lines— of the grasses that are barren yet a banner—expresses the *minimum* of being which was the only basis of hope in Chesterton's eyes:

> The wasting thistle whitens on my crest,
> The barren grasses blow upon my spear,
> A green, pale pennon: blazon of wild faith
> And love of fruitless things.

The opposites employed in the poem reach for each other like the opposing buttresses of a Gothic structure—Redfeather and the Knight, laughter and prophecy, common sense and mysticism, earthiness and holiness.

This melodrama is also, at one level, pantomime—Redfeather with flagon and sword, the Knight with his spear and withering plume, Orm with a magic fire that enlightens yet destroys (for fire is the Promethean-ambiguous blessing that can blight, as Orm's benevolence does).[1] But from under these crude masks there sound faraway rhythms suggestive of vast forces at play, like some

> soliloquy of God
> That moveth as a mask the lips of man.

From *behind* each figure comes the chanted meaning:

> So, with the wan waste grasses on my spear
> I ride forever seeking after God.

Ourselves would fade into those still white fires.

Weave we green crowns—how noble and how high
Fling we white flowers—how radiant and how pure. . . .

> impersonal
As God he grows—melted in sun and stars.

Yet the vision is not pantheistic. The blank verse moves to many different measures, and remains dramatic. The action, conflict, and climax are real.

A sure test of the poem's dramatic thrust is the long opening soliloquy. At first a weary chant, it becomes a scathing denunciation; then a promise of vision shines across the lines like a shaft of light; but, as consciousness of the rain and the horse's gait returns, the words are weary again, and coldly determined. This soliloquy destroys Cecil's claim that the barren grasses are mere tufts of Whitman, and that Chesterton's optimism was at one time a complete denial of evil. The devil is real in this poem; so are the ascetic's agonies:

Think you to teach me? Know I not His ways?
Strange-visaged blunders, mystic cruelties.
All! All! I know Him, for I love Him. Go!

CHESTERTON PARADOX

The play is a connected system of paradoxes, corresponding to the network of surprises in the nature of reality—the inner division and unity of things. All things share a common being, yet this existence is different from each thing's essence. Orm *is*, he shines with God's secret and inmost glory; but Orm is *Orm,* and therefore limits that reality. This kind of paradox is not a rhetorical trope but the structural form of all the play, dictating one's entire approach to its theme. In this way does paradox overshadow Chesterton's career from the outset. It must be assessed at its source.

Hugh Kenner has made the most complete and perceptive study of Chesterton's paradox. There is no better introduction to the subject than his division of this stylistic trademark into three major types:

1. *Verbal* paradox, meant to stimulate the reader by contradicting common ideas or reversing normal language.

2. *Metaphysical* paradox, based on a contradiction within things; asserting that all created things are only *analogously* existent, good, bad, large, small, etc. By combining several points of view, looking up and down, Chesterton achieves a many-sided complexity of vision. Here Kenner treats briefly the real center of his thesis—the relation between Chestertonian paradox and the Thomistic doctrine of analogy (a doctrine which carries the discernment of sameness in difference back to its metaphysical root—the presence of existence in all the separate existents).

3. *Aesthetic* paradox, arising from the inability of language to express reality "in the round," so that words name only aspects, meet only at certain points, overlap and clash, slide into equivocal or altered meanings. When Chesterton points out these limits of language—by sharply jerking a word back to its purpose, or deliberately using vague words where language cannot be precise, or combining words of several functions to catch an elusive truth in a trap sprung from several sides—he is using "aesthetic" paradox.

These distinctions are neatly made; they give a convenient symmetry to Kenner's book. But when he adduces examples, all the lines of careful division seem to dissolve. Under verbal paradox, he gives most attention to two examples. The first: "Blasphemy is not wild; blasphemy is in its nature prosaic."[2] This Kenner calls a mere reversal of a popular half-truth into its opposite half-truth. But he misses the point of Chesterton's specific and continuing attack on negation in its many forms. Chesterton claimed that denial as such is dull, because its final point of equilibrium is nothingness, the ultimate boredom of the abyss. He said this frequently, as in *The Defendant*:

> For in our time the blasphemies are threadbare. Pessimism is now patently, *as it is always essentially*, more commonplace than piety.[3]

The second example is: "There is nothing that fails like success."[4] Chesterton's specific point, here, is that the modern ideal of Success substitutes quantity and condition for that acceptance of the "mystical minimum" which is the basis for realism, humility, joy, and achievement.[5]

When the examples chosen to isolate "verbalism" from metaphysical paradox do not attain this end, the division into such categories seems a sterile exercise. Kenner is, in the end, forced to admit the metaphysical background to all the paradoxes. The treatment of "aesthetic paradox" becomes a maze of meaningless distinctions because Kenner tries to make Chesterton wield "aesthetic paradox" without engaging in the activities of the artist.

The center of the book—the treatment of metaphysical paradox—points the way to a just assessment of Chesterton; but Kenner's approach is not, in practice, metaphysical but epistemological. He refers to the Thomistic doctrine of the real distinction between essence and existence, between *quod est* and *ut est,* but he looks rather at the *processes* of analogous judgments than at the source of all their validity. He even uses as a working definition this "essentialist" formulation:

> Paradox consists in showing briefly and dramatically that a new line of reason will indicate a new point on the object.[6]

Such paradox *is* dependent on one's "line of reason" and can be used simply as a trick.

But suppose a searching mind were to discover that all created things have double roots; suppose one root were not a form, a concept, an essence—none of those differing aspects of reality which the mind can grasp and control as a concept, but a formless energy within and under all forms, making them act and be present. This aspect of things cannot be expressed by a shift of vantage-point, or merely added as another facet to several essential judgments. Because this non-formal *actus,* or urgency of reality, is formally inexplicable, it is always—to man's reason—an exception, not less an exception in any of its manifestations. Commonplace things are as odd, under this light, as rare things. The real oddity is that there *are* things at all. How is one to speak of tricks or types of paradox in the face of such a vision? Chesterton did not deal in many types of paradox; not in paradoxes at all. He saw one exception— Being—and it colored his talk about all beings.

An objection could be raised here, that I seem to "justify" anything that Chesterton says in the way of paradox. If Kenner's norms are not valid, what are the norms to be applied? The answer is simple: there are no special rules. All the norms of literary taste apply here—but they can only be intelligently applied after one has grasped the meaning and purpose of the rhetoric, the insight that is worked out through all the channels of his athletic use of language. *The Wild Knight,* for instance, is a poem in which every word points to a conflict—the meeting of opposites in Orm. When this is not the case (and in varying degrees Chesterton *will* fail of such integrity), then he is at fault—for a variety of reasons, but not simply for "paradoxicality." As a matter of fact, though *The Wild Knight* is not Chesterton's greatest work, it is the one with least faults. Nowhere else is the same care given to each line, not even in *The Ballad of the White Horse*.

CHESTERTON'S NIGHTMARE NOVEL

The Wild Knight is typical, and a guide to Chesterton's work, precisely because it was born out of his early bafflement. It is true that Chesterton does not mention it when listing the works which sprang from this crisis, but that is almost certainly because of its attacks on priestcraft and narrow dogma.[7] Instead, he cites *The Man Who Was Thursday* as the most complete expression of his youthful encounter with the aesthetes.[8] Although the novel did not appear until 1908, its dedicatory poem bears out Chesterton's memory of the matter. The story of his plight is indirectly presented here (not, be it noticed, as a private fancy of his own adolescence, but as an historic mood shared by many). Solipsism and Impressionism are the foes:

Science announced nonentity and art admired decay.

Stevenson and Whitman are the allies:

I find again that book we found, I feel the hour that flings
Far out of fish-shaped Paumanok some cry of cleaner things;
And the Green Carnation withered, as in forest fires that pass
Roared in the wind of all the world ten million leaves of grass;
Or sane and sweet and sudden as a bird sings in the rain—

Truth out of Tusitala spoke and pleasure out of pain.
Yea, cool and clear and sudden as a bird sings in the grey,
Dunedin to Samoa spoke, and darkness unto day.[9]

The novel has those qualities Chesterton ascribed to dreams: unity of mood and wild variety of incident.[10] Unreality overclouds Gabriel Syme, the story's hero, destroying and dissolving everything he reaches out for. This is like a story by Kafka, in which stairs melt into crumbling sand, and horses gallop but carry one nowhere. But in Kafka's tales the spell is never broken, whereas Syme takes an irrational courage into every chamber of horror and is rewarded by a final collapse in which *illusion* dissolves.

The unity of the piece is not only one of mood. There is method in Syme's madness. He climbs ordered degrees of unreason, until he reaches the top and is left alone, for a dark space, in his tower of insanity. The first fears are childish ones, mere grotesques of an imagination that has run wild. Professor de Worms is "the crooked man who went a crooked mile,"[11] the bogy man which our plastic mind can, by some mystery of idolatry, first shape and then fear.

But the next encounter, with Bull, is even more unnerving— the encounter with cold and impersonal thought. Syme is now the child who has lost his world of poetry and personality:

Syme was increasingly conscious that his new adventure had somehow a quality of cold sanity worse than the wild adventures of the past. Last night, for instance, the tall tenements had seemed to him like a tower in a dream. As he now went up the weary and perpetual steps, he was daunted and bewildered by their almost infinite series. But it was not the hot horror of a dream or of anything that might be exaggeration or delusion. Their infinity was more like the empty infinity of arithmetic, something unthinkable, yet necessary to thought.

Or it was like the stunning statements of astronomy about the distance of the fixed stars. He was ascending the house of reason, a thing more hideous than unreason itself.[12]

The tyranny of astronomy and cold science goes with another invasion of childhood, the banishing of romance in the name of "realism":

> About the Professor's make-up and all his antics there was always something merely grotesque, like a gollywog. Syme remembered those wild woes of yesterday as one remembers being afraid of Bogy in childhood. But here was daylight; here was a healthy, square-shouldered man in tweeds, not odd save for the accident of his ugly spectacles, not glaring or grinning at all, but smiling steadily and not saying a word. The whole had a sense of unbearable reality. Under the increasing sunlight the colours of the Doctor's complexion, the pattern of his tweeds, grew and expanded outrageously, as such things grow too important in a realistic novel.[13]

The next stage of Syme's fear is reached in his duel with the Marquis, when death hovers over him, ready to blot out all things:

> the fear of the Professor had been the fear of the tyrannic accidents of nightmare, and the fear of the Doctor had been the fear of the airless vacuum of science. The first was the old fear that any miracle might happen, the second the more hopeless fear that no miracle can ever happen. But he saw that these fears were fancies, for he found himself in the presence of the great fact of the fear of death, with its coarse and pitiless common sense. He felt like a man who had dreamed all night of falling over precipices, and had woken up on the morning when he was to be hanged.

He felt a strange and vivid value in all the earth around him, in the grass under his feet; he felt the love of life in all living things. He could almost fancy that he heard the grass growing; he could almost fancy that even as he stood fresh flowers were springing up and breaking into blossom in the meadow—flowers blood-red and burning gold and blue, fulfilling the whole pageant of the spring. And whenever his eyes strayed for a flash from the calm, staring, hypnotic eyes of the Marquis, they saw the little tuft of almond tree against the sky-line. He had the feeling that if by some miracle he escaped he would be ready to sit forever before that almond tree, desiring nothing else in the world.[14]

The next step into nightmare—that caused by the flight from the secretary—is more healthy but not less real. It is the fear of defeat—not mere death, but irrelevant death. The army that advances after the fugitives seems like the whole world in cry at their heels. But beyond this shared despair there is a "last and worst" fancy that comes to Syme alone. Fleeing through the mottled shadows of the forest, pursued by men in masks and supported by men who have just removed their masks, Syme begins to wonder if anything is fixed in dependable identity:

Was not everything, after all, like this bewildering woodland, this dance of dark and light? Everything only a glimpse, the glimpse always unforeseen, and always forgotten. For Gabriel Syme had found in the heart of that sun-splashed wood what many modern painters had found there. He had found the thing which the modern people call Impressionism, which is another name for that final scepticism which can find no floor to the universe.[15]

Graphically the novel presents that "suicide of intellect" which Chesterton would describe in his next volume, *Orthodoxy*. The various shapes and suggestings of unreal things have led at last to Unreality itself. There is nowhere else to go. Here Chesterton must end the story, as Kafka would, in the farthest reaches of the unreal, or rescue his hero somehow.

That rescue involves the archetypal drama which hovers behind this entire pantomime of chase and nightmare. "The Council" and the "Accuser" are, in the last scene, direct references to the Book of Job. The final chase through monstrous scenes, thronged with trumpeting and incredible beasts, is a glimpse of that animal world which Jehovah called up for Job. Syme is answered by the elephant, as Job was by Behemoth. These echoes multiply in the final chapter as the Sons of God shout for joy in the strange dance the Council witnesses. The parallels are finally established by Bull's quotation: "Now there was a day when the sons of God came to present themselves before the Lord, and Satan came also among them."[16]

Job's challenge to a meaningless world of pain was not met by the narrow rationalizings of his friends but by the answering challenge to battle which God issued. The whirlwind offers adventure, not explanation. If Job joins the war on chaos, about which the stars shout for joy, he must live with the mysteries of free will, suffering, and evil, not resorting to his friends' refuge of optimism. Chesterton called the Book of Job the finest proof that pessimists and optimists are both wrong.[17] And he gave his novel the same theme, making of optimism the last and most seductive temptation which Syme must meet.

The pleasant daydream of Sunday's banquet resembles the earlier stages of nightmare; joy is substituted for horror, but it is the paralyzing joy of a dream, where individuality fades into a central fire. Everything had been illusion; now everything is God. A single-textured optimism can only lead to a single-textured world—to pantheism, which all the fighters resent as a denial of their struggle. Sunday remains truly their foe insofar as he is Everything. As Chesterton said many years later:

> the ogre who appears brutal but is also cryptically benevolent is not so much God, in the sense of religion or irreligion, but rather Nature as it appears to the pantheist, whose pantheism is struggling out of pessimism.[18]

On the same page, Chesterton points to a *change* that overcomes Sunday, that figure of blind energy, of pure existential drive, when the last unveiling is reached. For Syme does rend this specious pantheism in the most violent manner. And only then does Sunday—the Lord's Day—become the Lord.

The Accuser, like Syme and the Professor, resents his scars; unlike them, however, he is seeking revenge, not explanation. He hurls at the others a taunt which Chesterton was all too familiar with, the ancient taunt of Job's diabolic afflicter—that the good have not suffered, that believers know no doubts and cannot deserve the reward of heroic rebels. Syme's answer—and Chesterton's—is brief, though it raises a thunderous echo. Syme shouts a denial out of his own experience. He has fought in the dark against all the forces in and beyond the world. He has been wrong and stupid, running down empty passages, taking journeys none of his fellows of the Council shared. He has known real isolation and a terrible solitude. The story of each man on the Council is equally heroic, sealed in his own incommunicable self. Being is an exception in each of its manifestations. It appears only in definite shapes drawn in the hardest lines against the background of nonexistence. Loneliness is the best proof of individuality.

Chesterton was just at this moment on the verge of writing *Orthodoxy,* which—growing out of his controversy with Blatchford—

would be his most complete statement of the idea of *creation*: creation means a sundering, a proliferation of individuals by the rearing of boundaries. God gave man glory and adventure by giving him free will, an independent path for his mind to explore. Existence God shares with us, at each instant, a living vein and open channel into his raging nature. But essence—identity—is ours. Man's life is caught in a tense dialectic on all levels, as *Orthodoxy* would demonstrate.

With a last touch of Job's audacity, Syme flings a challenge at Sunday, who has faded and grown vague in the twilight. His amorphous energy and dissolving outline seem to lift him above the struggle the others have undergone. But when Syme asks him if he is of their fellowship of battle a new note enters the distant voice as it thunders back: "Can ye drink of the cup that I drink of?" In *Orthodoxy* Chesterton would suggest, darkly, that the Trinity is a proof that God knows personality and dialectic in a higher form of pure action without suffering. Here he glances at the Incarnation, whereby *God*'s personality is established by His loneliness.

Chesterton saw that the simple existentialist is as unstable as the rationalist. The world of empty Forms leads to Platonic doubts and Schopenhauer's negations. But a worship of mere energy can as easily take a manic form, in Whitman's cheery effusiveness as in Nietzsche's dark worship of strength. Sunday is the god of Whitman.

THE ART OF CHESTERTON

The ideas in *Thursday* resemble those of the forthcoming *Orthodoxy,* and many would consider the first book as much an essay or set of arguments as the second. Is the novel form an extraneous decoration only, a distracting and unnecessary element? Cecil tells us that Gilbert took great pains with this tale, but regrets that it does not reach the stature of his first novel, *The Napoleon of Notting Hill*.[19] Before one can judge its merits, however, one must know *what* it is. Cecil complains that it lacks characterization. Now it is true that all the characters speak like Chesterton, that their differences are symbolic and functional. But a realistic character would destroy the whole framework of this myth. Nor do those solve the problem who make all the speeches delivered through different masks a mere set of essays: the last challenge to Sunday, the last thunders from that whirlwind, mean nothing outside the setting of the story, and that setting is itself a series of impressions, conveyed in colors and symbols and strange images.

It is not even accurate to call this a parable, for in that art-form the story has a logic and autonomy aside from the major parallelism it enforces. But here the story changes its entire character when symbols or intent are altered. This is more like a surrealist painting than like an essay. It begins as a political satire, quickly becomes a detective story, then an adventure of pursuit, a nightmare, a fantasy of loneliness, a myth of Nature, an echo of prophecy, a symbol of creation, a theophany; and each of these changes is vital to the movement and embodying of meaning; while all through this blaze of blurred forms run strands of humor and nonsense, allegory and argument, none of it extraneous or simply ornamental.

Such an extraordinary display of virtuosity (or verbosity) as *Thursday* brings us sharply against the problem of Chesterton's claims as an artist—not only the question whether he was a good artist or bad, but whether he was an artist at all. Here again, Kenner's thesis is better stated than most. According to him, Chesterton was a metaphysician too calm and unperturbed to feel the sensitive nerves of language as extensions of his own nerves. This raises difficulties already suggested—of sincerity or hysteria in Chesterton's high-flown rhetoric, of a sterile clash between what

Kenner calls the essential Chesterton and what everyone will admit is the obvious Chesterton.

But there are further objections arising from his early career, from works like *Thursday*: if Chesterton was not an artist, why did he begin thinking and writing in terms of colors and symbols? The balanced and complicated sentences which he had earlier imitated from Ruskin were more suited to exposition and metaphysics; yet, from the time of the Slade crisis, he began to drift into a literary counterpart of the painters' technique which he feared. He abandoned balance and stability for a rapid forward drive, rushing to a wave-crest of adjectives. Obscurely "tonal" words are daubed here and there in a manner thoroughly Impressionist. He tried to gain energy even at the deliberate sacrifice of clarity, and he praised this achievement of exuberance in Shakespeare, Rabelais, Dickens, and his other favorite authors. He felt some link between this style and the existential trend of his own thoughts. All of these developments are artistic and relate to a mode of communication radically different from the scientific methods of philosophy.

Not only did Chesterton begin his work by thinking through symbols and heraldic colors at the art school; whenever he approached a new insight, he did it by way of a symbolic or artistic form. His ideas always get their first expression in poems, narratives, or drawings. Belloc's collaboration with Chesterton is interesting in this respect. Rapidly inventing a novel, Belloc would come to Chesterton with the plot and characters still shaping in his mind. As they talked, Chesterton's pen gave substance to the shadows of Belloc's fancy; only then did Belloc write the novel, with the pictures before him. This says little for Belloc as a novelist (and indeed he wrote fiction only as part of his sad campaign for a livelihood), but it is a symbol of Chesterton's own mode of thought-through-images.

What Chesterton did for Belloc's novels, he did for his own books and essays. Msgr. O'Connor says Chesterton wanted to write a book on the Jesuits toward the end of his life.[20] He never wrested the time for this project from his ever-accelerating round of labors, but we might have guessed such a book was coming to birth from the three late poems on the Jesuits which are among his papers. Much of *Orthodoxy* is prefigured in *Thursday;* the issues on which the *Authobiography* focuses were first detached in the study of Stevenson; and the ideas finally brought to light in the book on Aquinas were first symbolized, thirty-three years earlier, in *The Wild Knight*. As one reads Chesterton's works in sequence, he sees that ideas are not merely decorated or disguised in the fiction and poems; they are born there, they come into being through these shapings of his imagination.

Of course, one can still believe that these were extra-artistic ideas, arrived at by a mere scribbling and doodling on stray pads, not fleshed and delivered from the creative throes which Kenner misses. Chesterton himself said that he could never keep flesh on his characters, that ideas kept wrestling their way out of such embodiments to fight naked.[21] But he kept writing the stories, even putting his views in narrative form when arguing or composing essays. Furthermore, certain symbols—the color grey, railway signals, twilight, swords—stimulated him in every context, in a way which depends on the mystery of expression, not only on the truths to be expressed.

The real process is reversed in Chesterton's statement. It is not a case of characters becoming ideas, but of his own dissatisfaction with abstract conceptions. Concepts always clothe themselves in color and come before him with weird faces. They never were nor could be convincing agents in a conventional novel. They are "characters" in the linguistic or heraldic sense, hieroglyphs of which he constructed a language that looks like a dance of ideograms. Chesterton was always uncomfortable with the arid essences of Plato; as if he felt, once more, the prison of solipsism rising around him. That is why ideas are plunged in circumstance and almost given personality in his writings.

The highest truth, wrote Chesterton in the Notebook, is always told in stories—a belief that worked deeper into his mind until it received final expression in the treatment of myth in *The Everlasting Man*. But many years before he analyzed the significance of stories as such, he sensed it and used it. In short, Chesterton *was* an artist. He may have been a poor one, but to say he was not one at all is surely perverse. The source of his vision, to be sure, was a metaphysical insight; but that is the spring of poetry in every authentic artist. Kenner himself is forced to treat Chesterton as an artist, since his critical instincts are sounder than his arguments. Though he intends to conduct an elaborate comparison with Thomas Aquinas in the matter of analogous vision, he quotes a commentary on Aquinas and then, in fact, forgets him. The operative and illuminating comparisons, everywhere, are to rhetorical doctors and theologians like Augustine and Tertullian, or to metaphysical poets like Blake and Joyce.[22] Yet Kenner can write:

> In a better age, with greater incentive for scholarship, and less pressure for immediate, continuous, and dissipating journalistic action, he might have been a principal ornament of the mediaeval Sorbonne. It is doing him the fullest possible homage to call him a splendid anachronism.[23]

METAPHYSICAL JESTER

Who can possibly desire scholarship of Chesterton? He did not simply lack the time to become a scholar; he *refused* to enter debate on facts, even when he knew the facts or could discover them with no effort. Had he become a professor—of the Sorbonne or any other university—he would have left encyclopedic learning to others and scattered his wisdom in a shower of epigrams, as Nietzsche did. And, indeed, Chesterton's method of teaching was not unlike Nietzsche's—parable, story, aphorism, pugnacious attack and challenge; all dramatic and rhetorical in structure, based on great knowledge and insight but never on the painstaking methods of the scholar. Both men were incisive, not exhaustive. The motive, too, coincides: to strike in upon the mind where it is least defended against reality, to give an existential insight which no formal reasoning or conceptual analysis could compass. *Zarathustra* resembles, in one sense, *The Wild Knight,* while on another level it works with the strategy of *The Everlasting Man*; and nothing more resembles Chesterton writing on Browning or Shakespeare than Nietzsche discussing Wagner or Sophocles. Of many detailed similarities, a striking one is the resemblance between the opening chapter of *The Everlasting Man* and the first sentences of Nietzsche's paper "On Truth and Falsity."

Chesterton came to his style, as Nietzsche had, by way of the prophets. But Chesterton even more than Nietzsche realized the dangers, to oneself and one's message, involved in the prophet's role, and he altered it, as Nietzsche did at times, to the stance of that other eternal figure of warning and instruction—the jester. Both men were *metaphysical jesters.* They became "mad" in the eyes of the world in order to speak from a totally detached point of view, one not logically demonstrable. The jester realizes that he must seem strange to others; this is what distinguishes him from a fanatic, from the *serious* madman. A deliberate exaggeration and self-mocking animation mark the man who works in this medium. For there have been others: Aristophanes,[24] Shakespeare in some of his comedies, even Rabelais; while the modern world is full of such jesters, successful or failing, of whom only one need be mentioned now (since Chesterton frequently compared their roles)—Bernard

Shaw. These and all other artists in this genre employ a heightened rhetoric and deceptive levity.

Once this is grasped, we have a set of norms for judging the mingled absurdities and confusion of *The Man Who Was Thursday*. This blend of Stevensonian adventure story, Dickensian grotesquerie, and Old Testament prophecy is completely personal and authentic, not a mere potpourri. The use made of varying styles and forms is *strategically* paradoxical—Job's drama in Soho, Stevenson's adventure in a metaphysical setting, a detective story with God as the criminal. These paradoxes are more important than any verbal paradoxes in the dialogue (which are, in fact, only meant to point up the underlying ironies). Through the shifting play of contrasts Chesterton achieves that glancing, elusive mode of statement which is the jester's trademark; not traveling in a straight line of exposition but cutting across the mind's activities to let light in directly, to achieve that metaphysical recognition which, the discursive philosophers assure us, is not discursive.

Chesterton's tales have the hard intent and the soft, ever-shifting outline of an Aristophanic fantasy, the high-flown bombast and quiet irony of Rabelais, the energy in scenes and words and characters which Shakespeare and Dickens could generate. But the surrealist, nightmare quality of his tales is more akin to Kafka's than to any other, a fact which C. S. Lewis was the first to notice.[25] Chesterton is forever deluging us with the quality called good humor. Kafka's strange magic derives from what can only be called his evil humor. In both cases, scenes melt into haunting pictures of a blinding philosophy; but Chesterton is blinded by a sudden light, and Kafka by a disintegrating darkness. Kafka's heroes become dogs, beetles, and prisoners at the blink of a blood-veined eye; Chesterton's become, in a twinkling, kings and heroes. One expresses himself in worms, the other in angels.

The mere mention of these two names on the same page will

be dismissed by many as whimsical. I do not mean merely that the comparison's result will be called invalid; the very act of comparing is considered gratuitous. Why should this be so? Chesterton answered this question in several places:

> The moderns, to do them justice, are not realists. They are not under any influence from the babyish notion that art should imitate life. But they are used to seeing life (in the modern books) exaggerated in the direction of pain or sensibility or mystery or delicacy or despair or candour or cruelty; they are well used to seeing life exaggerated in all these directions. But they are not used to seeing life exaggerated in the direction of life.[26]

> We understand a devout occultism, an evil occultism, a tragic occultism, but a farcical occultism is beyond us.[27]

Kafka's bestial visions are very effective symbols, arranged in startling order and stirring limitless processes of reflection. But Chesterton's similar visions are dismissed as aimless debauches of rhetoric because they lead to metaphysical insights which are not at present fashionable. Because most of our modern jesters are sombre and bitter, from Nietzsche to Kafka, Chesterton's fantasies are as idly underrated as Shakespeare's wildly comic visions were by the eighteenth century, or Aristophanes' by the era of New Comedy in Greece. Even Kenner affords examples of this radical misconception:

> The Father Brown stories, for example, with all their machinery of murder and repentance, and all their genuine moral interest in the fact of human sin that makes them unique among detective stories, are patently devoid of the intense dramatic life of *Crime and Punishment*.[28]

There is no adequate comment on this but Chesterton's own:

> The usual way of criticizing an author who has added something to the literary forms of the world, is to complain that his work does not contain something which is obviously the specialty of someone else. The correct thing to say about Maeterlinck is that some play of his in which, let us say, a princess dies in a deserted tower by the sea, has a certain beauty, but that we look in vain in it for that robust geniality, that really boisterous will to live which may be found in *Martin Chuzzlewit*. The right thing to say about *Cyrano de Bergerac* is that it may have a certain kind of wit and spirit, but that it really throws no light on the duty of middle-aged married couples in Norway.[29]

Going to Father Brown for the agonies of Dostoievski, going to Chesterton for scholarship, are perfect examples of the error Chesterton describes in that paragraph. Gloomy magic we will accept, but not the happy occultism which is a defence of being. We look for "modernity" and the popular pessimism even in the unlikeliest places and go away saddened when Raskolnikov is not found lurking in Flambeau (whose mere name should tell us how far these tales are in their intent from Dostoievski's). This is surely to limit literature, giving it a single value and function, a function determined by nothing more valid than one's own emotional preferences.

PART TWO (1900–1912)

Controversy

4.

THE SIGNATURE
OF STYLE

Chesterton drifted out of art school with much less in the way of settled plans than he had taken into it, but with a new purpose clear before him—to oppose with his pen that air of corrosive cynicism which followed on the Victorian complacency. His task, now, was to work out those energetic ideas which had been born in him. For four years he read proofs for publishers—first at Redway, then at Fisher Unwin. All this time his head was tumbling with poems and stories (which fill every inch of the Fisher Unwin office paper left in his notes). The stifling fumes of his enclosure in himself were clearing; and, to complete the emancipation from boyhood friendships and boyhood isolation, love for a quietly beautiful woman, pious somewhat in the Burne-Jones manner, seized him with a violence that makes one think of Dante. This love for his Frances was idealized, but not with the unreality of the Junior Debating Club dream. The private poems saved from the fire to which Frances consigned most of them, after Gilbert's death, show a healthy passion informed by the ideas which were intoxicating him.

With a sure instinct, Chesterton burst into print only after the proper incubation period—four years after the critical passage through art school—and won immediate acclaim. His style, so characteristic that it would be from this time on considered inevitable, is the sign that Chesterton had, by 1900, reached the inner balance and freedom which breathe through all his later work. No longer would he grope uncertainly, change styles; leave stories stranded, verses and aphorisms isolated, incapable of development or resolution (as so often happens in the notebooks). Swinburne, Isaias, Ruskin, Browning—the solemn chairman, the lonely young poet, the sad student of the notebooks—disappear, and Chesterton appears. The sense of self-achievement and style extends even to his appearance. It was at this time that he began to put on weight and acquire his signature-apparel—the cape, the swordcane. Those were not the remains of boyhood, but new things he had the courage and imagination to adopt as he reached maturity.

In 1900, the year he left Fisher Unwin, Chesterton wrote reviews in almost every issue of *The Speaker;* by 1901 he was contributing his weekly column to *The Daily News.* This launching of his journalistic career is usually associated with the Boer War and his alliance with the "Pro-Boers"—justly, for he met and impressed men of the Liberal press during those days of passion and quick sympathies. But it is not true that he entered journalism as a political commentator. His background was one of art school and publishing; he had written articles on famous painters in *The Bookman*; and though he was accepted on *The Speaker* as one who shared the paper's political views, most of the books he was given to review were of general literary interest. Even more to the point, his first series of articles, for which the subjects were not determined by assignment of the editor, had nothing to do with politics. This series was published as *The Defendant* and was a first statement of his constant theme—that even "commonplace" things are exceptional. On *The Daily News* he made frequent forays into the realm of politics, but always from this continuing position of defender and interpreter of ordinary things. His first public clash with Bernard Shaw was not over the issue of Socialism but of Shakespeare.[1] Even when he wrote about politics, he gave a deliberately literary "impression" of his subject, describing the atmosphere of certain men's patriotism, or the philosophy one must hold in order to support any program consistently.

In his early reviews, Chesterton was already laying the foundation for his vast body of literary criticism. A profound unity informs all these judgments, no matter how scattered or occasional, on literature. Contained in them, assumed throughout them, is a philosophy of criticism far in advance of Victorian moralism and decadent aestheticism. The basis of this criticism was laid in Chesterton's first book of essays, *The Defendant*. Chesterton insists, in his defence of penny dreadfuls and of detective stories, that literature is a real object, good or bad. Many critics seem to assume that unless a work is well done, it is not done at all; unless it means something new or esoteric, it signifies nothing. This bias is only an aspect of man's eternal blindness to the reality of commonplace things. But Chesterton knew that all beings are, strictly speaking, exceptional; and he realized that every piece of literature is basically an oddity and marvel—a proof of man's eternal ache to say things and find answers.

TWELVE TYPES

This approach to literature has, of course, become a common tenet of recent criticism. The word, aside from its function as a sign, is also a *thing*. Since I. A. Richards, the analytic philosophy has taken over literary criticism and made of the symbol, of the poem, of the artifact, an autonomous field of exploration. Modern critics have emphasized the word's isolated action. Chesterton arrived at the same awareness by a totally different route—not through Kantian emphasis on knowledge as a human construction, but by an existential insight which kept *both* the word's meaning *and* its mode of existing operative, in a state of tense struggle and reinforcement. This awareness of the artifact's own reality was very rare in 1900; and it was the profundity of Chesterton's realization of these first facts about literature which sometimes made him look shallow and hasty. He did not take the ordinary critic's approach, discussing schools, influence, etc. He approached art from the side of metaphysics, looking to the artifact's own mode of existence. The jaunty carriage and brisk step of Byron's poems were more important to Chesterton than the sentimentally despondent words. And if we look at the volume in which the Byron essay appeared, *Twelve Types* (1902), we shall find that its method is basically that of stylistic analysis. Chesterton denies that Carlyle was tortured by a fundamental disbelief, because he could joke with the cosmos.[2] Discussing Rostand, he finds the man's spirit and message in the fact that he uses not only verse but *rhyme* in drama. Rostand did not *say* man's life is poetic to its roots; he showed it by making rhymes echo and chime through long dialogues as naturally as the sexes answer to each other, or as day responds to night.[3] Pope's carefulness is exciting, not dull, because his verse-form contains its own challenge; dramatically he must continue to hit the mark.[4] The norms that are applied, in all these cases, Chesterton makes explicit in his essay on Tolstoi:

> An artist teaches far more by his mere background and prop-
> erties, his landscape, his costumes, his idiom and technique—
> all the part of his work, in short, of which he is probably
> unconscious, than by the elaborate and pompous moral dicta
> which he fondly imagines to be his opinions.[5]

So Chesterton discusses "the white light of morning" in the short tales of Tolstoi the artist and contrasts this world with the cramped universe of Tolstoi the moralist.

A priori criticism of Scott usually involves an admission that he is a great novelist *despite* his static descriptions and extraneous detail. But Chesterton sees, in the pacing and precision of Scott's style, that such details is at the very heart of his romantic method, that Scott enjoyed a confrontation, a landscape, a weapon as such. One should go to Douglas Fairbanks for swordfights, but to Scott for the Sword.[6] This is criticism of the highest order, flexible on every level of form and style because fixed at its metaphysical roots.

Yet Chesterton has always been accused of turning criticism into propaganda, of using an author as a peg for his own views. Even Cecil thought his brother was a good critic only when discussing authors with whom he agreed. Julius West repeated this indictment (along with most of Cecil's judgments),[7] and recent study has not gone beyond stale reptition of the charge.[8] This implies that Chesterton could understand only what he knew before, and that the artist's unique means of expression were inconsequential to him. But nothing could be farther from his actual practice than his ideological approach to art. Praise of things for their separate merits was his only "ideology," and this led to an appreciation of each note and inflection for its own sake.

The first major statement of this charge against Chesterton is typical. Cecil calls the Byron essay in *Twelve Types* "the worst essay, I think, that Mr. Chesterton has ever written." But Cecil's own suggestions for revision reflect his devouring interest in politics and involve more enthusiasm for history than instinct for poetry.[9] In other words, he takes just that personal bias into criticism of which he accuses Gilbert. The same thing is often true of Cecil's successors in this indictment; never has ideology more completely dictated critical response than in the automatic dismissal of Chesterton's works from serious consideration.

Another early test of Chesterton's critical ability came in his first clash with Shaw on the subject of Shakespeare. Shaw had just reaffirmed before the world that Shakespeare often wrote potboilers to please the crowd and make money. He proved this by alluding to Shakespeare's lack of positive message and "social conscience." In other words, Shakespeare did not preach.

Chesterton, after pointing out the Puritan nature of Shaw's arguments, went on to attack their critical basis. Shakespeare had the love of words and expression as such. He loved to roll or savor words, as an artist loves mere color or the sculptor mere marble. There is in such artists a first love of the medium itself as a *thing* before it becomes a sign. Shakespeare, of course, can activate the signifying potentiality of words as few other poets can. But it is because he, more than any poet, realized the double nature of words, as signs but also as things, and because he felt more deeply the double function of art, which is to mean but also to be, that Shakespeare stands on two legs, as it were, and combines all the excellences of poetry: wild and natural expression with farthest formal significance, sheer verbal beauty with deft relevance of phrase. He is fully exercising his own first act—to be—when he not only stirs in a word all its meanings but activates all its separate musicality and magic. These two aspects of the word are not to be divorced in Shakespeare, as Shaw claimed, distinguishing verbal felicity from serious purpose or meaning:

Mr. Shaw says that in manner nothing could be done better than "As You Like It," but in matter he himself would never do anything so bad. When I read this, I saw suddenly how simple is the whole mistake. I can only draw Mr. Shaw's attention to the fact that "As You Like It" is poetry. What can anybody mean by talking of the matter or manner of a poem? I will give Mr. Shaw three lines out of "As You Like It" from the exquisite and irrational song of Hymen at the end:

> There is a joy in Heaven
> When earthly things made even
> Atone together

If the words "When earthly things made even" were presented to us in the form of "When terrestrial affairs are reduced to an equilibrium," the meaning would not merely have been spoilt, the meaning would have entirely disappeared. This identity between the matter and the manner is simply the definition of poetry. The aim of good prose words is to mean what they say. The aim of good poetical words is to mean what they do not say. When Shakespeare says (in one of the long philosophical speeches which Mr. Shaw does not quote because they do not happen to be pessimistic),

> For valour is not Love a Hercules
> Still climbing trees in the Hesperides,

it is difficult, or rather impossible, to use any other language to express what he conveys. You cannot convey a sense of sunrise and an ancient hope and the colours of the ends of the earth.[10]

BROWNING

Such quick and glancing criticism in the journals led publishers to ask for monographs on various authors. The first commission came from John Morley, who asked Chesterton, in 1903, to do the Browning volume in the "English Men of Letters" series. This was considered an honor, since most of the volumes were written by scholars and members of the academy, while Chesterton was a young journalist who, a short time before this, had not been qualified to enter either of the universities. But Chesterton did not alter his method in this first monograph, or attempt "authoritative" interpretation. The book is what his essays were—stylistic analysis, quick and glancing, incisive but almost haphazard.

There have been two interpretations (both wide of the mark) of this intransigence in style—that Chesterton could do no other, and that he wanted to shock the staid by an impudent "freshness." Cecil upholds the second view, assuring us that his brother had "fluttered the dovecote" of criticism, an achievement Cecil always over-valued. But the majority of critics is with the first view.

The factual errors in the book have become famous, through anecdote and exaggeration, yet most of them were in the matter of accurate quotation, and these do not represent a failure in scholarship. They could represent many things—idiocy, impudence, or malice—but not lack of scholarship. It takes no scholarship accurately to quote a poem in one's own language, a poem which is the subject of the essay. To judge this failure by the norms of scholarly endeavor is futile. Kenner regrets that Chesterton had not the time (and the mediaeval atmosphere) to make his philosophic work scholarly and non-journalistic. But here was an opening into the academic or literary world, offered a young man whose career was not yet established in a definite mould.[11] It was his first attempt on this scale; no others existed, to set a pattern or prejudice his readers. Had Chesterton desired acceptance on the terms Kenner describes, he could have achieved it—or at least made his bid for it—in this single venture. The fantastic view of Chesterton as a natural phenomenon, as someone unable to work in any but a single mode, is inadequate here, as Cecil's reaction to his brother's performance indicates.[12] This was a crossroad.

In *Browning* Chesterton wrote a long essay with facts misstated and lines misquoted. He did it deliberately. Why?

In his reviews of biographies Chesterton had stated, from the outset, that style and significance matter more to mankind than simple record of event.[13] Now Browning, in the years when this book appeared, was an almost perfect case for Chesterton to test these views on. The Browning Society had become as obscurely learned in the poet as the poet was in certain quaint areas of research. These enthusiasts not only quibbled about facts and details; they read their own mental processes into their hero's work and called him a scholarly "metaphysician." Chesterton's thesis is that Browning is "a poet, one of the few men who have never written a line of anything but poetry,"[14] and especially a romantic poet of love. Few would quarrel with that judgment now, though it was a paradox at the time; yet few realize how Chesterton's instinct in the matter is connected with his method.

Chesterton begins the book with a few comments on the dispute concerning Browning's ancestry. The ingenuity of biographers had made each new finding or hypothesis significant of something, for facts are endlessly plastic to such treatment; the same ingenuity could adjust any facts to some predetermined meaning. Chesterton, on the other hand, wants to know what was significant to Browning. He studies facts from within the poems, "looking out." He studies Browning's middle-class origins by studying the man's own view of middle-class respectability. He considers the external world only in the traces it has left in his work.

But, we might ask, why did Chesterton add error to impression in his criticism? How could he misquote the poems in which he is absorbed, from which he looks forth? The answer may seem subtle, but anyone who has written any kind of criticism will recognize that it is both sound and, basically, simple. Chesterton did not invite or defend error, but he opposed what everyone who writes knows is a source of distortion. Usually a quick re-acquaintance with one's subject, even if it is a re-acquaintance with things long familiar, is necessary for the expository writer. But it is a necessary evil in the case of the critic; one is too close to the subject, looking for quotations, evidence, and "proof" in poetry, instead of retiring to a point of vantage where one can *receive* evidence, naturally, from the large shape and development of the work. The difficulty lies in the reconciliation of this first, unhurried and unbiased receptivity with the closely detailed work necessary to the task of conveying one's insights to others.

Chesterton had an extraordinary advantage in this regard. His memory for literary passages was prodigious, the source of almost as many anecdotes and legends as his inability to remember dates and practical schedules. Furthermore, he managed usually to write only on authors he had been closely acquainted with all his life. I think it safe to say no one had read the works of Dickens or Browning or Ruskin or Stevenson as thoroughly as he. The values he found in these authors he did not try to establish from a search through other critics, secondary sources, or contemporary history. He would not even search the books themselves again. His mind had already sifted the sources of his impression, retaining the most salient features. That is why Chesterton quoted poets from memory: he would not surrender his total and frequent experience of the poem to a false re-encounter with the lines, in an air of utilitarian search for "quotes," nor try to assess them out of the wider context. This was not a matter of laziness; he tried to prevent Dorothy Collins, his secretary in later years, from looking up references, pinning dead facts onto his living re-creation of a shape he had glimpsed in the mass of an author's output. As he said, early in his career,

> I quote from memory both by temper and on principle. That is what literature is for; it ought to be part of a man.[15]

Chesterton's total code in this matter was actually very strict, and he underwent a good deal of misunderstanding for it. His motives can be gauged from the estimate he made of others who attempted the kind of criticism he had set up as his own ideal. One such estimate, though lengthy, is important and worth quoting:

> This is a conscientious book because the author has kept awake to write it. The hardest kind of work is really to work with one's head, not with one's pen or spectacles or paste-pot or scissors or British Museum reading ticket. To write down no word that does not mean something; to write no sentence without a point to it; to echo no mere fashionable phrases; to pick living adjectives; to select real analogies; not to pad by so much as an inch; this is really to work hard, and this is how Mr. Chesson works when he is at it. One can read through the narrative and trivial parts of Cruikshank's life in this book with the certainty that the author's mind will be fully present in every sentence. He does not write the pompous parts of the book and leave the rest to write itself. . . . For it shows (what is much rarer than many people fancy) a strong literary sense of honor. Here is a little book, claiming only to be a slight bi-

ography, likely to be used as a mere table ornament. There are five or six first-class critics now drawing large salaries who would write such a book without taking any trouble at all to earn their money, except the trouble of being accurate—which can be delegated. It would be so easy to write a readable and flowing account of Cruikshank, full of all the unconscious modern dogmas. . . . Such a book would have been accepted; it would have been praised as much as I am now praising this. But Mr. Chesson, out of his own intellectual integrity, prefers to *think* his way through the book, to stud every other sentence with some sincere conviction or some sincere doubt. That is the sort of accuracy and the sort of conscientiousness which we really want to encourage. It is not dishonest to write a new life of Cruikshank with a false date for his birth, for that can be learnt in an encyclopaedia. But it is dishonest to write a new life of Cruikshank with nothing really in it at all except what exists already in the encyclopaedia. It is not dishonorable to put some private error into a book, but it is dishonorable not to put any private truth into it. We writers are paid to cut off bits of ourselves, and we must deliver the goods, if they be pounds of flesh. . . . Here is a man who puts big thoughts into a small book. Here is a man (one may even say) who puts important thoughts into an unimportant book. If once writers can be urged to that sort of industry, English literature is saved.[16]

The kind of criticism Chesterton admired is written, most often, on the Continent. Malraux's criticism, or that of Rilke on Rodin, of Baudelaire on Delacroix, has the same marks as Chesterton's—a personal reading of symbols in a highly charged rhetorical atmosphere, where metaphysical issues are soon reached and discussed through the medium of art. These efforts, carried on at this level, are not a propagandist's or ideologue's misuse of art; for art is meant to open these dark realms to "wild surmise."

One of the greatest examples of this sort of critical activity is Nietzsche's *Birth of Tragedy*, which sustains a division and polarity by a complex dialectic of language; its rhetoric shows the same paradox and heightening of strain to effect balance which is everywhere at work in Chesterton. Antithesis and epigram serve the same function in the work of these two because they were both metaphysical jesters—one clad in a motley of night-shades, the other in a blaze of jostling colors.

It must be admitted that Chesterton could not live up to his high critical ideals in his first monograph. The book makes three major points. The first is simply that Browning was a poet, not a philosopher. This is a point which needs no laboring at a time when Donne and Eliot are reigning poets; when Edith Sitwell agonizes with Pope as earlier generations did with Shelley, while Yvor Winters condemns Pope for founding the romantic school. But the age fed on Tennyson did believe Browning a crabbed, obscure, and complicated thinker. Chesterton shows that Browning had a purely aesthetic taste for the forms and filigrees of language; that he worked always in the romantic vein where, unless emotion enlightens, everything remains dark. But, though Chesterton stands on firm ground here, and strikes home when he says Browning loved obscurity itself as an artistic form, like a labyrinth, he presents, prominently in the earlier pages, two contrary but equally erroneous interpretations of Browning's "obscurity."[17] He obviously sensed that Browning is *not* complicated, and then "made a case" for his instinct in the matter. The inconsistency came from his failure to accomplish his own purpose. The book is more broken up by chronology and system than his later ones; he tries to "fit in" all the major events of Browning's life, all the marks of his pen, and this divides the analysis into artificial compartments in which misleading distinctions arise.

The second center of emphasis in the book is Browning's relish for the grotesque—a taste Chesterton completely shared. Both men understood that the existential act can be more manifest—when *presented* as an act, by assertive and dramatic thrusts—in ugly things than in beautiful forms, loved for their static symmetry.[18] It is only one of those misleading distinctions already mentioned which made Chesterton separate "obscurity" and "ugliness" throughout the book. They are aspects of the same trait in Browning.[19]

The third point to which Chesterton directs his attention is Browning's "Liberalism." The dramatic monologue represents, in Chesterton's eyes, the advent of "free speech" to poetry. Everyone has a case. Anyone may be the carrier of truth. In such a metaphysical "democracy" Chesterton recognized his own instincts.[20] But Browning's monologues are greatest, not when they present that entire empathy which Chesterton stresses,[21] but when they achieve empathy with irony—so that we see a man from several points, all the points fixed. There is no relativism in Browning's best satirical monologues; nor in "The Ring and the Book," where the points are multiplied to a confusing quantity, but all the more firmly fixed because of this increase in the angles of vision.[22] Chesterton had grown up with Browning and written his early poems in imitation of him. Here he recalls those poems and that tutelage; this is the Liberalism of his boyhood, which rejected dogmas and fixed creeds, putting in its last major appearance.

In the last analysis, therefore, Chesterton's *Browning,* though lively in manner, was a failure. Not free enough of conventional forms, it introduces misleading compartments, distinctions, and interruptions, so that the whole question of "obscurity" is intolerably obscured. The book's defence of optimism and Liberalism leaves out the balancing elements in Browning's work. We must remember, however, that if Chesterton failed, it was because he could not reach the mark on that set of critical scales which he erected in this first volume. He bungled the book but created a form.

Chesterton's next monograph was *G. F. Watts,* done in 1904 for the "Popular Library of Art" series. Watts had captured Chesterton's admiration as early as 1895;[23] and this admiration was confirmed during Chesterton's struggle with Impressionism, since it is the forthright blaze and thrust of Watts that Chesterton praises. Few share that taste now, but it is impossible to deny that Chesterton's praise is tasteful.

The importance of the book, however, derives from its discussion of art as a separate language. Chesterton toyed often with the idea of a color-language; here he tells us that art is such a new tongue, exploring new realities, capturing things in its subtle net which no other set of symbols can compass. Because all signs fail to exhaust the reality we deal with, art's visual "language" fills in important gaps and opens important realms where verbal language fails. The passages on the limits of language[24] and on the harmony between thoughts and things[25] are among the best he ever penned. They show us how he could "argue" for years with Impressionist pictures.

The treatment of art as a separate language is an excellent critical approach. It avoids the literary fallacy which makes painting *follow* words, reducing it to the symbol of a symbol. But it also avoids the error of more recent critics, who assign to painting an impossible sterility of meaning—the status of a non-conveying symbol. To give art this kind of isolation is, literally, idolatry—the worship of a thing as an "absolute" divorced from all contact with reality. Chesterton realized that painting, because it is a unique language, can perform in its own sphere all the functions of language. One can explain with it, drawing diagrams for Euclid or the Underground. One can write sermons with it. One can also write poems in this strange "tongue"—and it is this last function which lifts painting to the level of serious art; where it acts, not as a symbol of other symbols; nor as a meaningless symbol, a sign pointing nowhere; but as a unique medium of contact with reality.

DICKENS

Chesterton's next book of criticism was published in 1906: *Charles Dickens*.[26]

Eliot and Trilling have both praised Chesterton's critical work on Dickens; but Orwell accused him of manufacturing a Catholic Distributist Dickens.[27] Cecil, too, thought his brother's sympathy with Dickens was political.[28] He was perhaps misled by the rapturous overture to the *Dickens*, one of Chesterton's unrestrained tributes to the French Revolution. But Chesterton's thesis is that the Revolution came to Dickens as a lift and heightening of the spirits, not as a political creed or program. "Dickens was not even a politician of any kind."[29] His novels ridicule reformers as frequently as they denounce the guardians of established system; and for the same reason. He did not know how to distinguish good and bad political or economic systems; he knew only who were bad men.[30] It is true that Chesterton always praises Dickens' "democracy"—but only as he speaks of Scott's,[31] or, in later years, of Francis of Assisi's and Louis IX's. "Democracy" was from the first a trans-political concept with Chesterton, though it was some time before he realized this (and a longer period before he would admit it). The democracy of *Thursday* or *The Wild Knight*, like that of St. Francis, is not a theory about monarchy or republics. It is a metaphysical view of being's value in all its manifestations. It is on these grounds that Chesterton calls Shelley an aristocrat and Dickens a democrat, though Shelley was far more strictly republican in theory.[32]

When dealing with Chesterton, the approach through politics is misleading in almost every instance, but never more so than in the case of Dickens. The seed of Chesterton's Dickensian criticism will be found in his *Bookman* essay of 1903 and in the *Daily News* article for February 8, 1902. These essays consider the attack then being mounted against Dickens' *exaggeration;* and it is this discussion of exaggeration, involving as it does the problems of "realism," caricature, symbolism and the entire nature of art, which unifies the book. The chapter on the revolutionary era, for instance, is introduced simply to describe the enthusiasm and "exaggeration" of the period in which Dickens began to write.[33]

Modern critics, shaken by Dostoievski's profound respect for Dickens, have hastily re-read him and discovered symbolism and psychology beneath the sentiment and slapstick. They are now saving great portions of the man, as they save other romantic artists, by giving qualified approval to his later work. The same thing has happened to Verdi's last operas and Delacroix's impressionistic developments. But there is always a hopeless air about such resurrections. He who does not like wild pictures of wild horses is never going to live on the divorced energy of color in Delacroix; there is too much he must ignore, and the strain will show. The man who does not like *Trovatore* can only like *Otello* for the wrong reasons and for a short time. The same thing is true of the moderns who try to extract thin slices of Dostoievski from the earthy mass of Dickens.

Chesterton knew from the first that Dickens' greatness lay in his subtle use of symbol. He does not praise the Dickens characters or satire or humor as such. He contends, rather, that the characters *are* two-dimensional,[34] the humor wild and farcical,[35] the

cheerfulness almost suffocating,[36] and the pathos terribly senti-
mental;[37] only adding that these detached judgments are irrelevant. The aspects which are abstracted and given tags like
"character study" and "satire" cannot truly be evaluated apart from
their use in the whole work.

Dickens does not simply exaggerate his characters, "blowing
them up" as photographers say. He blows up his readers. He stuns
us so that we notice, in the magic light of such drunkenness, those
eccentricities which go everywhere unnoticed. Proof of this lies in
the interest Dickens arouses not only in every minor character, but
in every single piece of life's furniture—the locks that gurgle in
their throats, the moon-faced clocks, lurking furniture, rusty
anchor-watches sunk in depths of waistcoat:

> The date on the door danced over Mr. Grewgious's, the
> knocker grinned at Mr. Scrooge, the Roman on the ceiling
> pointed down at Mr. Tulkinghorn, the elderly armchair leered
> at Tom Smart.[38]

There is a Dickens landscape, a Dickens meal, a Dickens door-
knocker—even a Dickens Christmas. All this is due to "the true
Dickens atmosphere in which clerks are clerks and at the same
time elves."[39] This atmosphere of pugnacious appreciation makes
all things and all men interesting. There is an undercurrent of enjoyment even in the sections descriptive of horror and sorrow, just
as there is enjoyment of odd and repulsive characters. This is not a
morbid taste, or a love of sad lives because they are sad, but a love
of life because it is life, of things as things, of people as miracles.
Dickens likes fog, which causes discomfort; but he likes it only because it impinges on one everywhere, makes one fully conscious of
one's own existence.[40] The Dickens ideal is to be glowing inside
with wine and chafing outside against the fog, because such tension stretches man to the effort of recognizing that there is a thing

called *reality*. Even his sombre later work is sustained by a pugnacious vitality of opposition to all the evils that hover around Bleak
House or the Dombey Company or the Dorrits' prison. The famous fog of *Bleak House* pulsates with a roaring indignation that
is itself a hymn to existence, a challenge issued to evil.[41]

Heightening of human awareness is effected by several kinds of
strain, notably by tragedy. But there is another heightening, more
commonly experienced yet more elusive, rarely expressed in art—
felt, for instance, in the company of friends on a truly joyful occasion. This is not semiconscious complacency but a *tense* joy, of
which Christmas is the universal symbol, though the experience is
more personal and elusive than any public occasion can of itself
suggest. These are the occasions when everything seems a little
more real, a little sharper in outline and richer in color, when
"every man is a caricature of himself."[42] This rare thing Shakespeare could call up as powerfully as he summoned the night mist.
It was part of Chaucer's wide gamut. And in this area of excellence
Dickens can walk even with these poets. The thing seems pecu-
liarly English. Pastoral poetry is ancient, yet there is no *As You
Like It* but in England. The picaresque novel, the caricature which
is grotesque through love and not through cruelty, the kindly
horseplay of tavern and ballad, the "comfortable" laughter of the
English, form a single and unequaled thing.[43] Rabelais has the out-
rageous zest, but his humor is always edged and Gallic. Perhaps
the best way to see what England has contributed to humanity
in this respect is to read Bergson on humor, and then turn to
Dickens.

Chesterton did not have to search around the periphery of
Dickens' work for psychological symbols or profound understanding of persons and issues. He did not isolate some element in his
art—realism, social criticism, or some other quality now in fashion—and praise it where it occurred. There lay at the heart of
Dickens' novels a "farcical occultism"[44] which uncovered the ener-

gies of joy and fueled all the vital worlds he created. That is why Chesterton calls *Pickwick* the central expression of Dickens' art; the primal inspiration of Dickens is at white heat throughout it, giving its formlessness the same unity—a unity of energy, not of pattern—which an explosion has. This first, "formless" novel is like the creation of Light before the stars.[45]

Because all Dickens' people and events and properties are symbols working together, Chesterton does not defend Dickens against the charge of exaggeration; his greatness lay in just this exaggeration, variety, eccentricity, humor—in an energy not caring to justify itself on "practical" or useful terms; in energy unexplained, and a causeless joy:

> His art is like life, because, like life, it cares for nothing outside itself, and goes on its way rejoicing. Both produce monsters with a kind of carelessness, like enormous by-products; life producing the rhinoceros, and art Mr. Bunsby. Art indeed copies life in not copying life, for life copies nothing.[46]

The endless creation of ever wilder grotesques came from Dickens' love of life in all its farthest manifestations. All his eccentrics came from this center, making Dickens, in the judgment of Edmund Wilson, the most creative English artist since Shakespeare.

After the publication of his *Dickens* in 1906, Chesterton was asked to contribute introductions to the Everyman re-issue of the Dickens novels. Over half of this series came out in 1907, the rest appeared in the following years. In 1911 they were collected in a single volume, *Appreciations and Criticisms of the Works of Charles Dickens*. This volume is more disjunct than the monograph,[47] but it is not inferior to it. The introductions do not simply repeat and expand comments in the first book. Their method is different, more technical. Chesterton does not deny that the plot and form of the story are mere framework, often, for the enclosed sketches;

but because Dickens infused life into every object he touched, the frame is as lively as the picture.[48]

Chesterton's view of the novel, expressed in his reviews,[49] is that it is not a single form but in potency to many forms. And Dickens' sense of variety makes him cast his stories into ever-varying shapes and gives to each novel a characteristic atmosphere,[50] an atmosphere at once greater than the novel's formal perfection (for Dickens' is the creative rather than the controlling art), yet suited to the general tradition of the form. Thus Chesterton discerns, as one of the sources of Dickens' strength, an instinctive sympathy with the most popular and eternal forms of literature, whose virtues he incorporated in his tales: the picaresque novel,[51] melodrama,[52] romance,[53] realism,[54] the picturesque setting,[55] ghost stories,[56] popular satire,[57] the utopia,[58] the nightmare,[59] the detective story.[60]

Though the approach is different in this book, Chesterton arrives by every avenue at the same nucleus: exaggeration, energy, "the primum mobile,"[61] a force so occult with irrepressible energy that Dickens' words seem "dipped in dark nonsense"[62] as in some hidden pool of Dionysos:

> a Dickens character hits you first on the nose and then on the waistcoat and then in the eye and then in the waistcoat again, with the blinding rapidity of some battering engine.[63]

Chesterton's criticism of Dickens did not start with his two books, nor end with them. Even when he was in school he had to explain a Dickens reference in one of his reports to the J.D.C.[64] He knew large portions of the novels by heart. He played Sam Weller in a masquerade, and presided as judge over the trial meant to solve the mystery of Edwin Drood.[65] The chair at Dorothy Collins' attic desk is Dickens' own, presented to Chesterton by the Dickens Society. Chesterton used symbols from the novels whenever he spoke in argument or explanation. Unquestionably, then, there was some bond of sympathy between Chesterton's critical and Dickens' creative mind. What was the source of this sympathy?

If Chesterton approached art with a bias, it was a bias for variety, for things in their peculiarity. He praised "otherness," by virtue of which separate things hold their unique measure of being. He praised Scott because his novels go deep into detail, and Dickens because his work towers high into absurdity of exaggeration. There is no higher qualification for the critic than this "bias," for it is a bias against bias. It allows one to see what particular authors intend and to appreciate what they communicate.

Dickens had the same appreciation for variety as such, based on a sense of life's fathomless energy. Such energy could only be expressed in "turgid and preternatural types" because it does, in fact, transcend types and forms. Dickens exaggerates beyond the limits of formal possibility because he is speaking of purer action and energy than belong to the order of essences. Chesterton points out that the novels are timeless in their technique; they deal with an eternal instant of energy.[66] Dickens is, in fact, a creator of myths rather than of novels.[67] His characters have become part of our civilization because they were fashioned out of the ancient stuff of folklore. Pickwick is the ancient of days: in age he arrives at youth and his own springs.[68] Sam Weller is a more moral Puck, the pure spirit of Irony which keeps men unbroken under the unbearable.

Such agreement and personal bias do inform Chesterton's criticism. In Dickens he saw a great unconscious witness to the truths he dwelt on always. In the miraculous bores he saw the mystical minimum; in the appetite for life which no suffering can dull, he saw that gratitude is the source of morality; in the formless perfection of Pickwick he saw that being is more important than essence. He saw Creation in such endless creativity. It is true that Dickens did not see these things himself, that the creator is less conscious than the critic—more conscious, rather, of *things* than of even the most pointedly existential theories. But Chesterton answered beforehand the objection of those who would call his criticism tendentious; and, in the process, defined the office of the critic:

> Criticism does not exist to say about authors the things that they know themselves. It exists to say the things about them which they did not know about themselves. If a critic says that the *Iliad* has a pagan rather than a Christian pity, or that it is full of pictures made by one epithet, of course he does not mean that Homer could have said that. If Homer could have said that the critic would leave Homer to say it. The function of criticism, if it has a legitimate function at all, can only be one function—that of dealing with the subconscious part of the author's mind which only the critic can express, and not with the conscious part of the author's mind, which the author himself can express.[69]

BLAKE AND THE VICTORIAN AGE

William Blake appeared in 1911, part of the same series for which *Watts* had been written, a series therefore in which Blake the engraver and painter was principally to be considered, rather than Blake the poet. But Chesterton directs his attention to the visionary, the mystic, the madman—a course which Blake would have approved of, whatever the editors made of it. They had, in fact, little cause for complaint: this is probably Chesterton's best piece of criticism. *Dickens* is a larger book in every way, with more brilliance and variety, more personal insight, and more error. Compared with it, *Blake* may have what Chesterton called a "narrow perfection." Nonetheless, it has a finish that belongs to no other piece of criticism he undertook.

This is not because of a sympathy in viewpoint. Chesterton was, it is true, drawn to myth, biblical grandeur and prophecy, moral parable and allegory. He had written as a seer, and used the simple aphoristic style. But Blake put these devices at the service of a vision far removed from Chesterton's own.

The book does not enter into the endless theories and interpretations of Blake's prophetic works. Chesterton never used his purely critical instincts so simply; ignoring other critics, and the niceties of the systems which Blake constructed, he looks simply at the style and finds there the secret of the man, his temper and type of mysticism.

The book's structure is its highest merit. Chesterton opens with the comment that a man's biography should begin at the beginning, when earth was sundered from heaven. Those who think Chesterton guilty of "cute" remarks may think he opens an entire book with one; but that sentence is actually a statement of the book's architectural plan. Leaving the larger issues for a moment, Chesterton sketches the major lines of Blake's life: his training under Flaxman, his experience of successive patrons, his response to the varying conditions and stages of his life. Then he asks whether Blake was mad. *No* is the answer to several formulations of this question: he was capable always of practical management, of logical discourse, of contact with the whole range of human realities and outside fact. He was not a fanatic about his visions. He took them, in a very matter-of-fact manner, as truth; and lived with them simply, as wise men do live with truths. But several things jar in this general harmony: his inability to work at a thing without crippling it somehow, the involuntary repetitions of poor lines in his poetry—dark chants, not put there at the urging of his artistic sense but of something alien. Here Chesterton touches the nerve of the matter. Blake is a better poet when his "spirits" are not interfering. He never speaks gibberish except when commanded to; he worked carefully and classically in his better poems and in all his engraving and visual imagery. On this evidence, Chesterton, without doubting the reality of his spiritual experiences, calls them a crippling influence on Blake's artistry—an influence alien, though not finally predominant.

The strengths and weaknesses of Blake's mind were related to the achievements and failures of his age. Chesterton, romantic though he was, respected the manliness and firm lines of the eighteenth century. Pope and Johnson were among his favorite authors, and he describes the Roman air of public life and humanism which made the age of reason great. But this elevation of the intellect sent instinct and religious feeling into subterranean and sinister channels: Cagliostro, Mesmer, Swedenborg, and the Freemasons appealed to a perverse and anarchic appetite for mystery, caused by the bland rationality of the period. Chesterton has great respect for Swedenborg, as for Blake; but in both he sees a stridency and unbalance caused by the fact that they were rebelling against the temper of their time.

Yet Chesterton will not put Blake in this rebel camp when he considers his work as a whole. The strongest thing in him was reason and clarity, as anyone can see who looks at his clear-cut lines or the syntax and rhetoric of his poems. Chesterton, contrasting his draughtsmanship with that of the Impressionists or the Rubens-like "expressionists" whom Blake attacked, describes his vision as Platonic, gnostic, *defined*. He contrasts this feeling for hard individuality with Oriental mysticism, which seeks to deny variety and the separate person, pooling things in some simple unity, dissolving the forms into one Light or one Darkness. In other words, Chesterton returns to the moment of creation, when earth was sundered from heaven.

Blake's "portrait" of Newton shows a giant figure naked under the sun, drawing hard forms upon the earth. That is the kind of picture Chesterton has etched—looking first at Blake's merely factual biography, then at his place and surroundings in time, and finally at the timeless aspect of his work. This is Blake rendered in the style of Blake.

The Victorian Age in Literature (1913) can justly be considered the last of a series. Fourteen years elapse between it and the appearance of his next long essay in criticism—*Robert Louis Stevenson;* and six years after this, *Chaucer* was written, the last book Chesterton devoted to an artist.

According to Chesterton, the literature of the Victorian age was conditioned throughout by the fact that poetry was severed from life by the utilitarian rulers of history at this juncture. Rebellion was driven into the politically sterile world of exotic poetry, and the burghers of England coldly came to terms with the ancient rulers of privilege. Middle-class religiosity and economics were joined to aristocratic political forms, and the Victorian Compromise effected. Chesterton sees the course of letters shaped by a series of attacks on this compromise. Romanticism, humored as an impractical and inconsequent amusement, kept asserting its right to speak of real things and to overthrow existing values. Dickens, Ruskin, Carlyle, Arnold, Newman—all were praised as stylists, poets, and "characters"; then ignored as politicians, critics, and teachers.

Chesterton begins his actual criticism with the novel, tracing its distinctive notes with that largeness and sense of distance which came from his refusal to work close to or clamp down references. The first fact that distinguishes the nineteenth-century novel from its manly sources in the eighteenth century is the feminine atmosphere which grew up around it. This does not mean merely that Jane Austen, the Brontës, George Eliot, Ouida, Mrs.

Oliphant, and others wrote novels. The period seemed to encourage feminine qualities even in male novelists. Prudish restraint and lack of militarism are signs of this; and these link the novel to that general toning down and compromise which the middle class effected. But the real origin of this trait, according to Chesterton, is the fact that the nineteenth-century English novel was a study of character on the most idiosyncratic level. (On this basis he goes so far as to rank Browning with the novelists.)[70] The male mind is abstractive, symbolic, poetic. The female mind, far from being airy and over-pure, is practical, intent on single persons and the thing at hand. This feminine character is that of the novel in England (as distinguished, for instance, from the Russian novel in the nineteenth century): it dealt in differences and subtleties of character rather than issues of time and eternity:

> Once the divine darkness against which we stand is really dismissed from the mind (as it was very nearly dismissed in the Victorian time) the differences between human beings become overpoweringly plain, whether they are expressed in the high caricatures of Dickens or the low lunacies of Zola.[71]

In the last chapter of the book Chesterton at last confronts two things which he had kept suspended in his mind for some time. Previously he had upheld the nineteenth century's spacious Liberalism, yet attacked the decadent eighties and nineties as a reaction against the old Liberals' serious ideals. He had not faced the problem that the decadents, though enemies of the Victorian morality, were produced by it. Their art for art's sake was a drunken variant of the stern age's commerce for commerce' sake, science for science' sake. But in this chapter he realizes that his twin creeds—Christianity and Liberalism—had practically destroyed each other in their nineteenth-century English forms of Protestantism and Benthamism.

His comments on the decadents are concerned with their artistic claims, not with the diabolic significance he once found in their work. The artifacts produced by this school are valid, but only when seen from one evanescent point; they have a narrow compass, so that nothing could be more ill-suited, aesthetically, than the illustration of Malory by Beardsley.[72] Light stirred in the *fin-de-siècle* twilight, taking two forms, socialist and imperialist, when the works of Shaw and Kipling appeared. Gilbert admits here what Cecil had borne in upon him by argument—the unintended influence of Stevenson upon the imperialists.[73]

The Victorian Age is marked by great caution and fairness: Dickens, Browning, Stevenson, and Chesterton's other heroes are discussed with full consciousness of their faults, while even Wilde and Beardsley are praised for what was strong in both men.[74] The extracts often quoted from this little volume are even more misleading than such isolated citations normally are; the book is a masterpiece of arrangement, of suspension and counter-tension, whereby names are lifted in large webs of inter-reacting influence. Almost everyone who has mentioned the book quotes or refers to Chesterton's cameo analyses of his favorite authors—Ruskin, Dickens, Browning. But he is equally good on Newman, Arnold, and others. He sees exactly how the apparently opposed qualities of Newman—intellectual lucidity and emotional richness—reinforce each other, giving urgency to every explanation, to every extension of a Newman period:

> The quality of his logic is that of a long but passionate patience, which waits until he has fixed all corners of an iron trap.[75]

Thackeray is often introduced into Chesterton's pages only as a foil to Dickens, but here he contrasts the "magnesium blazes" of Dickens with Thackeray's evocative magic:

Thackeray is everybody's past, is everybody's youth. Forgotten friends flit about the passages of dreamy colleges and unremembered clubs, we hear fragments of unfinished conversations, we see faces without names for an instant, fixed forever in some trivial glance; we smell the strong smell of social cliques now quite incongruous to us; and there stir in all the little rooms at once the hundred ghosts of oneself. For this purpose Thackeray was equipped with a singularly easy and sympathetic style, carved in slow curves where Dickens hacked out images with a hatchet.[76]

There are as many examples of this instinct for style and its meaning as there are names in the book. One example chosen from the many will conclude this chapter.

In *Heretics* Chesterton had criticized the Rubaiyat's attitude toward wine; but he praised FitzGerald's style for "combining the gay pugnacity of an epigram with the vague sadness of a song."[77] In *The Victorian Age* he extends that critical judgment when discussing the Rubaiyat:

> its most arresting quality is a combination of something haunting and harmonious that flows by like a river or a song, with something else that is compact and pregnant like a pithy saying picked out in rock by the chisel of some pagan philosopher. It is at once a tune that escapes and an inscription that remains. Thus, alone among the reckless and romantic verses that first rose in Coleridge and Keats, it preserves something also of the wit and civilization of the eighteenth century. Lines like "A Muezzin from the tower of darkness cries" or "Their mouths are stopped with dust" are successful in the same sense as "Pinnacled dim in the intense inane" or "Through verdurous glooms and winding mossy ways." But

> Indeed, indeed, repentance oft before
> I swore; but was I sober when I swore?

is equally successful in the same sense as

> Damn with faint praise, assent with civil leer
> And without sneering teach the rest to sneer.

It thus earned a right to be considered the complete expression of that scepticism and sensual sadness into which later Victorian literature was more and more falling away; a sort of bible of unbelief. For a cold fit had followed the hot fit of Swinburne which was of a feverish sort: he had set out to break down without having, or even thinking he had, the rudiments of rebuilding in him. . . . The nineteenth-century sceptics did not really shake the respectable world and alter it, as the eighteenth-century sceptics had done; but that was because the eighteenth-century sceptics were something more than sceptics, and believed in Greek tragedies, in Roman laws, in the Republic. . . . But these later poets did, so to speak, spread their soul in all the empty spaces; weaker brethren, disappointed artists, unattached individuals, very young people, were sapped or swept away by these songs; which, so far as any poetic sense in them goes, were almost songs without words. It is because there is something which is after all indescribably manly, intellectual, firm about FitzGerald's way of phrasing the pessimism that he towers above the slope that was tumbling down to the decadents. . . . [78]

The quotation is incomplete, on both ends and in the middle, because I do not wish to give the impression of a separate piece from what is only the woof of a larger design. Here we can see, though, how Chesterton weaves: the echo of epigram in the style *is* a sign of some eighteenth-century virtue in the poem, since the eighteenth century resounded with Rome and the older, more chiseled paganism; not to be confused with the effeminate delicacy of second-rate Swinburnes.[79] This is always the way Chesterton the critic goes to work—quick not only to recognize the distinct tenor of an artist's phrasing but to see through this sacramental word the ultimate *verbum* of a man.

5.

A GRAMMAR OF LUNACY

In 1901 Chesterton married; in 1909 he moved out of London to Beaconsfield. These dates frame what may be called his golden years on Fleet Street. A publisher's reader exploded suddenly into that incessant talk and laughter, overflowing in all directions, which stunned Fleet Street and all of London. The distinguished author who edited *The Clarion* found himself wondering out loud how he had become so totally embroiled in debate with a man not yet thirty years old. Bernard Shaw let it be known to all that Chesterton was his favorite foe. Chesterton seemed not only to have appeared from nowhere but to be omnipresent—entering every controversy, known in every pub along Fleet Street, lecturing everywhere. His name leaped out at readers from the pages of every kind of journal and paper—academic, religious, political, partisan, obscure, trivial, absurd.

The first thing which struck those who watched Chesterton's emergence was his mirth. His early doubts and morbidities, his externally sterile years as a publisher's reader, his uncertainty about career and the task to be done—all these clouds which hung over his early life had been dispersed by 1900; they vanished so completely that men would later have difficulty in believing they had ever passed over him. He came before the world as a jester with a word for all, for the wise and the foolish; and wise and foolish listened. He gained wife, fame, enemies, experience, money, and weight in a swirl of activity made almost feverish by the sudden contrast with his obscure and static years. At first sight he seems merely to have been swept along by this heady conflict with Wells, Shaw, Blatchford, Campbell, and others. But there was an instinct in Chesterton which made him follow the inner logic of the role he had, from the same instinct, assumed.

In his first *Speaker* articles (republished, as we have said, as *The Defendant*), Chesterton took the most trivial and despised things—penny dreadfuls, slang, detective stories—and proved their unique value, their truly "ultimate" value, by pushing them back to the edge of nothingness, limning their merits against that background. Some early book reviews from *The Speaker* and *The Daily News* were next republished, in variously altered forms, as *Twelve Types*. These, too, are defences—of antithesis and the satiric couplet (Pope), of romance (Scott), of asceticism (Francis), of rhyme (Rostand), even of scepticism (Charles II).

THE RHYTHM OF THOUGHT

In these first books, and in his early reviews, Chesterton already used a recurrent rhythm of development. He begins by discussing an oddity or strange aspect of his subject, treated with what seems pure whimsy; then he stumbles "unexpectedly" across a serious issue involved in the oddity; an argument follows, conducted as a dialectic cross-fire of objections; which climbs gradually onto a loftier plane of rhetoric, to reach a towering peroration. In a typical case, reviewing on its appearance Butler's translation of the *Odyssey*, Chesterton jests about Butler's claim that a woman wrote the poem; he suggests, in the light of this version, that Butler really believes it was a charwoman. The issue that is discovered here is the modern distrust of the heroic, an attitude criticized on several planes; and the rhetorical peroration sweeps to a vision of some hero returning to the crowded room of striving and ambitious suitors for fame, one who can lift and draw the heavy bow of Ulysses.[1] This resembles the full organ of Chesterton's conclusion to things like the "Defence of Penny Dreadfuls," or the Rostand essay in *Twelve Types*.

This rhythm of development remained operative in Chesterton's best work. The whimsical opening is not an accident or journalist's trick; it *is* Chesterton's response to reality, a response of wonder at the oddity of being. And, in their address to others, these opening comments have the mark of the jester, of one who comments on the immediate situation with a detached irony and objectivity of amusement. Nor is the rhetorical release at the end of the wave's movement mere appendage. It represents the moment when, by argument and irony and laughter, Chesterton has reached the point where he can use the mantic tone of the notebooks, pouring out his praise of existence without fear of the egoism, the sentimentality, the fanaticism which haunt the prophet.

In this paradoxical rhythm, moving from joke to jeremiad, paradox is fully deployed only in the central, argumentative section. There one senses battle even when Chesterton is not belaboring some named opponent. Some have claimed that Chesterton could only write *against* people, and he gave the impression, throughout his early career, that he was always attacking other men's positions because he had none of his own to establish or defend. But he had begun by arguing with himself. Long before he met foes of the caliber of Shaw, he had pursued the long and involved arguments within his own mind which led him at last against a blank wall. This taught him the barren nature of logic when it is used as anything but a set of procedural rules. He was a terribly effective logician, but he wrote some of his most lucid passages to prove that logic is a weapon of destruction or defense, not a tool for building.[2] Logic considers the necessary relations between concepts, but it cannot set this entire machinery of interrelated essential notes against a background of being and nothingness. That is the reason Chesterton called it a comparatively barren form of dialectic.

Chesterton's own internal conflict had revealed to him another kind of struggle; this was a creative conflict, and it led to a process of thought radically different from the circular machinery of logic. The Chestertonian dialectic is a transition from mere syllogistic exercises to this creative conflict of metaphysical paradox. The first process he analyzed in *Orthodoxy* as "the suicide of thought." The second he studied under various names—mysticism, poetry, magic, and fairy tale; but primarily as *paradox*.

THE BLATCHFORD CONTROVERSY

A fine example of this dialectic is that formative controversy, which filled so many columns of so many journals in 1903 and 1904, between Chesterton and the editor of the socialist *Clarion,* Robert Blatchford. Chesterton attacked some of Blatchford's statements in his *Daily News* column; Blatchford noticed this, and responded in kind. Soon each was in pursuit of the other on his home ground. Then Chesterton ran a special series of five articles in *The Commonwealth* as part of this increasing campaign, and the debate further ramified into whatever journals were available to the participants. Like the endless duel in unlikely places which Chesterton was about to describe in *The Ball and the Cross,* this controversy was disjointed yet continuous. As Chesterton remarked,

> No doubt there is something a little bewildering at first about a discussion leaping in this way from journal to journal; but all reforms seem unfamiliar, and when Mr. Blatchford has produced his crushing reply to this in "The Electrical Times," and I my dignified rejoinder in "Nuggets," people will have begun to get in the swing of things.[3]

Finally, in 1904, when Blatchford instituted a series of articles in *The Clarion* which should defend the Christian case against his own assault, Chesterton contributed four articles—more than any other of the defending spokesmen—which summed up his growing argument. The whole series was reprinted, under an eccentric title, as "The Religious Doubts of Democracy."

Chesterton's first article in this series, "Christianity and Rationalism," takes Blatchford's logical denials of revelation and makes of them logical demonstrations. This is admittedly a tour de force, meant only to show that Blatchford's arguments are themselves a forcing of logic to a task it cannot sustain. Blatchford used the methods of history and psychology (instruments of shadowy terror in that afterglow of Darwin and the Higher Criticism) to discredit Christianity, proving by "what happens" what *cannot* happen, invoking process against exception. He tried to make logic predetermine fact. This is the barren dialectic, and Chesterton deftly reduces it to absurdity.

In his second article, "Why I Believe in Christianity," Chesterton moves from the first to the second kind of dialectic. The determinist lives a set of contradictions, professing irresponsibility but acting on the assumption that the will is free. The Christian takes this conflict into his theory and admits paradox, saying that we are linked to God directly (and so determined), yet linked precisely by God's determination that we be free. Derived existence and real identity do mysteriously conflict; but this conflict—however hidden from the processes of logic—is generative. Mystery is answered by other, corroborating mysteries: we know that man is ultimately good, though immediately evil—pure in his source, though corrupt in his more narrowly autonomous self.

The third article, "Miracles and Modern Civilization," establishes the difference between the two dialectics—that which explains the processes of the universe and that which explains the presence of the universe. Miracles, of course, are opposed to the processes of nature, to the "rules" established periodically by scientists: but they are not infractions of the higher principles which deal with the *presence* of the universe, since that presence is itself a miracle, a standing contradiction and exception.

The fourth article, "The Heroism of the Slums," is an *ad hominem* argument directed at the editor and readers of the socialist paper in which this series appeared, showing that determinism is a weak foundation on which to base reforms of any kind.

Maisie Ward finds in these articles, though I cannot, a clearly stated belief in Christ's divinity (a belief which Chesterton had earlier treated as unimportant).[4] In his *Daily News* column for Dec. 19, 1903, Chesterton answered four questions Blatchford had put to him, and the first two run thus:

Are you a Christian? Certainly.

What do you mean by Christian? The belief that a certain human being whom we call Christ stood to a certain super-human being whom we call God in a certain unique transcendental relation which we call sonship.[5]

The answer is as carefully worded as it is brief, and we must therefore take as intended the opposition between "human being" and "superhuman being." In the controversy itself, Chesterton wrote that Christ "had a strange psychic energy of which we know nothing."

Maisie Ward not only cuts the four articles to three but describes them as a "sketch of some elements of Christian theology."[6] This seems to me to mistake their aim, and to run counter to Chesterton's own judgment of their significance:

That this stage may be understood, it must be realised what the things I was defending against Blatchford were. It was not a question of some abstract theological thesis, like the definition of the Trinity or the dogmas of Election or Effectual Grace. I was not yet so far gone in orthodoxy as to be so theological as all that. What I was defending seemed to me a plain matter of ordinary human morals. Indeed it seemed to me to raise the question of the very possibility of any morals. It was the question of Responsibility, sometimes called the question of Free Will. . . . It was not that I began by believing in supernormal things. It was that the unbelievers began by disbelieving even in normal things. It was the secularists who drove me to theological ethics, by themselves denying any sane or rational possibility of secular ethics. I might myself have been a secularist, so long as it meant that I could be merely responsible to secular society. It was the Determinist who told me, at the top of his voice, that I could not be responsible at all. And as I rather like being treated as a responsible being, and not as a lunatic let out for the day, I began to look around for some spiritual asylum that was not merely a lunatic asylum.[7]

Baffled by the barren logic of the rationalist, Chesterton moved onto a different plane of argument. Instinctively he had done this during his first encounter with solipsism; now he was conscious of his action, and defending it. The emphasis is metaphysical throughout; Chesterton is not defending faith as a supernatural principle, but "paradox" as a higher use of reason than logic—the normal and healthy employment of the mind.

Before we leave these four articles, which are thoroughly typical of Chesterton's early controversies, we may ask what the contemporary reader made of them. Though Chesterton always "scored" brilliantly, he seemed ultimately to be playing a game. The reason for this impression is that Chesterton was not simply arguing with Blatchford. Blatchford set the dialectic in motion, but, once moving, this process followed its own inner dictates, setting up poles of creative opposition. This polarity of Chesterton's arguments was easily mistaken for mere juggling from one hand to the other. This suspicion would grow in volume and intensity until Chesterton was forced to devote the whole of *Orthodoxy* to the explanation and defence of his method. But even before we examine that defence we can see that Chesterton's dialectic works according to internal laws and is not a string of debater's tricks. This explains the sharp cut and thrust of Chesterton's rejoinders, yet the complete absence of personal enmity or any baser heat of debate. Ideas fight *each other* in his mind, as the symbolic characters do in his novels.

At this stage, however, we can ask why Chesterton explained yet disguised the nature of "paradox" by clothing it in motley. The answer is simple: Chesterton was not a philosopher, nor did he want to be. He was a defender of philosophy, which is quite another thing.

Philosophy, being a scientific discipline, can assign order to all things within its competence. Neither God nor primal chaos escapes its sweep and purview. But, like all other disciplines, it cannot order itself. Just as one must stand above science to weigh its ultimate significance—and rise above poetry, or prayer, or ping-pong, to assign them their place on an ultimate scale—so one cannot answer "what good is it?" of philosophy except from a point of judgment situated above philosophy. It may sound rash to demand such a lofty eminence, but men have in fact always felt the need for it and held that certain persons stood upon it. St. Paul contrasted "the wisdom of this world" with a higher knowledge, and all men have in practice felt a distinction between philosophy and wisdom. Dr. Johnson, for instance, was not trained in the science of philosophy, but he defended that discipline with his own humanistic wisdom. Prophets are the only men who by their office have been such legislators for philosophy; prophets, and their reverse image—jesters. St. Paul, it will be remembered, said the higher wisdom seems folly when weighed on the lesser scales of this world.

Now Chesterton began his career with the ideal of opposing pessimism and praising existence. He began with several allies, as he thought—Stevenson, Whitman, Browning. But poets have strong preferences in their praise of existents, and Whitman praised even nonexistence when the whimsy took him, as in the lilac-rhapsody on Lincoln's death. When Chesterton engaged in actual debate, he began searching for a philosophy or religion which would praise existence as such, "on principle." But philosophers were not listened to by the world in which Chesterton moved. Therefore he made it his business to convince men that philosophy is more important than the physical sciences, theology more exciting than blasphemy, orthodoxy more practical than heresy.

As a jester, Chesterton made his paradoxical stance conscious and emphatic, telling "efficient" men they could succeed only by becoming theorists. On this level his argument was a pragmatic one. And here we run up against Margaret Clarke's objection to Chesterton, that already discussed in the introduction. She claims that his early writings were not truly Christian but gnostic in their insistence on results. This contention, like most criticism of Chesterton's paradox, is a more perverse oxymoron than he ever constructed. Chesterton, romantic and the friend of forlorn hopes, who edited the journal of what was manifestly a defeated cause, could never have been a millenarist looking for an earthly reward. But the evidence Miss Clarke adduces, before becoming paradoxical, has real import. She sees obvious facts which many have overlooked. It is true that *Heretics* and *Orthodoxy* are not examples of Christian apologetic. *Orthodoxy* is, on one level, personal apologia and defence; its further aim, along with *Heretics*, is to help re-establish certitude and philosophical realism against the flux of progressivism and scientific relativism. Chesterton's Christian apologetic was written much later.

Chesterton's argument in these two books *is* pragmatic. He is not stating a particular philosophy, he is defending philosophy itself. Those who do this are always discussing the *use* of human knowledge (or frequently, as in Paul's case and Nietzsche's, the uselessness). Prophets are totally concerned with practice, and faith submits philosophy to the same pragmatic test which all created things must meet, of final usefulness *sub specie aeternitatis*. The jester, then, in a court of efficient scientists and self-sufficient artists, must especially insist upon the practical value of theory and dogma. But this value is not measured in terms of worldly "success."

Chesterton announces his pragmatic purpose in the introduction to *Heretics*, where he tells the parable of a monk who is a practical man because a metaphysician. Chesterton is not claiming that the monk's philosophy is right, but that the monk is right to be a philosopher. The moderns, who forswore dogma in the name of progress, worshiped strength and success—Shaw and Wells in the Superman, Kipling in Imperialism, Whistler in art. These men were brilliant and sincere, but they were impractical. Men will not strive in a great birth-pang of the Superman; they only transcend themselves by trying to become more profoundly human. Men will not love their country and improve it by complacently thrusting it upon others. Nor will they succeed in art by studying their own poses in a mirror, but by looking outwards toward reality.

Chesterton attacks many "heretics" in the book, but all for the same reason. Men try to broaden themselves by attacking the family, Christmas, jesting, or drink, in the name of travel and knowledge, solemnity, hygiene, science—in short, by sacrificing lasting values to the immediate gains of "progress" and relative improvement. But they narrow themselves and fail to touch the human nerve whose responses work real transformations. The worship of success is arrogant and unscrupulous, while real achievement is worked by humility and fixed ideals. Science claims it can improve man by studying probabilities, but religion transforms man by making him accomplish impossibilities. The gravity of science and neo-paganism, of politics and business, is efficient only as a destructive force; to build and lift things, men need an almost supernatural levity.

Heretics was meant to be, and is, a defence of philosophy. But in combining and reshaping *Daily News* articles which should enforce this theme, Chesterton included of necessity his reflections on other things that preoccupied him at this period—especially ritual and romance, for he was moving toward the High Anglican positions on the liturgy and Modernism. Nonetheless, Christianity is defended only incidentally in this book, and as an extension of its theme. Faith, hope, and charity are called "inventions" of the Christian body, whereby it proved psychologically broader than the reasonable pagan systems.[8] Chesterton explicitly refuses to deal with Christ's claim or words. His subject is "historic Christianity with all its sins on its head; I take it as I would take Jacobinism, or Mormonism, or any other mixed or unpleasing product."[9] This policy is observed throughout the book. Speaking of Shaw's golden rule that there is no golden rule, Chesterton says, "I am not discussing now with any fullness whether this is so or not,"[10] and goes on to say that idealism *accomplishes* more than such cynicism. Christ's offering of wine is contrasted with Omar's on a purely natural level, as celebration opposed to medication. Christianity is praised for its common sense, its understanding of man's needs. The monk of the parable is not called a mystic; he is practical because concerned with theory. To this paradox and parable of the monk the book returns, in the last pages, and finds its goal.

ORTHODOXY: THE BARREN DIALECTIC

Orthodoxy—written three years later (1908)—takes a longer journey, toward a higher goal. In the first book Chesterton forswore all argument beyond the pragmatic prelude to philosophical speculation; in the second he writes, "I wish to set forth my faith."[11] This personal apologia was made possible because the book represents an arrival. No longer is Christianity a hypothesis, as in the Blatchford controversy, or a fine code of common sense, as in *Heretics*. It is "my faith," and the Church's authoritative character is the last link—or, rather, the anchor—to the chain of argument. *Heretics* was a recasting of separate reviews and articles, united by a single theme but not by an advancing strategy of argument. *Orthodoxy*'s eight long chapters are progressive and continuous, and they reveal something new: not respect for religion, merely, nor religious instincts, but a firm religious faith. The parable which opens the book is not of a hypothetical monk's practicality but of Chesterton's personal discovery.

In the introductory chapter, Chesterton presents his faith as an answer not to all men's arguments but to his own dilemma and needs—especially his need for romance. He finds in romance the higher dialectic of paradox—the quest for things at once ancient and new, the need for exploration and return, for Troy and Ithaca.

Yet he renounces, in the second chapter ("The Maniac"), the dialectic he means to discover. He will make his way thither through the barren dialectic of the solely logical mind. The traditional religious quest opens with the problem of good and evil; discovering both good and evil within himself, man rises to God from a realization of personal sin. But this is an existential journey. The question whether man is good or evil is only a part of the question whether *being* is good or evil. Original sin and man's corruption raise all the problems of the Manicheans and nihilists, planting us solidly in the realm of metaphysics. The "moderns" had in Chesterton's day denied the validity of metaphysics, and the experience of sin, and the distinction between good and evil. Chesterton decides, therefore, to meet them on their own terms. If sin is not a test and origin for the study of man's relation to reality, then madness is. The existential discussion led to beatitude or damnation. The essentialist dialectic is logical, and should lead to truth or error. The final error is that which not only distorts things but destroys the instrument for reaching truth. To err means to go wide of the mark, and the last error is mental aimlessness, the complete unstringing of the bow. Chesterton takes this test as apt for the logical dialectic; and by this test it is proved barren.

Isolated reason, what Chesterton calls the pure promptitude of the mind, is sterile. It can prove anything because, with its complete impartiality, it can choose any hypothesis to work from. That is why madmen's arguments are so unassailable on the level of logic. The more vigorously logic prosecutes its own internal pursuit, the greater is the danger of its turning away from direct experience and fact. Its arguments may be perfect, but the perfection is narrow and circular. The philosophers who defend an absolute materialism or an absolute idealism are using the madman's detailed reasoning; no contradictions or exceptions intrude into this perfect circle, because direct experience of different levels of reality is not taken as its own test. Logical consistency is more important to the rationalist and the madman than the immediate reality of fact.

Chesterton's next chapter, "The Suicide of Thought," asks why reason cannot meet its own test. It is not because the intellect is a useless tool. Chesterton does not attack the mind but comes to its defence: pure reason is irrational reason, the use of an instrument against its proper aim. The mind is constructive, as those mediaeval thinkers realized who called logic an art as well as a science. Syllogisms are pieces of architecture; the mind must take the materials for this manufacturing process from life, through man's entire perceptive apparatus. When reason takes upon itself the task of entire discovery and construction, it makes discovery impossible. A sculptor who wants all the credit for his work is a bit vain if he is only jealous of his teachers or his forebears. But if he is jealous of the marble and refuses any help from it, no statues will ever receive his proud care. So of the mind. When pure reason asserts that it will accept nothing which it cannot justify on its own terms, it destroys itself.

Descartes wrote *Cogito ergo sum,* beginning his journey in the chamber of his own intellect. Because he did not look out from that chamber but at it, his journey never got under way; and man is still sitting inside a narrow room cogitating on cogitation. If we *are* only because we think, then we are what we think, and all things are what we think or do not think them; the lunatic *is* God. Rationalism's attack on faith becomes an attack on reason: "With a long and sustained tug we have attempted to pull the mitre off pontifical man; and his head has come off with it."[12]

Chesterton recognizes several stages along this road, or several degrees of exhaustion in this endless round of effort. The mystique of evolution and progress came from this substitution of process for perception. When men were left with nothing but the process of cogitation, they hoped something would come of it if it merely continued long enough. They could live without fixed anchorage in reality by simply waiting for the future or pursuing the processes of time. But this only led to an acceleration of that centripetal force that denies all outlet to the mind.

Another hope for escape was offered in pure volition, taking Nietzschean-existentialist forms. But because this was merely an escape from Cartesian intellection, it remained a reflection of it, opposed only as things are when reversed in a mirror. Rationalism is the ally of all unreason. In his motion of mere escape from reason, Nietzsche had to deny all perceptive tests and fixed norms of fact; but this takes away the point of the will—the grip and exclusion, the creative and destructive choice. Nietzsche's worship of will is Dionysian, simple ecstasy and expenditure in the void. It gives the will no goal, it carries the will nowhere. Such expenditure of will, as of intellect, is self-destructive. Dionysos is the god of dissolution.

The barren dialectic has been pursued to a standstill. It can go no farther; in fact, it has gone nowhere at all. Progress, evolution, free thought, and lawless will are clearly not moving forward. It is time to go back—to the beginning.

ORTHODOXY—THE HIGHER DIALECTIC

The higher dialectic—no longer of mind with mind, but of mind with fact—is opened in the next chapter, "The Ethics of Elfland." The mind deals in necessity. Given the number system, all the table of its later relations and maneuvers *must* follow in a strictly determined way. Given both premises, the conclusion *must* follow. This mental action can become a mental appetite: men forget that conclusions are made to *follow,* but not to *be.* They transfer the rules of the mind to external processes. Then, adding fallacy to fallacy, they discern necessity where there is none—for instance, in repetition. Because an apple tree always produces apples, the mind assumes that it *must* do so, without having any real grounds for asserting this necessity. One can say that certain chemical components of the tree result in what he sees resulting; he can discuss more and more of the operative elements in the genesis of apples. But all this is only a more detailed description of the process. To say that X and Y do such and such is only a more complete and lengthy way of saying that apple trees produce apples. As Ruskin said, men look at the stuff that produces green leaves, give it the Greek name for "green leaf" (chlorophyl), and think they have explained everything. But description prolonged or repeated forever is not a proof of necessity. Sooner or later, the mind must confess that it is dealing with a fact it did not invent but simply found. At this point, the tide turns against the insane rationalism of the first two chapters, and sanity returns.

Given matter, it acts according to its nature, says the scientist; but what necessity was there for our being given matter, asks Chesterton, opening a new level of mystery below the talk of inevitability and "law." Necessity belongs to the realm of determined things, of *definition,* but there is no discernible necessity for the presence of the things to be defined. Repetition dulls our wonder at things but does not make them intrinsically less wonderful. The sun *happens* as freshly now as on the first day of its rising. The mystery of that "first act" is not dispelled—or even touched—by all the successive theories about the sun's secondary actions and wanderings. As St. Augustine said, the birth of any baby is far more miraculous than the resurrection of Lazarus.

The intellect is not self-sufficient and enclosed, but one member in a "give-and-take," in an endlessly reflecting and reinforcing dialectic. Trees stand not by virtue of a scientific formula but by a mystery outside the mind. The fairy tales are right. Trees stand by magic. Once the world has been sundered from the mind, it becomes elfland. If repetition is not determination, perhaps it is conspiracy. At any rate, it does not "follow" on anything as a "conclusion." It is, to "pure reason," inexplicable (or, as modern existentialists would say, absurd). We have escaped the prison of the mind.

But existentialism was not for Chesterton merely an escape or release. We have seen his criticism of Nietzsche, who fell from the rationalists' vacuum into the void of Dionysos. Chesterton escapes the mind in order to enter the world, to achieve and reject things. The tree's presence is inexplicable, but it *is* limited by a certain form, or it would not be a tree at all. This is the second fairy-tale truth—that condition and limit are necessary for the preservation of being. An appreciation of the importance of limit, of being's dependence on defining form, explains to Chesterton his first conception of the world in terms of endearing diminutives. Compared with Being's boundless act, all beings we know are small in compass and possessed on sufferance, an infinite good in a finite container. "I hoarded the hills."[13]

This concept of limit is further developed in the next chapter, "The Flag of the World." In protecting the forms and vessels of existence, in guarding the boundaries of the universe, man exercises a kind of metaphysical patriotism. Optimism is the fault of the cosmic jingo, and pessimism of the cosmic traitor, men who think of the world as the subject of simple praise or blame. But the cosmic patriot's attitude is complex, reflecting the dialectic of reality: he sees that the world *is,* and he loves that; then he can attack faults and praise merits in the scheme of things without losing that first loyalty to reality. This committed criticism and lover's reform is more like the wife's attempts to change her husband than her plans for changing the furniture—at once more violent and more tender. Christianity establishes this first loyalty and correspondent criticism, as can be seen in her distinction between the resignation of the suicide and the resolution of the martyr.

As the mind sunders the world from its own processes in order to find reality, so God sunders the cosmos from himself, giving man identity, individuality, something belonging to the unique person. But this otherness could not be without a sameness, without the Being we derive directly and continuously from His own deepest Act. Thus all existent things deserve a first unbounded loyalty, and then a strict vigilance of control; like Redfeather facing Orm, we can attack the world in the name of the world, defending Being against the individual distortion which beings can effect.

In chapter six, "The Paradoxes of Christianity," Chesterton derives an ethics from this dialectic view of reality. The pagan ethic created by Plato and Aristotle had been one of moderation. But that accepted by the Christian world is marked by fierceness because it is paradoxical, a thing of "love and wrath both burning"— the love directed to existence, the wrath to the perversion of existence. One *can* love the sinner and hate the sin, both violently; or be deeply humble because of one's failings yet toweringly proud of one's existence. The mystery of courage is such a paradox: a self-forgetful love of existence, opposed to the cold calculation of "advantages." The brave man loves existence enough to accept it gladly even in the straitened conditions of danger. He will "be a man" even if he dies; he will lose his life to save it.

The Aristotelian ethic is one of calculation and the golden mean, not of such flaming concomitants. It tempers pride and meanness to a reasonable median because it is based on a formal and not an existential metaphysics. Dilution and moderation are not the appropriate response to the wild act of existence. The dialectic between activity and form in things should be echoed by distinct but intense responses in man—heights of pride and depths of humility balanced and sustained by creative tension and response, not simply diluted. This is the ethic by which we must judge Christian saints (extravagant hybrists by the pagan norm, their flaming love and humility shattering the level of safe compromise among the virtues). By it we must judge the entire history and art and achievement of Christendom, a thing of energy and tension, like the sprung and sustaining arches of Gothic, which leap higher and stretch wider than the balanced lintel of a Greek temple.

ORTHODOXY—DIALECTIC IN POLITICS AND THEOLOGY

The next two chapters apply this ethic to politics and theology: "The Eternal Revolution" criticizes those who would reform the world by pursuing some simple "progress." Reality is a pattern of dialectic tensions, and one must have a total ideal in order to understand it and improve it. One must believe that it is worth improving yet in need of improvement. Thus every rebellion is a conservation: one preserves being by perfecting its vessels, not by simply destroying them.

Chesterton's activity as lecturer and controversialist brought him into contact with the "New Theologians" of England, who were "broadening" Christian doctrine in the direction of brotherhood and a vaguely inclusive church. Chesterton had been tempted toward this benevolent pantheism, predisposed to it by his boy-hood exposure to Stopford Brooke and George Macdonald. In the same year in which *Orthodoxy* appeared, he presented this boundless benevolence as the last temptation in *Thursday*. Now, in the chapter called "The Romance of Orthodoxy," he argues that the liberalizing theologians do not liberate. In removing form and definition, they make *personal* assertion meaningless. Man's relation to God arises from the dialectic of creation: he is a derived yet individual being. But this status is dissolved by syncretism. In seeking brotherhood and removing barriers, the Modernists remove identity and find there are no separate brothers left to love. What God sundered men try to join, making the danger and adventure of free men impossible. Even God they would bind in chains, removing miracle, dogma, and His personal intervention from their religion. Orthodoxy and dogma show that man's life is a story, not a mere pooling of things or mechanical flowing of things. It sees even God as a triune blaze of seeming contradiction, of dialectic without loss or complexity. The Incarnation and Crucifixion are more wondrous the more impossible they seem. The doctrine of original sin strikes every man low, but only to lift him into God's council, a conspirator in the saving rebellion of a greater Prometheus.

The attack on Modernism leads to the final stage of the book's argument. In "Authority and the Adventurer," Chesterton gives the true test of reality, opposed to the test of pure logic with which he opened the discussion. Man must finally judge life not by rational explanations or logic, but by *consonance of mysteries*. The miracle of a tree, of the mind, of the will, form eventually a *pattern* of miracles. We have seen this dialectic pattern, this continuing paradox, at work on all levels of reality. The Christian faith proves its validity by reflecting all of these mysteries, corresponding to them, linking them, without destroying them in the false simplicity of an invented system. This wisdom does not reduce all things to mind or spirit or matter or God. It accepts and answers reality in a living dialogue.

At this point Chesterton asks the question which marks the decisive nature of the book. Why not take from Christianity its good elements, its "inventions," its common sense, without submitting to its authority and discipline? "This is the last question,"[14] though this was the first time Chesterton faced it directly.

Because the Church conducts a continuing dialogue with reality, the Christian wisdom is not a group of ideas among which men can pick and choose. Its total, unexpected, improbable correspondence with reality is what gives it validity. It is authoritative in its total texture, with the authority of confirmation by reality, not merely by selective argument. It is a continuing, self-balancing thing, fixed yet developing—not a teaching but a teacher, "speaking not as the scribes and Pharisees but as one having authority." Under this dynamic tutelage, Chesterton learns from the Church as a child does from his father, by daily contact and spontaneous interchange.

It will be seen that Chesterton's idea of authority as the seat of dialectic is like Newman's idea of the development of doctrine.[15] Both men answered the Modernists by saying that real development is only possible where there is something worth developing, inexhaustibly rich in undiscovered ramifications, yet fixed enough to be continuous and to afford a frame of discovered and certain reality. It is precisely doctrine that develops, for doctrine is stable enough to benefit by the fluctuating course of mankind's fortunes. Doctrine gives men the ability to work with assurance in an ascertained reality. It can use whatever good things man comes to command in the successions of history because it has in itself norms for judging such inventions. It can assert the acquired force of the past in accepting or rejecting recent things. It has life because it draws on a complexus of thoughts, experiences, stresses, institutions, habits, and inner tensions. In contrast to this living wisdom, doctrinaire systems—which spring up and die daily by virtue of what Newman called Liberalism's "anti-dogmatic principle"—are not balanced by complexities, not checked by the multiple restraints of reality. They do not have that total concern for man, and experience of men, which the personal, supernatural authority of Christ gives to the Church, the living Teacher.

It is true that Chesterton's reflections had so far brought him only to Newman's starting point, the Anglican Church: fourteen years elapsed between *Orthodoxy* and Chesterton's submission to Roman Catholic authority. But *Orthodoxy* marks the climax of all his early controversy. By a very rapid extension of his concept of paradox, and a supreme exercise of his critical instincts,[16] he had reached in 1908 that position which became so familiar to the world that men forgot this was the goal of a long journey, not a permanent and static thing. *Orthodoxy* was written, and reached, by the intense process that went on at all times in Chesterton's mind, the process that had at first unbalanced and then strengthened his dialectic genius. Paradox had led to orthodoxy in Chesterton because the paradox was not simply irresponsible nor the orthodoxy simply static:

> When next you hear some attack called an idle paradox, ask after the dox. Ask how long the dox has been in the world; how many have believed in the dox; how often the dox has proved itself right in practice; how often thoughtful men have returned to the dox on theory. Pursue the dox; persecute the dox. In short, ask the dox whether it is orthodox.[17]

Such paradox is stabilizing, the energetic opposition of things which leads to balance in Christian ethics; and orthodoxy is a dynamic thing, the authority and personal guidance of that "che *move* il sole e l'altre stelle."

6.

THE DEFENCE OF

NOTTING HILL

The most baffling part of Chesterton's mind is that which was persistently turned toward politics. In other fields he was elusive and ironic of set purpose, the jester playing hide-and-seek with meaning in order to be caught. But in this arena he was confused by terms and masks, as he confesses in his *Autobiography,* protesting against the veil or haze that descends upon men who enter the toils of government.[1] His was the Gallic mind, judging by creeds and theory,[2] so that the compromise and bargaining of politics went on in a world literally invisible to him. It is with some justification, therefore, that men have avoided any serious treatment of his political writings; why try to chart a course where a man was simply set adrift? But it is impossible to ignore certain abiding tenets of his political work, because they were a symbolic expression of his metaphysical insights.

One book alone deals meaningfully with Chesterton's political thought—Cecil's anonymous study, written in 1908, drawing much of its emphasis and proportion from the running debate which had been the early life and education of both men. Cecil had none of the artistic or metaphysical preoccupations of his brother; politics was his passion. He had, by 1908, thought himself out of the middle-class Liberalism of his home into a "Tory Socialism" still contradictory but surprisingly balanced for a man whose interests were so pointedly practical. He would become a Roman Catholic five years after this book was published, and already he was shouting back to his brother to catch up with him. Much of the book is spent trying to convince Gilbert that he is no longer a Liberal, that he is clinging to the term through a combination of loyalty, wishful thinking, and mere refusal to think—but primarily through loyalty to his first creed and the source of his early ideals:

> That fundamental conservatism, which, as I shall endeavour
> to show, is a key to his maturer opinions, was even then strong
> with him, and, by a paradox as wild as any that he has pro-
> pounded, it kept him and keeps him faithful to the Liberal
> party.[3]

This was a shrewd analysis, confirmed by all later events, and even by Chesterton's own admission.[4]

It is difficult to overestimate the naïveté and purity of Chesterton's first Liberalism. He approached the assumptions of his youth with that demand for theoretical consistency which we find at every stage of his development. There was a strange glamour about the ideas which hovered beneficently over the world into which he was born—progress, enlightenment, expansion and freedom. Chesterton took what was vaguely assumed and sharply asserted it—that Rousseau had revealed men's equality to a world which had never heard the news, that Napoleon shattered a universal tyranny and freed the nations. Liberalism was to him both a creed and a party; he made no distinction between them. Gladstone was a hero and half a saint,[5] Chamberlain a villain and almost a devil.

As Chesterton learned a little of real politics, and felt the foundations of his Liberalism crumbling, his reaction was like that of the new theologians who thought Christianity would be washed away unless they rescued it: he invented a series of "higher Liberalisms." This tendency causes a great deal of confusion, as time goes on and Chesterton's "Liberalism" becomes more markedly individual, until the label is finally misleading. It seemed, before long, that he was supporting "the Liberal tradition" only because it was a tradition—that is, only for conservative reasons.

Just what did Chesterton mean by Liberalism in this first stage of his career? The ideal of comradeship and a belief in man's equality are not a political program but a personal ideal, more akin to Charity than Republicanism. In *Browning* he defined Liberalism as the guarantee of freedom in speech and worship. In another place he summed up the Liberal program under three points: equality, self-government, and freedom of religion.[6] He never seems to have had any clear ideas on the machinery of representation which would best insure self-government, though he was in favor of restricting the power of the House of Lords, principally as a gesture against "aristocracy." He seemed to want a party which should fight only on transcendent issues, and he entered the world of journalism at a time when he could give a messianic tone to the Liberal opposition to the Boer War.

THE BREAK WITH LIBERALISM

Chesterton dated his break with the Liberals from the Insurance Act (1911), but confessed that the spirit of the party—its little irritations and nagging opposition—had repelled him for some time before that date.[7] The truth of the matter is that Chesterton reached a peak of expectation and hope at the party's great victory of 1906,[8] in which Belloc entered Parliament; and his disillusionment kept step with Belloc's growing distaste for the niceties of political maneuver. This reaction would have come to both men, idealists and logicians impatient of compromise, no matter what their party affiliation; but the Nonconformist support on which the Liberals depended was especially disenchanting for men of their Catholic instincts. Belloc hurt his career with a breezy disregard for the Puritan stand on licensing laws, female suffrage, and religion in education. Chesterton took an even more intransigent position on these subjects.

It is not difficult to date the altering of his attitude toward the Liberal party. *Heretics* (1905) concluded with a firm profession of party loyalty. Three years later, in *Orthodoxy,* he protests that he still believes in Liberalism, even if he can no longer believe in Liberals.[9] In *Shaw* (1909), he regrets that the democratic revolution of modern times was not balanced with the reaction that might bring out the best in both movements: without such dialectic discipline, rebellion merely extended itself into an aimless optimism about progress, "a dreary hope."[10] In 1910 he wrote the drinking song which mocked George Cadbury, and was forced to resign from the *Daily News.*[11] When Belloc and Cecil collaborated on *The Party*

System (1911), Chesterton believed their thesis that Commons was as undemocratic as Lords, and despaired of understanding or influencing parliamentary politics. The year before that, in *What's Wrong With the World,* he had already turned from the consideration of the Public House (his own name for Westminster) to the private home.

But Chesterton continued to support the "higher Liberalism" of *The Wild Knight* and *Thursday*—the belief that God gives each man a secret dispatch for battle and rebellion in the world. From the time when aesthetes and nihilists seemed, in his youth, to control the stars, Chesterton considered human virtue a rebellion against the Prince of this World. Man is in exile and under tyranny—but the tyranny is not from outside him. Man's real fight is against original sin; and this revolution is a restoration, a rebellion which conserves:

> To the orthodox there must always be a case for revolution; for
> in the hearts of men God has been put under the feet of Satan.
> In the upper world hell once rebelled against heaven. But in
> this world heaven is rebelling against hell.[12]

A man who thought in dialectic patterns as Chesterton did had in time to see that simple "rebellion" is as meaningless a term as "optimism." Rebellion and conservation are correlates, meaningful only when united in dynamic balance. This ideal had already been expressed in his novels—in *Thursday's* conspirator-policemen, radical champions of order; in *Notting Hill's* new-old world, a kind of 1984 mediaevalism; in the sceptic and the mystic of *The Ball and the Cross,* who are the reforming intellect and the remembering heart of man.

Orthodoxy is full of arguments for tradition and dogma as the only bases for reform and freedom. Man must have a fixed ideal in order to alter evil conditions. He even says that Liberal is a misleading term in modern argument, since it stands so often in favor of bondage rather than of liberation.[13] From this time forward, his own use of the term would be one of those paradoxes he acted out on a large scale. He described Shaw's role as "revolutionizing the revolutionists,"[14] and he played an analogous role in the courts of Liberal opinion—*The Daily News* and *The Daily Herald*—until the jester was driven out of the court. He was a jester who told Liberals they must give votes to their own ancestors as well as to slum-dwellers, that they must study history and love national traditions in order to be effective revolutionists, that they must become dogmatists before they could be iconoclasts. He had discovered the substance of that which he first sought under the labels of democracy and rebellion; and, since the terms were crucial in the contemporary arena, he continued to use them, showing others who felt the needs that first drove him what solid ground could be reached through this haze.

Chesterton's romantic love of "rebellion" was, like his taste for exaggeration and the grotesque in art, an attempt to express being's dynamism and novelty. This is the reverse of the schematic programs and essentialist patterns of modern social reformers. And because the existentialism was theological, the rebellion was part of God's ancient battle, waged when he came back "Conqueror of Chaos in a six days' war."[15] The deepest radicalism is a *return* to roots, not simple deracination; the most wide-sweeping revolution is that encirclement of the earth by which Innocent Smith simultaneously comes home and discovers the New Jerusalem. Chesterton's "liberal traditionalism" became a dialectic concept which grew in complexity and value; as he put it, the Christian God is both Zeus and Prometheus, the ruler and the rebel:[16]

The term "reactionary" is generally used as a term of offense, just as the term "progressive" is used as a term of praise; but only once in a hundred times is either of them used so as to convey any meaning or truth. Yet though the words have become a mere hackneyed cant, they have their proper use. Progress means persistence in the direction of one object maintained for a considerable period; reaction means some upheaval of disgust or contradiction, which overthrows the recent persistence and appeals back, perhaps, to its opposite. Thus we might truly say that English poetry from Cowley to Akenside progressed towards clearness and metrical accuracy. And we might truly say that Coleridge's *Ancient Mariner* was a reaction against this progress, the writing of a mere mad ballad in order to show how much more life there was in old barbaric mysticism than in the recent easy-going rationality. Progress happens, in short, whenever men can endure one tendency for a long time. And reaction happens whenever some particular men can endure it no longer. These definitions are simple but I think them comprehensive. A progressive is always a conservative; he conserves the direction of progress. A reactionary is always a rebel.[17]

"Liberal" and "conservative," the most misleading terms in the modern world, sadly need the dialectic treatment Chesterton regularly gave them. Those who worship progress must, as he pointed out in *Heretics,* worship power and success; whence the totalitarianism of the "Liberal" twentieth century. On the other hand, men usually exercise their freedom in a reverence for the past; which explains the antiquarian loyalties of all romantics. The sterile separation and false simplification of the terms Chesterton analyzes have led to endless evils—the belief that freedom means formlessness, that progress means homogenization, that "conservatism" means stark repression, that "liberalism" means beneficent and omnipresent regulation. Bereft of the broader visions of saner periods, modern men fight for these arid caricatures of human life, without any sense of the real shape of man's conflict. It was precisely his instinct for freedom and liberality and humanism which drove Chesterton to a reverence for the past:

> Man is like Perseus, he cannot look at the Gorgon of the future except in the mirror of the past. All those who have tried to look at a fixed future directly have been turned to stone. The human heart has been petrified in them. The old Calvinists, with their predestination and necessity, were turned to stone. The modern scientific sociologists, with their anthropology and absurd eugenics, are turned to stone. They make amusing statues. It is utterly useless to talk about enlarging one's mind with visions of the future. The future does not enlarge one's mind in the least. The future is a blank wall on which I can paint my own portrait as large as I like. If I am narrow I can make the future narrow; if I am mean I can make the future mean. I cannot make the past mean. I cannot make St. Catherine of Siena mean. I cannot make Plato narrow. In the past I have real antagonists, men certainly better, braver, or more brilliant than I. Among the dead I have living rivals. In the future all my rivals are dead because they are unborn. I know I could not write "Paradise Lost," but I could easily write a "Utopia" very favourable to the sort of poetry I can write. I know I might not die as bravely as thousands of Christian martyrs or mediaeval knights, but it is quite easy for me to say that future society will have eliminated religious dogmatism or military peril. This explains almost the whole of the modern fascination for the future, its scientific essays, its more credible romances. We are fleeing from the faces of our fathers, because they are faces. We are attracted to the future because it is what is called a soft job. In front of us lies an unknown or unreal world which we can mould according to every cowardice or triviality in our own temperaments. But if we look back at our fathers, as they gather in the gate of his-

tory, we see it like the gate of Eden, described by one of them in verse which we cannot imitate: With dreadful faces thronged and fiery arms.[18]

THE NAPOLEON OF NOTTING HILL

Chesterton frequently meditated on the romance of Robinson Crusoe and of all "desert island" literature—the restriction which gives to everything a terrible value. Every stave rescued from the ship must serve as tool and weapon and toy. He advised people to get snowed up in a cottage or stranded in a railway car, so that they could realize for a moment the value of the actualities they shuffle back and forth every day. He took the same attitude toward everything, even addressing the cosmos in diminutives; looking at it against a backdrop of non-being, so that he might "hoard the hills." He liked to work in the smallest corner of his home; and he kept an unpretentious menage all his life.

This was, of course, an instinctive (and later a conscious) homage paid to "the divine democracy of things." The existential value of each slightest object is literally boundless; being is being, whatever the quantities in which it is served up. The same respect for men, each an isolated miracle, beings which can be conscious of being, constituted Chesterton's political "democracy." But he saw in the Imperialism of Chamberlain and Kipling a worship of quantity rather than of individual beings—an essentially futile quest, since there is always more of any "more" that might be added to the Empire. As he looked at other political theories, he saw in almost all of them the rule of quantity—in the mathematical systems of reform, the dehydrated programs and schemes. As always, his ideas first shaped themselves into colors and narrative, and in 1904 he wrote the book which he always considered his basic statement of political belief—*The Napoleon of Notting Hill*.

Here, at the springs of his thought, we see clearly that Chesterton's democracy transcended particular political forms. Adam Wayne, the suburban Napoleon, has a thirst for diversification, for hierarchies and liveries and separate sanctities. But these are not advanced as parts of a system, of a neo-feudalism. Rather they indicate a revolt against the voracious appetite for Systems. He realized that the mechanical, utilitarian, quantitative schemes were even more the danger of twentieth-century politics than they had been in the Victorian era. Fascism, Communism, and Socialism have borne out that judgment.

Notting Hill's struggle takes place in the future and is on one level a satirical response to Wells' scientific fantasies, in which the union of political and scientific machineries causes the dwarfing of man. Chesterton suggests that some imp of perversity will rebel under the shadow of this threat—that insanity which unbalances the mind only to restore the dialectic of sanity. Auberon Quin is Chesterton's greatest attempt to be fair to his old enemies, the aesthetes. When reformers have made the world a utilitarian nightmare in which men are killed to effect the neat outcome of some social theory, the suppressed whimsy of man will give to imagination that license which had previously been reserved for the efficiency experts. Those who think nothing worthwhile but making an empire will give way to those who think of nothing but making a pun. Something else must be added to this autonomous imagination, something which will turn the pun into a poem, and that is the local patriotism of Adam Wayne, who hoards one hill—that most unlikely place, Notting Hill—in defiance of the vast systems which will make of that crossing a network of rails and wires. Quin stands with Wayne because of a Ruskinian preference for grass as compared with railway tracks; but Wayne is asserting the value of the person against social pattern—man as an end, not a means to be used in some scheme of quantitative improvement. He is saying that a true consideration of man is always, to some extent, a view of him in his separate and many-sided reality. All ranks, hierarchies, nations, and neighborhoods are meant to guarantee this isolation, to prevent the blind treatment of men in the mass.[19] This is what is meant by the Englishman's boast that his home is his castle—a motto which contains the entire theme of *Notting Hill*. It is also the source of the American ideal of federation, of the Greek belief in the Polis as the natural field for human expression and achievement. Wherever a man stands, it is true that

> For every tiny town or place
> God made the stars especially

Spiritually, Notting Hill is the center of the cosmos; the stars were made for Adam Wayne—not for him to possess, but as decoration for his home.

This book was dedicated to Belloc, who had the same local patriotism, but for a place contrasted in every way with Chesterton's first home:

> You saw the moon from Sussex Downs,
> A Sussex moon, untravelled still,
> I saw a moon that was the town's,
> The largest lamp on Campden Hill.

But this very diversity reinforces the book's theme—that men must articulate their separate personalities, disregarding the promise of efficiency following on uniformity; and that it were better for them to die as men than to perform as machines:

> And when the pedants bade us mark
> What cold mechanic happenings
> Must come, our souls said in the dark,
> "Belike; but there are likelier things."

Likelier across these flats afar,
These sulky levels smooth and free
The drums shall crash a waltz of war
And Death shall dance with Liberty;
Likelier the barricades shall blare
Slaughter below and smoke above,
And death and hate and hell declare
That men have found a thing to love.

These are not barricades thrown up by the reasoning of a Robespierre, to bring a logical system to birth; they are the grotesque weapons of Notting Hill, used by a man who defends his home and person with a blind rage for being. Adam Wayne is Provost, and Quin is a monarch; but these positions are not at issue, nor is any political philosophy implied by them. The struggle is on a mythic level altogether more profound, as the last chapter demonstrates.

WHAT'S WRONG WITH THE WORLD

Six years after he had written the *Napoleon*, Chesterton finally developed his political theories in a sustained argument. He wrote *What's Wrong With the World,* moving from the assumptions of the novel to the assertion that property is the bastion of freedom. The book has not the dialectic density of *Orthodoxy;* it is linear, and the forty-nine short chapters are so many steps taken down a carefully hedged path. The first part is "methodological," a satire and penetrating criticism of sociology's methods. He attacks the fallacy of treating society as an organism. Then the doctrine of *Heretics* is repeated in this context: only an ultimate theory can be immediately practical; we cannot know what man most profoundly desires to effect until we know something of what he *is*.

In chapter six we are told that the starting point for all practical consideration of man as "political" is the family. This is the society which "society" is only invented to protect. Here man is man because of the interplay between man and woman, adult and child. Here man shapes and is shaped; escapes the limits of mere competition with his equals and finds completion with his opposites. Unfortunately, the sociologist, even when he sets out to protect the family, often ends by destroying it in the name of some instrument of reform, sacrificing the end to the means.

The other major divisions of the book are devoted to the elements of the family—the man, the woman, and the child. Under the last two of these headings he puts in context his regular arguments on feminism and education. The section devoted to man seems included for reasons of symmetry rather than of necessity. Here equality and comradeship are praised, in contrast with "Caesarism" or the denial of every man's essentially masculine role in the world, that function which his position in the family clearly gives to him but which is ignored by all schemes and systems that treat him as a pawn of the state, the recipient of doles. Healthy conversation among men is always based on a presumption of equality, even when it is competitive; which is the meaning of the golf handicap. The psychology of male company is described with great subtlety in chapter two, where the Greek stress on beauty as a determinant in male relations is analyzed and the cult of the superior man exposed in this unhealthy example.

In the next section, Chesterton, who had been carrying on a running battle with the suffragettes, stated again his view of the sexes. Sex was always, for him, the expression of that dialectic which sustains life; and his comments on the psychology of sex are very acute. He notes, for instance, that the "iciness" which is called an affectation in the seventeenth-century laments over cruel mistresses is an expression of a deep truth about woman, whose most terrifying power is the refusal to respond to man. The skirt he sees as a symbol of this cloistered aloofness and veil around woman. Man's sexual response to woman is presumed and almost automatic; but woman's can be withdrawn, even permanently withdrawn, for the aura around the virgin is something as old as man's history. The suffragettes try to impress men by destroying their own power in this respect, by using masculine assertiveness to gain their own ends. The modern isolation of "frigidity" as a psychological aberration disarms woman in the same way: as so often happens in the modern world, a vast and multiform instinct is reduced to its single most insane form, then expelled from the human balance of things.

On every level—relation to the child, to the home, to each other—the sexes best supplement and support each other when they are kept most distinct. They are most apposite when most opposite. Jobs and the vote, as Chesterton admits, do not automatically destroy femininity. But those who were advocating these reforms at the turn of the century used arguments and raised ideals which would destroy woman's distinctive role. Certainly the ideal of competition (rather than complementarity) has by now reached an intensity never before felt in history. The results, in terms of divorce, delinquency, and psychological maladjustment, are clear to anyone with eyes.

Sex is the bond of society because it is the antithetic principle that leads to harmony as opposed to uniformity. Chesterton saw that modern politics undermines the family at a very deep level because it opposes the concept of diversity. Always a democrat in his insistence on the equality of men, he saw that the leveling egalitarian is the person who destroys equality by making everyone compete on the same arid plain of endeavor, where any pre-eminence is absolute. From this follows all the absurd talk of "freeing" woman, or of her "equality." Man and woman are equal because different in their entire function and purpose; on this difference is built all agreement:

> Our God who made two lovers in a garden,
> And smote them separate and set them free,
> Their four eyes wild for wonder and wrath and pardon,
> And their kiss thunder, as lips of land and sea;
> Each rapt unendingly beyond the other,
> Two starry worlds of unknown gods at war. . . .
>
> Make not this sex, this other side of things,
> A thing less distant than the world's desire.
> What colour to the end of evening clings,
> And what far cry of frontiers, and what fire
> Fallen too far beyond the sun for seeking,
> Let it divide us though our kingdom come;
> With a far signal in our secret speaking
> To hang the proud horizon in our home.[20]

Man and woman bring the horizon into the home, combining intimacy and distance. The modern concept of competition instead of complementarity has reduced sex from this structural principle of antithesis running through all of society to a separate "instinct" that must be pandered to, assuaged, or clinically "treated." Chesterton indicates that sex is not overemphasized in modern life, but underrated; it is unmanageable, and flares out with dark intensity because it has been forced into too small a compartment. No wonder Freud found it stalking the mind, when the mind had driven it out of the social framework. Bentham and Marx, the factory and the commune, the "purely economic" society, have led to Freud and the purely sexual subconscious.

In the section on the child, Chesterton returns to *Heretics*, where he had stated the absurdity of "pure methodology" in education. Men try to pass on good things to their children without deciding what is Good. Paul Shorey used Chesterton's rapid statement of this argument to sum up the Socratic foundation of educational theory.[21] The comparison is one of those which are strengthened, not weakened, by closer study. Chesterton's objections to the ideas of "drawing out" a child, of "encouraging expression" as the aim of education, are devastating, and have gained point since they were written. Chesterton had only seen Herbert Spencer's statement of the error; we have seen the Deweyites' practice of it. As usual, Chesterton is weaker when he comes to practical suggestions, as in his remarks on the public schools of England.

The last part of the book is a brief statement of the case for distributed ownership. The role of all three members of the family— man, woman, and child—is best protected by a separate integrity of the family, an integrity guaranteed in society by the possession of property. Though this is supposed to be the book's conclusion, goal of all its arguings, the discussion is hurried and uncertain. Distributism was not yet born in 1910, though its component elements were taking shape. In 1912 Belloc would finally state in integrated form what he had been piecing together, and give a standard term to the world's discussions—*The Servile State*. In 1925 a less elegant tag was invented for the program of "The Distributist League." Chesterton's gravitation toward these partially defined ideas was still vague in 1910; though they would eventually receive from him the loyalty he had offered to the Liberal Party.

CECIL CHESTERTON

Though he learned little from the actual political arena—and perhaps because he was not sensitive to this kind of contact—Chesterton was deeply influenced, throughout his early career, by his friendship with three men—Cecil, his younger brother; Hilaire Belloc; and Bernard Shaw. Gilbert did not go to a university, so no teacher ever swayed him. Whitman and Stevenson were of the kind which does not form practical disciples (as Nietzsche's works made a disciple of Shaw). The one literary force of any weight with Chesterton—Ruskin's political and economic writings—was diluted by Chesterton's objections to Ruskin's aesthetics. Thus, in certain practical areas, he learned willingly from the three men he most respected among political figures of his day. We have something of the measure of his talents when we note the fact that he needed and accepted such influence only in the area of politics. Only here did he feel a lack of direct confrontation with reality; he tried to establish contact indirectly through men in whom he sensed a grip of the facts.

Cecil was more politician than author, and he had the wisdom to realize this. The courage he showed in the clash with Lloyd George and Rufus Isaacs over Marconi shares (see p. 188 below) was that of a man who knows he is playing the game of politics; using the pressures and undergoing the risks of men who exercise power. Gilbert misconceived the entire case by thinking that the sole test to be applied was the enunciation of truth. To this extent, Cecil involved Gilbert in things he was not fitted to understand; but Cecil was still learning about politics as he taught his brother. He would have taught him much more but for his tragic death. Cecil would not have been discouraged by the drudgery of politics, as Belloc was. Unfortunately, Gilbert felt himself the heir to his brother's voice and task; whereas, if Cecil had lived, the two men's careers would gradually have drifted apart. (Sir Thomas Beecham, who helped finance *The New Witness* from his personal funds, devotes a chapter of his autobiography to Cecil, "the finest journalist of his day." Belloc, discussing the state of English prose style, answered simply, "Cecil Chesterton is dead.")

HILAIRE BELLOC

The second, and predominant, influence of this period was the strong charm which many felt almost as a bewitchment spread by Hilaire Belloc. No wonder this man captured Chesterton's imagination. He loved France and the Gallic virtues, yet was solidly, through and through, English; more so than Chesterton. Because of his girth, because of his ready and armored wit, Chesterton is often compared to Samuel Johnson. But Belloc possessed the real ingredients of the abrupt Doctor's greatness: logic, pride, piety, and a fear of death. Both men had the pagan poetry in their bones, of rhetoric, and conquest, and the love of that which they must lose. They clung tenaciously to a Christian faith superimposed by logic on a native Roman earth. They each hid a dangerously sensitive mind under bluster, nursing their wounds, remembering the checks given their careers, looking anxiously to their position in the future of letters. Both men were tender and rude, assertive yet frightened, eccentrically learned; and both had the magnetism that belongs to men haunted.

Chesterton and Belloc met during the Boer War, when they were both writing reviews for *The Speaker*. Chesterton's Liberalism was already tottering; he was vaguely socialist in his sympathies, since the socialists gave him some of that salvationist mystique which he needed in his devotion to a party. Then Belloc came upon the scene, as he did in the meeting Chesterton described by adapting a few lines from Macaulay:

> The furious Frenchman comes with his clarions and
>   his drums,
> His tactics of Sadowa and his maxims of Jean-Paul.
> He is bursting on our flanks, grasp your pikes and close
>   your ranks,
> For Belloc never comes but to conquer or to fall.[22]

Belloc had the piety for local things which Chesterton missed in the Liberal Party. He had helped found a paper in 1899 to oppose the *fin-de-siècle* weariness which Chesterton felt called to combat.[23] He shared Chesterton's respect for France and the Republic; Belloc's first historical study was of Danton, who had been made to deliver one of those monologues which Chesterton wrote for *The Debater.* And Belloc already had several economic and political theories which could easily be fitted to Chesterton's instincts. Above all, Belloc had the poet's and the pagan's reverence for real things. He was, in fact, too "poetic" to write any but the shortest poems. His love of concrete things made him compose in separate lines; he could not think in terms of total structure, as his book on Milton shows. His finest essays, like that on "An Unknown Country," are written around the haunting quality of single verses; his tragic appreciation of life lay in a single-minded grasp upon things. Shaw captured his spirit perfectly when he said Belloc clung to Sussex earth with both hands. This was an attitude Chesterton admired, as an expression of the value of being; but it was not one which came naturally to his own volatile and detached mind.

In each of his many tributes to Belloc, Chesterton emphasizes his realism and firm roots. In the *Autobiography,* he praises his friend's poem "The Rebel," which sketches a clear plan of battle in the very hottest blaze of hatred. The plan and rhetoric of that poem Chesterton used as the model for Marcus' reply to Alfred in *The Ballad of the White Horse,*[24] and much of Belloc went into his picture of the Roman who has taken root in England—who gazes over clouded downs, whose vines tie him to his own earth, whose faith grew out of hard doubt, who quotes a Latin psalm at the height of battle.

The friendship was firm, despite trial; but the admiration was one-sided. Belloc's severely classical taste made Chesterton's style unpalatable to him; he admitted that he had not read many of his ally's books, and the evaluation he wrote of him in 1940 confirms this. But in the first years of the century, when both men lived in London, the two were a devastating pair in any debate—one haughty and capable of great oratory, the other genial and witty; one Catholic, the other Anglican; one a French citizen with a History First from Oxford, the other a journalist who was admitted to the wars of the academy. As early as 1905 Shaw called them a single phenomenon, the Chesterbelloc.

But most readers have forgotten that Shaw used that term only to point out how unnatural was the union of these two men:

> Chesterton and Belloc are not the same sort of Christian, not the same sort of Pagan, not the same sort of Liberal, not the same sort of anything intellectual.[25]

He regretted that positive direction was being given to the lumbering Chesterbelloc by "Hilary Forelegs," Chesterton merely following the lead of this lesser man (as Shaw thought him).

Belloc exercised his influence on Chesterton in three areas. The first was that large field where Chesterton was uncertain of himself, comprising almost the whole of politics and economics. Here the influence borrowed from and gave strength to that other hold upon Chesterton, admiration for his brother, since Belloc and Cecil agreed in temperament and conviction; they collaborated to produce *The Party System* in 1911 and to found *The Eye Witness,* later *The New Witness,* as part of their campaign against political corruption. Belloc's respect for Cecil's courage and pen were far stronger than his esteem for Gilbert, who followed the lead of his brother and his friend in this attack on the party system. Belloc's developing opposition to the Whig historians, his emphasis on ancient Rome, his argument that England was made decisively Roman in her centuries of occupation and that Prussia had not shared this benediction of civilization—all these were views Chesterton came to share, along with a new esteem for peasants and monarchs.

And when all these strands were joined in the persuasive volume *The Servile State,* none was more completely persuaded than Chesterton.

The second area of influence was that anti-Semitism which Belloc had caught in France. Belloc himself kept much of the breezy humor of exaggeration in his attacks on the Jews (which rang far otherwise in those pre-Hitler days); the same thing can be found in Johnson's snorts at Scotland. Chesterton, on the other hand, was too seriously concerned with ideas to harbor merely emotional prejudices. His temptation was always to make men into symbols of their own ideas; and when once he had met the type of the Jewish financier, the symbol was deeply fixed in his mind. This judgment was fed from the one real source of prejudice in Chesterton—his personal loyalty. Samuel and Rufus Isaacs were the men who, in government and business, gambled and won against his brother. This one involvement in the deadly wars of finance and politics cut deep into Chesterton's life. It is no accident that his fiercest and most effective piece of satire was directed against F. E. Smith, the charming orator who had been Belloc's rival at Oxford, and who had prosecuted the Marconi case against Cecil.

The third point of contact between these two men was the Catholic Church. But here the influence was not at all that which has been suspected. It is not unusual to hear that Belloc "converted Chesterton." Whereas, if there was any effect, it was a deterring rather than an impelling force. Belloc was desperately sincere in his religion; but the Faith was something he held by conscious effort and in defiance of his emotional responses. He was pagan metal in a Christian mould; and the reluctant, Marc-Aurelian metal never cooled or set in the mould, so that the retaining forms could be removed. His mental element remained liquid; formless fears and doubts, and brooding on mortality, moved always under his acceptance of the Christian dogma. Because of his own absorption in this struggle, he often misread the reactions of others to the Papal claims: he saw persecution wherever he did not find acceptance. He felt that his own failures, from the loss of an Oxford fellowship to the loss of all channels for his writing, had been caused by a hatred for Rome. When Chesterton later escaped this onus, Belloc claimed it was only because he was a convert.

Chesterton came from that section of the English people whose entire fault was a shapeless tolerance, and he never endorsed Belloc's sense of persecution. When he was told that people like his parents were principally motivated by a hatred for Catholicism, he silently ignored the statement. Belloc, whose sincerity did infect most of his friends, obviously broached the subject of Catholicism with Chesterton; there is a letter of 1907 referring to their "discussion" at Oxford and commending Chesterton's doubts to the Blessed Virgin.[26] But this was not politics or economics; Chesterton did not admit pressure of any kind on this subject. His failure to respond convinced Belloc that he was merely romantic in his attachment to Catholic culture, for Belloc peremptorily told Msgr. O'Connor to ignore Chesterton's sick-bed call for a priest in 1914; and in 1922, when Chesterton finally entered the Church, he confided to Baring his entire astonishment. Msgr. O'Connor felt that Chesterton had Belloc in mind when he complained, in his book on conversion, that Catholic well-wishers often put off troubled souls by their solicitude.[27]

As a matter of fact, the two men saw little of each other after Chesterton moved out of London in 1909. Belloc would go out to Beaconsfield to get the illustrations for his novels, after his temperamental intransigence had made it almost impossible for this great prose stylist and master of epigram to find an audience. In 1936, when Chesterton wrote his *Autobiography*, he made one chapter a splendid tribute to his friend; luckily he did not live to see that brave man's final and useless phase. Belloc had always feared death, loneliness, the loss of friends and of landscape and of wine; he knew all these things at the end. The last photographs of him are like tragic poems in their effect, the etched record of folly and greatness.

BERNARD SHAW

The other figure of principal importance for Chesterton was Bernard Shaw. Maisie Ward can hardly credit the review of *Heretics* which called Chesterton a disciple of Shaw; but this, if a misleading comparison, is not an absurd one. Many saw a resemblance, in compression, paradox, and epigram, between the established dramatist and the rising journalist. What is more important, Chesterton and Shaw were fascinated with each other, as their voluminous descriptions of each other indicate. Even in their obvious contrasts there was a certain symmetry, like the precise reversal of a man's image in his mirror. Defining his own role as a metaphysical jester, in the introductions to *Orthodoxy* and *The Well and the Shallows,* Chesterton defended his position by considering the parallel stance of Shaw. The Irishman wore a flamboyant motley of vanity, as Chesterton did of humility,[28] the motley of men whose aim and technique were similar—*ridentem dicere verum.*

Both men sensed their profound resemblance—Shaw when he spoke of Chesterton's Gallic fury of logic, Chesterton when he described the detached Shavian intellect, in terms he would later use of his own mental quandary, the crisis of the Slade School days. He fought, in Shaw as in an *alter ego,* that dangerously rapid mind which can go deeper into an argument until it disappears, like some snake swallowing itself. Chesterton wrote frequently of Shaw as he was to describe his own crucial period, analyzing the mind's power to accelerate indefinitely until it loses contact with reality, encountering the "nemesis of wit; the skidding of a wheel at the height of its speed."[29] Shaw's logic was nimble because unweighted with the nameless loyalties and yearnings of the man who is more than a mind. He was a passionate Irishman, but without patriotism or a native earth. His passion was subsumed in intellection.

Thus the witticisms, from either side, on beer and beef were not mere horseplay. Chesterton recognized in Shaw a dangerous self-sufficiency of the intellect which demanded a vegetarian's austerities as its symbol. When Shaw tried to answer the charges of Puritanism by confessing to orgies of musical appreciation more abandoned than the alcoholic's wildest flings, his very manner of confessing this as some kind of "secret drinking" proved that he felt it a betrayal of the Platonic purity of his mental operations.[30] The same conflict ran through the debates on Shakespeare, whose lush words and largesse seemed nearly obscene to Shaw. Here was precisely the kind of intellect whose cold manipulations of life would become the worst threat to the twentieth-century state. Shaw's importance among the Fabians, and the Fabians' importance in this century, have proved Chesterton wise in his choice of a foe.

The book on Shaw appeared in 1909. It is not to be considered with his essays in literary criticism, for little is said of the plays; it constituted merely another rejoinder in the endless debate, concentrating on the cold kindness, the fury of intellect, in Shaw. The Shavian wit is far removed from that humor which is an admission of weakness, binding a man to his fellows.[31] The usual criticisms of Shaw are unjust, but there *is* a unique scorn in his barbed witticisms—not that of pride, but of a lonely intellect not shaped in the common folly and blind wisdom of ordinary men; he would not share the "great doom of laughter."[32] Shaw tried to love progress instead of men; his asceticism was an attempt to "purge the old man," but in the name of Nietzsche's Superman. In other words, Shaw lacked precisely that which Chesterton admired in Belloc—*pietas*, the reverence for one's ancestors, one's earth, one's contact with being on all sides. Chesterton's attitude toward both men was determined by the presence in the one, and the lack in the other, of this anchorage in existence. The friendship with Belloc faded somewhat; that with Shaw continued to grow, and was rich to the end. But Chesterton had taken the measure, when first he met them, of the force which drove each man; and he never changed his judgment of Belloc's pious regard for history and Shaw's disloyal flight into "progress."

7.

PATTERN IN PANTOMIME

When Chesterton was immured in theoretical doubts, the sheer drive of a good story became for him a kind of final *argument*, the proof in action that existence is an adventure, that man's value, even dimly reflected in the antics of a puppet, is unquestionable. This is why, at the art school, the thrust and speed of Stevenson's narrative brought Chesterton back into contact with that *existence* which arguments had thinned or dispersed. The Notebook has three entries on the subject of stories, including this:

> There is too much tendency to turn your life into an essay.
> I propose to make mine a story.[1]

Later he rhymed in the manner of Browning these lines:

MAN

This his head's glory is:
He, be he strong,
Some way a story is,
Some way a song.

Stevenson offered Chesterton a *via media* of escape from the opposite exaggerations of nihilism and optimism. The concept of adventure is that of a good thing endangered, a thing only to be saved by risk. In *Orthodoxy*, Chesterton explored how compactly this attitude sums up the proper relation of man to existence: being is an undoubted good which is challenged by indubitable evils; only by fighting for the one and against the others can the value of existence be realized. This is the truth expressed in those stories which imply on each page that "men, even ordinary men, want in the last resort, not life or death, but drums."[2]

NOVELS

Chesterton's own stories are metaphysical pirate tales. The "bloody pirate's sloop" of *Lepanto* is straight out of *Treasure Island*. The chase and struggle of changing identities in *Thursday* recall both *Ballantrae* and the Jekyll-Hyde fantasy. These are tales, not of life or death, but drums; rather, of swords. It is almost impossible to find a volume of Chesterton's tales without a sword that is somewhere unsheathed in the action. This pugnacity repels some, and raises the suspicion that Chesterton's love of literary battle was an escape value through which were dissipated the tensions which his airy cheerfulness could not resolve. The animosity which he did not express in personal contacts rushed out in these unreal dreams, dreams which are themselves unhealthy, whatever good effect they had in the balance of Chesterton's own mental state.

But the actual stories do not fit this neat explanation. There is no hatred or simple release of antagonisms in the novels, no beating of figureheads with the obscure energy of Quilp. Chesterton's own words about St. George and the dragon mislead us here, for there are no dragons in his stories. Even when an Orm appears, he is not introudced merely to be slain. He is the medium of St. George's vision. This complication and reversal of roles cuts across the melodramatic simplicity of the plot's outline. Especially in the lengthier novels, the sword is not simply a shining weapon with which to cut the slimy scales. For one thing, there are always two swords in Chesterton's best novels—the clashing blades which are God's scissors, shaping the world.[3]

Chesterton's earliest novels were *The Napoleon of Notting Hill* and *The Ball and the Cross,* the first written in 1904, the second in 1905 (though it did not appear in book form until 1909). In both stories, an extended conflict is developed—between Quin and Wayne, between Turnbull and MacIan. The significant feature of both conflicts is that they are not clashes of good and evil, but sustained encounters between opposed principles, each correct in its own sphere, yet each in need of the tempering influence of its opponent. In *Notting Hill,* the antagonists finally recognize that their separate flames of genius are in reality the "two lobes in the brain of a ploughman." Isolated, Wayne's iron devotion easily becomes a cruel fanaticism, just as Quin's levity of unconcern can become a cruel aestheticism; but, joined, they achieve that flying balance and poise of stress which is praised in *Orthodoxy.*

The same kind of struggle is even more thoroughly pursued, in *The Ball and the Cross,* through every analogue of man's life. Turnbull and MacIan try to duel, but they are interrupted at every turn by the simplistic philosophies which forbid this dialectic clash and complexity. Because one figure is devout and the other an atheist, one should not make them hero and villain.[4] The devout fanatic stands not for religion but for faith, for poetry, for superstition. Turnbull, on the other hand, is the spokesman of reason, science, and the hard demand for proof. The novel is like its French scene, "where reason and religion clash in one continual tournament."[5] By exactly balancing these two approaches—that of reason and that of poetry—Chesterton presents a more profoundly integrated picture of mental balance than he was later to do in *Orthodoxy.* In that essay the folly of "pure reason" is contrasted with the sanity of the poet's instincts. In the novel, the wild beliefs of legend and myth, the blindness of the multiple gods, are also felt as a danger. Theologically, the absolute claims of faith and reason in their own areas of competence are sustained with a subtlety that the Schoolmen would have appreciated. And while the two heroes struggle to achieve the balance of sanity, the insane opinions of those who would separate them are effectively satirized. These modern philosophers stand always for divorce, for simplification; they are intellectual pacifists, afraid of the unleashed energy of such combat between poetry and reason. They do not see that these spirits are truly destructive only in isolation, in the unnatural separation which breeds rationalists on one side and irrational existentialists on the other. This terrible isolation is the dream which tempts, and nearly defeats, each warrior.

The crossing swords are directed by a third thing which makes the conflict possible by containing its potential resolution. That thing is represented by the hidden monk whose fighting is over.

This spirit of debate and mysticism—for he is both theologian and hermit—had been flung onto the pinnacle of St. Paul's, and there he underwent the supreme division and inner tension which brought him peace. His crisis had been so acute as to seem unreal, with an absurdity at once increasing and dispelling fear. Descending through this unreal dream, he discovered the earth as some strange new planet. His moment of simultaneous resignation and clinging apprehension has given a poise to all the polarity which men must sustain in order to keep their balance. He reaches the only true state of peace, that of the Wild Knight:

> It seems almost as if there were some equality among things, some balance in all possible contingencies which we are not permitted to know lest we should learn indifference to good and evil, but which is sometimes shown to us for an instant as a last aid in our last agony.[6]

This vision of the equal value of existence in all its vessels is contrasted with all the false pacifisms that would separate the book's heroes. The monk found peace only in division. When he argues with Lucifer, he upholds the cross because man, like the cross, is an eternal collision;[7] immediately after this argument, he is forced to embody such conflict at its highest pitch of tension. Only then does he arrive at the principle of union in division, since he has tasted the one experience which is man's victory: "The cross cannot be defeated . . . for it is Defeat."[8] The metaphysics of real relations teaches us that two things can only be related through a third thing which is their base, and that is the role of the monk in the creative dialectic of Turnbull and MacIan. As Hegel sensed, only to go astray over the mathematics of his discovery, all dialectic *is* fundamentally triple. One of the Father Brown stories is written around this insight. In "The Duel of Doctor Hirsch" Father Brown realizes that the approaching duel is impossible because the opponents are opposite in every way, even in insignificant ways. This kind of opposition is barren because there is no point of contact between the fighting elements; and in that truth the solution of the mystery lies. The "foes" are unreal—a pretense carried out by one man with and without his disguise.

DETECTIVE TALES

To the Stevensonian adventure story Chesterton soon added the detective mystery as a frame for his narrative. His fascination with the form dates from after the Slade crisis, but it became as great as his interest in pantomime, adventure tales, and the toy theater. His first detective tales, written in 1904, were pieces of mere whimsy—*The Club of Queer Trades*. But Basil Grant, the detective, enunciates the view of evidence which Father Brown was to follow for years:

> I never could believe in that man—what's his name, in those
> capital stories?—Sherlock Holmes. Every detail points to
> something, certainly; but generally to the wrong thing. Facts
> point in all directions, it seems to me, like the thousands of
> twigs on a tree. It's only the life of the tree that has unity and
> goes up—only the green blood that springs, like a fountain,
> at the stars.[9]

Though he spoke ill of detective stories in his 1900 "Defence," Chesterton was bound to change his attitude. In the defence he says they arouse wonder and put mystery back into the drab streets of London. But the appeal of the mystery tale is deeper, and reaches in the direction of Chesterton's own interests, since every good detective novel is built on paradox. Suspense must go against *doxa,* betraying suspicion. Furthermore, the technique of such tales is one of progress through negations to assertion. Elimination of possibilities is the detective's method, and it is a lively parable of the fact that truth can be found by a process of destruction. This dialectic which creates by destroying was unfolded throughout Chesterton's first union of Gaboriau's and Stevenson's techniques, *The Man Who Was Thursday,* where a series of "suspects" are almost literally eliminated, since their identity and total reality disappear. And the last assertion is the more absolute for its expression in negative terms, like the negatives in which Aquinas couched the predications of God.

The detective novel which followed *Thursday,* in 1912, was actually that first novel which Chesterton tried many times to write during the Fisher Unwin interlude between the Slade School and Fleet Street. *Manalive* was first intended as the adventures of Eric Peterson, aesthete and decadent nihilist, who finds his way out of the depths he had sounded. This story was carefully planned as a new variation on the detective romance, and Chesterton's notes on the subject are important evidence of the way he invented the skeletons of his stories. The entire sketch is interesting, and it even contains the seed of *The Surprise,* Chesterton's third and last play; but the opening words will suffice here:

> I think this might be called a new kind of novel, approximately defined as the romantically philosophic: *i.e.,* a story in which modern thoughts are typified, not by long arguments, but by rapid, symbolic incidents—an allegoric comedy.[10]

The story was originally to move through chambers of horror, suggesting the experiences of art school and solipsism; but this program had been fulfilled in *Thursday,* and a corner was turned at that point, a corner whose permanent monument is *Orthodoxy.* By 1912, the peak of Chesterton's early career, these horrors had faded, and he had the artistic good sense not to attempt describing them again. He changed the form from a detective investigation to a mock trial as absurd in its trappings as the trial in Alice's Wonderland.

Manalive is Chesterton's happiest novel; there is little conflict in it, only a release of parables that had run under his thought for some time: the need for revolution as a return to one's self, the opposite thirsts for renewal and preservation which are only satisfied when they are *simultaneously* fulfilled. The staleness and the rebirth of "Beacon House" are made palpable in all the improbable series of events. The satire is a bit heavy, but Smith is given a sufficiently varied gallery of anti-types: financiers and scientists and Irish melancholics, Russian and French revolutionaries, and a Chinese conservative. The political point of the novel is very important: Smith not only wears the insignia of both parties on an election day, he rebukes the larger opponents of history in much the same way. The stolid French shopkeeper (who had saved the endangered men in *The Ball and the Cross*) is treated as harshly by Smith as the Russian revolutionary, even as harshly as the aristocratic lady and the Chinese priest who would preserve culture by turning a nation into a museum. The need for balance and controlled conflict—for harder commandments and looser conventions—is expressed in the whirling yet stable adventures of Smith. Julius West, making a rather obvious charge of improbability, misses the logic of the entire parable when he asks where Smith's lawyers got their documents.[11] The answer is given in so many words by the book: Smith's wife, Mary, had them. Even the difficulty of collecting them is explained by the character of Mary; for one of the finest touches of the story is saved for the last chapter, in which Mary finally speaks—only to reveal that the wild poet of gesture is wedded to the most prosaic sort of woman, who allows his escapades as she would the collecting of stamps or snakes. The need for balance and correction is something Smith feels as well as his opponents.

In two places, Chesterton's own memoirs and Msgr. O'Connor's, the source is given of Chesterton's most famous paradox—the innocence of Father Brown. The negations of Christian asceticism—the innocence and denial of experience symbolized by celibacy—are exaggerated in the clumsy figure and absent-minded actions of the dumpy priest. But these negations lead to knowledge. The innocent man sees, the humble man perceives things in the right perspective. An eccentric like Sherlock Holmes cannot judge human problems because he is not himself placed in the center of humanity.[12] That is why Holmes must measure and magnify the trivial deposits of a man's passage.

The first Father Brown story—*The Blue Cross*—is like the event which gave rise to it; it only concerns the knowledge the priest has gained in the confessional. But the later stories revolve around the doctrine of *Heretics* and *Orthodoxy,* the idea that humility is the root of knowledge. This is a common-sense argument, not strictly theological, and the fact that Father Brown is a priest did not mean much in the stories written between 1910 and 1914. Father Brown wore a collar for the same reason that he wore rumpled clothes and a blank expression—because one does not expect shrewd knowledge of the world from a priest, just as one does not expect it from a moon-faced dumpling of a man. The first series was interrupted by the war, and Father Brown did not reappear until 1923, after Chesterton's entry into the Church; this second series, comprising the last three of the five volumes written, gave deeper meaning to Father Brown's innocence, as we shall see.

The success of the stories was merited. For one thing, their brevity was an advantage. Chesterton's technique of juxtaposing

vivid symbols was always rapid, and he had obvious difficulty
keeping a long story in motion. Even in the Father Brown tales he
symbolically tells the story several times. One is not supposed to
follow clues so much as to read an heraldic device which foreshad-
ows the story's point—the French cartoon which gives away the
fury of the guillotine;[13] the set of mirrors that presents beforehand
the mystery of self-knowledge through self-ignorance;[14] the dum-
mies which suggest the real men we treat as automata.[15] Social
satire, comedy, and debate give the complication necessary to detective stories; but the secret at the core is simple, as it must be in
all such mysteries.[16] The priest is only a marionette, but the puppets act out entertaining and deeply significant parables. By giving a moral significance to the action, Chesterton avoided the
anti-climax and mere dispersal of interest which is the danger of
the detective novel's concluding pages.[17]

DRAMA

Chesterton's first period of narrative fecundity reached its climax
in his first play. Shaw practically forced Chesterton to write *Magic*,
and his knowledge of the theater and of Chesterton were both vindicated when the play was put on. Drama is a thing of conflict, and
all of Chesterton's thought was dialectic. Drama is a compressed
and heightened form, a ritual of action and symbolic words; and
Chesterton's critical mind worked always in symbol, preferably in
symbolic narrative. His abrupt repartee and gesture often seem too
thin, too rapid in the leisurely-paced, introspective form of the
novel, but they are perfectly suited to the stage. Suspense and sensationalism are the stock-in-trade of Sophocles and Shakespeare, so
that Aristotle called the high point of every play a reversal.

The prelude of *Magic* sets the play's tone; but its function was not only to plunge the audience into a mist and agnosticism about fairies. That is more aptly effected by the shallow dialogue of the rationalists than by the brief meeting of two shadows. George Moore objected to this prelude as a non-functioning ornament; but his misreading of the play appears in the fact that he regrets the love between the conjurer and the girl.[18] He thinks this makes the conjurer too solid, in a play whose atmosphere should be misty and transcendental. But the conjurer is far from this airy irresponsibility: his magic is all too solid and crushing a burden, his flesh too real. This is the only realistic hero Chesterton ever imagined, because he is the only hero who sins, credibly, before our eyes.

The prelude is a parable of the love that is awakened in the scenes that follow. It resembles the Don Juan myth which Shaw inserts into a conventional comedy—an interpretation of the real issues moving under the brittle conversation and actions, the "simple" comedy of manners. The meeting of the conjurer and the girl represents that stirring of trust and doubt about each other which Shakespeare presented in the false battle of Beatrice with Benedick. Both Chesterton's characters later confess that their fairy tale was false; they knew it was not a meeting of elf and child, but of man and woman. This confession is at once a recognition of each other and of themselves, of their human love. The mist is not for a miracle, but for the supposedly conventional situation of drama—the obscure meeting of man and woman across the gulf that separates them.

The conjurer's magic is never associated with anything misty. It is as solid as sin, because it is a sin. The master stroke of the play is that which turns the red lamp blue. There is no movement of a wand, no whispered incantation. The conjurer does not stir at all; but matter suffers change under his own spiritual alteration. Sin as a simple *fact* has never been so effectively put on the stage. This theatrical magic of Chesterton's makes possible that filling of the stage with devils which is so weird, even as we read it, in the last act. The first climax was a simple change of color among motionless actors. In the last crisis, men actually leave the stage, surrendering its center to unseen actors. The very flippancy and absurdity of the dialogue accents the invisible forces at work in this play—from the incantation of love, through the invasion by devils, to the resolution which is also an exorcism.

The play is, in some sense, a climax in Chesterton's life; and, as fits such a completion, it serves almost as a résumé of his movement up to that point. The magician is the only man who possesses the truth, and he purchased this knowledge by going into the abyss, by knowing what devils prey on men. Even more important, his greater knowledge makes him actually the greatest sinner on the scene. The others are stupid; but they are, for that very reason, innocent. However sharp the colors and crises of this drama, it possesses what all the grimy things which clutter our stage claim and never achieve, a ruthless realism. The man with faith is not automatically saved, nor ever happy; he has a higher knowledge, and therefore he is the tempted and caducous agent in the story. His morning headaches after dabbling in spiritualism were a literal part of Chesterton's own experience that left a deep imprint on his life.[19]

The other characters reflect Chesterton's experiences, also, and the stages of his development. The knot to be untangled in the action is the madness that has come upon a young fellow who would explain everything. This is the stuff of *Orthodoxy*'s argument and the Slade experiences. The doctor espouses a less fanatic but equally narrow belief in science. The girl who believes in fairies but not in devils has the poetry which *Orthodoxy* praises; she is Lady Olive from *The Wild Knight,* but there is a deeper criticism of her belief in innocence. She almost loses her lover because she doubts his sin. The Anglican clergyman, a Modernist who defends tradition and healthy drinking and history, who revels in the poetry of *Job*, takes the same approach which *Heretics* expounded. The Reverend Smith does not have a literal faith in any set creed; the sinner must teach him to believe in the devil.

By the time *Magic* reached the theater, it ran concomitantly with another drama which tore Chesterton away from the stage and art and criticism—the trial of his brother. He left the stage for the courtroom, and he never really returned.

8.

RHYME AND REASON

Chesterton's favorite reading from childhood was the poets—Isaias and Job and the psalms, Shakespeare and Browning and Swinburne. His taste was catholic, including Pope as well as Shelley, though he was always faintly irritated by Milton's inhuman epic. Very soon he had begun his own versifying, interspersing ballads modeled on Scott with his first romances and fairy tales. The next two stages of his work have already been mentioned—the sprawling monologues in *The Debater* and the attempt to put the Notebook's aphorisms into rhymed form. The poems of his first volume of importance, *The Wild Knight*, arose from that effort, and they mark the end of his specifically poetic ambitions. After this first volume of such promise, he became a jester in verse as in prose.

The Wild Knight includes poems like "The Fish," which Chesterton had been working on since the Slade days. "By a Babe Unborn," which the *Autobiography* relates to his struggle to burst out of his own mind, is a concentration into verse of the story he had variously recast, then published, as "A Crazy Tale." The binding theme of the volume is Chesterton's universal theme of praise for existence, but the nightmare-separation from the world of reality is still vividly remembered. In eight poems we find the fate of the outcast depicted, becoming at its most intense moments the final loneliness of an unregarded death;[1] while in two poems solipsism is directly described.[2] To Kenner's thesis it might, therefore, be objected that Chesterton *was* writing from his own experience, and of things he had intensely felt. But this response is too pat. The threat Chesterton felt was of madness, and the response is intellectually defiant, that is, argumentative. Argument rarely leads to good poetry; it would finally divert Chesterton from the course of the poet. But in this first volume, the intention and the workmanship are a poet's.

Diffusion, a Swinburnian laxity and facility, were the faults Chesterton had inherited from his early work; but we can see here his conscious opposition to this drift. He strives for a tight and pregnant simplicity, and often achieves it:

THE SKELETON

Chattering finch and water-fly
Are not merrier than I;

> Here among the flowers I lie
> Laughing everlastingly.
> No; I may not tell the best;
> Surely, friends, I might have guessed
> Death was but the good King's jest,
> It was hid so carefully.

The entire volume shows an attempt at verbal asceticism which did not last. Swinburne's influence is still here, but in a very short flower of the sea; Browning's, too, but in a very short monologue. The greatest resemblance, strangely enough, did not arise from direct imitation. These poems, like Blake's, are very fierce auguries of innocence, their rhetoric patterned after that of the prophets, as in the poem whose first two lines are a paraphrase of Isaias' opening distich:

> To teach the grey earth like a child,
> To bid the heavens repent.

If the lion does not exactly lie down with the lamb, "The Donkey" moves surprisingly like the Tyger, and "The Fish" and "The Skeleton" are also of this company. Another brief poem traces the world's vitality into the narrow chamber of a seed, and discovers there

> God almighty, and with him
> Cherubim and Seraphim,
> Filling all eternity—
> Adonai Elohim.

Even more important than these stylistic considerations is the fact that many of these poems achieve insight without argument—an attainment difficult enough to one of his critical cast of mind, and one which he never made his own during the many years after this first book appeared. The poem to St. Joseph is an example:

> If the stars fell; night's nameless dreams
>   Of bliss and blasphemy came true,
> If skies were green and snow were gold,
>   And you loved me as I love you;
>
> O long light hands and curled brown hair
>   And eyes where sits a naked soul;
> Dare I even then draw near and burn
>   My fingers in the aureole?
>
> Yes, in the one wise foolish hour
>   God gives this strange strength to a man.
> He can demand, though not deserve,
>   Where ask he cannot, seize he can.
>
> But once the blood's wild wedding o'er,
>   Were not dread his, half dark desire,
> To see the Christ-child in the cot,
>   The Virgin Mary by the fire?

The poem does not hinge on intellectual paradox, but on a real emotional ambivalence: Chesterton sees rather than understands man's conflicting instincts—that sex is fruition and expenditure, that virginity is barren yet has in itself some holiness. The poem's structure is perfect, rising to one climax, then reaching a deeper climax and mystery. The symbols are theological, as in Blake's work, but the reality is analogously physical and moral and mystical and mad.

METAPHYSICAL MINSTRELSY

But other poems in the book, especially the exercises in political rhetoric, show that paradox was driving out the autonomy of direct emotional vision. This is not to say, as Kenner does, that philosophy was driving out poetry. It may have been poetry that was receding, but the new element was not philosophy. "Paradox" is constructed of the same symbolic stuff in Chesterton's verse as in his novels, and it must be judged by the same norms. Chesterton ceased to be a poet, in the conventional sense, but he became a rhyming jester. His later volumes, except for one poem which was in itself a book, were mere collections of his occasional verse written for the newspaper or for his friends. They are haphazard collections, and include things which are merely topical and things which are worthless. Three things Chesterton could write, those three which Shaw could not[3]—a love song, a war song, a drinking song. They are songs rather than poems, spontaneous as some feudal bard's "journalism." It is extraordinary how completely Chesterton's talents did express themselves in the manner of a jongleur. His drinking songs have less argument in them than any of his later verses; they arose from a deep enjoyment of his role as a truly festive Feste; for only the metaphysical jester can escape the melancholy of all other clowns. If we add two more genres to the list, both entirely in keeping with the minstrel's repertoire, it will be complete—satire and carols.

Haste and extravagance are marks of the jester's style—for it is not a mere lack of style. Even in *The Wild Knight* we can see this new mode of song coming to birth. One of the solipsist poems, in which the poet tries to escape a horrible world wherein everyone bears his own recurrent countenance, ends with these lines:

Then my dream snapped: and with a heart that leapt
I saw across the tavern where I slept,
The sight of all my life most full of grace,
A gin-damned drunkard's wan half-witted face.

There is a jolting bathos in the revelation of the poem's scene—as if the nightmare had been caused only by whisky fumes; but Chesterton had to admit this setting in order to make a drunkard the vision of grace, as Orm had been in another context. There is in the relishing of this extreme contrast a humor that is answered by the vivid, even gaudy, violence of the last verse. This is not poetry, but it is artistic in its aim; it is a metaphysical joke. The minstrel is laughing, and especially laughing at himself.

Chesterton's ability to play with pictures brightly picked out was simply another aspect of his central rhetoric of jest. Yet if it be granted that Chesterton was that kind of wild and logical symbolist which I have called a metaphysical jester, many objections to this kind of writing remain: for instance, the claim that it is merely philosophy in disguise. But we have already considered this claim in the case of Chesterton's novels, and found it baseless. A more serious charge is that such a rhetoric of ideas is "propaganda" in the modern sense of intellectual seduction.

Propaganda is not art; neither is it education of an honest sort. Propaganda is that bastard form of art and instruction which sugars a doctrine with colors and forms not integral to it or to the artifact used for this indoctrination. But Chesterton did not build an argument, then stick it all over with figures of speech. The symbols came first to him, as his real form of expression. These are always apt symbols, carrying their own meaning; there is no previously formulated expression of the ideas to which they must be fitted. They are the expression. We have seen this in the case of colors, which had a symbolic urgency which was activated in many ways, but always from within. Chesterton felt the symbol's vitality before he knew what it signified. Even persons and events—Joan of Arc, Lepanto—were symbols to him before he understood what they might symbolize. The figure of the white horse, too, had haunted him in various guises long before he thought of it primarily as Alfred's horse. If anyone thinks he is a mere propagandist, let him say what explicit concept or course of argument that white shape is meant to promote. An honest mind will soon disappear into the depths of that richest of Chesterton's symbols.

Chesterton's verses are those of the court fool, who does not pretend to make things as sane men do. The characters in his novels are not symbols of men, like Hamlet, but of ideas, like Zarathustra. Such a jester stands outside propaganda, the illegitimate use of art *ab extra,* in the same way that the satirist does. Oblique comment is the jester's mode, as syllogisms are the technique of the logician. A propagandist can use attractive but fallacious syllogisms, as he uses appealing but inept symbols. But this does not mean that the real logician or satirist or jester is a propagandist.

The proof that Chesterton was not a propagandist is that he ceased trying to write poetry and fiction of the conventional type. He forswore the quiet stories and self-contained nonsense verses which he had first excelled in. His first slim publication, *Greybeards at Play,* distorted the form of nonsense verses by inserting satire on decadent artists and philosophers.[4] He had the good sense not to attempt this again, and I think he grew to dislike his one essay into "pure" nonsense.[5] His work from that time on has a uniformity of texture which Chesterton sustained so well that men forgot it was artificial. It is reasonable to say that his artifact is worthless, but it is simply absurd to claim that it is not an artifact.

But if the verse be called a metaphysical minstrelsy—neither philosophy nor propaganda—other criticisms can still be adduced. For instance, an *a priori* argument against such verse is that its blatant and over-vivid coloring forbids all subtlety and makes deli-

cate insight impossible. But jugglery is entirely a matter of delicate balance; and, as Chesterton frequently insisted in his comments on pantomime, even an exaggerated phrase or gesture can
"act out" what is shadowy or deep-hidden. The poem in which
Christ's double role is described—he is Zeus; he is Prometheus—
is projected as a whirling pantomime of the eagle and the vulture,
cornfields and chasms, daylight and fires in the night.[6] Yet the
concept is a delicate one, nowhere else in Chesterton, nor in any
other writer, given this uniquely illuminating expression. One
cannot make the eagle and vulture mere trappings for the statement that God is both order and act. Such abstract words, or any
multiplication of them, do not express what Chesterton says.
There is no other way of saying it: God is Zeus, God is Prometheus. Similarly, there is no other way of saying what he says of
the Virgin in "The White Witch"—that Mary is an anti-
witch, who drives out all the evil phantasms which the image
of Hecate—of that deepest of human perversions, the woman of
evil—has spread in the imagination of men since the dawn
of time.[7]

Even single lines have this ability to say much in a simple and
direct stroke. The entire map of Europe is sketched in *Lepanto*, so
that a single brush-stroke fixes, in this heraldry, France:

The shadow of the Valois was yawning at the Mass.

The cobwebby assonance is overdone, as the slumbering heaviness
of "Sloth" is overdone in a mediaeval carving; but the exaggeration
touches depths that careful statement often does not reach.

Mediaeval art is aptly brought in here—heraldry and the windows and the stiff chasubles and the gold everywhere. We have
long since overcome the misconception, held for centuries, that
only chiaroscuro can achieve subtlety and open man's soul. The

density and richness of a window are complicated by the very brilliance and multiplicity of colors. Every Gothic cathedral wore motley. That dazzling multiplicity is what we have noticed already in Chesterton's tales—the jostling suspension of all colors in the scheme. The same technique is used in the poems. All the issues of liberty and Europe's fate are traced in the whirl of *Lepanto*'s colors, and then the whole thing is set in a comic frame which deepens the significance and interrelation of the historical sections of the poem. Chesterton looks backward from Quixote, using the comic knight as a means of understanding the hopeless, victorious knight of Austria.

Another objection, tangential to those just considered, is that such obvious and crude rhetoric as Chesterton used is easily reeled off by anyone with a modicum of talent. The fallacy at work here should be recognized. The juggler's art may not be worthy of exalted attention, but it is not easy. No one ever juggled by accident. It is an art, and it takes practice. The same is true of Chesterton's symbolic juggling of words and colors. Even in its simplest form this is a difficult thing. It may be a waste of time to write drinking songs; but when good ones are written, they are written only by skilled artificers, like Horace and Shakespeare. Where are the swarms of men succeeding in this easy pastime?

Chesterton certainly considered facility a part of his task as a minstrel; not simply a temptation, as it is for most poets. It is a mistake to think there is no asceticism in the immediate volley, as in the six years' chiseling. The asceticism lies in the difficulties undertaken, the willingness to accept any challenge. Look through the collected poems and notice the variety of forms Chesterton used: sonnets, triolets, ballades, odes, blank verse, couplets. His ballad forms are often deceptively simple in appearance. He tried one difficult metre in his first volume, with little success. It was used in a poem devoted to the praise of Woman. Many years later he used the rhythm again in a fine tribute of the Virgin:

> And a dwarfed and dwindled race in the dark red deserts
>> Stumbled and strayed,
> While one in the mortal shape that was once for immortals
>> Made, was remade.[8]

His early ballad of Gibeon, otherwise worthless, is a panting obstacle course of feminine rhymes. He frequently used the rhyme-scheme of *In Memoriam*. All this is tour de force, admittedly; but tour de force is by definition that which is not easy. And, like another master of tour de force, Chesterton as he ends the refrain thrusts home, not only in symbolic poems like "Lepanto" and "The Monster," but in the acerb verses on F. E. Smith and the Bishop who called St. Francis flea-bitten, in the brilliant translations of Dante, Du Bellay, Guérin.

THE BALLAD OF THE WHITE HORSE

Because Chesterton was a true balladeer, he could use certain traditional forms with a spontaneity and sense of the form's genius which is denied most poets by their very acuteness and personal accent. This was true not only of the drinking song but of the Christmas carol. Because of this, it was possible that Chesterton could write one kind of poem which would not be only jest or tour de force. He could retain his loose and rapid spontaneity, yet work to a larger plan, polishing and reshaping its parts. He could stitch together the ballad stanzas as the original singers had done at the dawn of epic, when the stories of Robin Hood and Roland were fashioned from the old, sporadic material to a new and larger pattern.

Chesterton's instincts led him to this form, and they did not fail him in the choice or execution. This was his most serious artistic endeavor, and he made the attempt but once. For at least four years that we know of he worked on *The Ballad of the White Horse,* the only example in his career of such extended labor and delayed publication. More than this, he used symbols, stanza forms, and words which he had been collecting in his mind for years. The white horse had been his private symbol of chivalry since the time when he owned a hobbyhorse of that color; an inn sign, a canvassing trip in Wiltshire, a honeymoon memory—these and many other experiences had been stored in the symbol's energy.[9] The first two lines of the finished poem were the inspired opening of a boyhood poem on Moses. One of Alfred's prayers had come to Chesterton in his sleep, and was copied down, in the first person, many years before the ballad appeared.[10] We can see the changes made in one section of the ballad by comparing it to the "Fragment of a Ballad of Alfred" published in the *Albany* for 1907, four years before publication of *The White Horse.*[11]

Chesterton's fascination with the ballad form dated from his school days, from the time when first he read Scott and Macaulay. A paper he delivered to the J.D.C. shows that he soon went to the original English ballads.[12] Discussing them in this paper, he praises especially their vigor of epithet and "signature phrase" which can bring a character to life at one stroke. Many of the figures in *The White Horse* are picked out in this vivid manner: the deserted king, for instance, is "Alfred of the lonely spear." One of his own first ballads, sung by the minstrel in a story written at the St. Paul's School, resembles the strain of the melancholy minstrel, Elf:

> Softly and silently
> Sail the fair Valkyrs,
> Spirit-receiving ones
> Whispering to warsmiths . . .

Bending their bright course
Laden with thane-spirits
Up to high halls
Where with the wise Woden
Baldur the beautiful
Reigneth for Right.

Whenever Chesterton's ballad is brought up, the inevitable comparison is with Coleridge's "Rime." Maurice Baring, in his review of *The White Horse,* remarked that Chesterton told a vivid story as well as Coleridge but did not let the tale alone carry the theme.[13] He thought Chesterton's ballad was, for this reason, less "authentic." But this is the one point on which the more recent poem has an unquestionable superiority. Coleridge's theme is not more complex and exalted than Chesterton's, but it is less "popular." Chesterton works from popular sentiment, as the ballad must; his poem is full of patriotism and the spirit of a single landscape:

He sang of war in the warm wet shires
  Where rain nor fruitage fails,
Where England of the motley states
Deepens like a garden to the gates
  In the purple walls of Wales.

Coleridge filled the English ballad with Oriental horrors, but *The White Horse*

Seems like the tales a whole tribe feigns,
  Too English to be true.

Chesterton recaptures, moreover, that moment when the primitive ballads were woven together to become national epic. His poem is the record of a war from the heroic age; epic boasts and similes, a national hero, the hushed eve of battle and the screaming day that follows, make *The White Horse* echo the tales of Roland and Henry V as well as of Robin Hood. Coleridge's ballad, on the other hand, is a weird voyage into the self, its introversion making the "authentic" heroic note impossible.

The local scene and fiery patriotism do not limit *The White Horse*. The vale of Alfred is England, and England is Christendom, in the poem. The "triple symbol" mentioned in the prose introduction is an interpretation of the elements in the English greatness—Saxon, Celtic, Roman. But they are also symbols of that complexus which Chesterton described in *Blake* as the formula of Western man—pagan poetry, Roman order, and Christian religion. Chesterton always insisted that Christianity did not drive out pagan things but subsumed them even in growing from them. There is a real conflict between poetry and reason, faith and doubt, the supernatural and nature, but this dialectic is life-giving, not destructive. This is the meaning of Colan, Eldred, and Marcus, united by Alfred, in the van of the English armies. In *The Everlasting Man* Chesterton would again describe a triple dialectic, considering three stages of history—not chronological stages, simply, but co-existent levels of human reality. First there is "minimal man"—child, savage, artist, god among the beasts. Then there is civilized man, giving law to the nations and searching the heavens. Finally, completing and ordinating the former elements, without banishing them, there is Christian man, exiled citizen of the City of God.

Against this Christian balance and complexity come the barbarian forces of simplification and destruction. The Danish heroes are merely the Christian thanes simplified, isolated from the balancing discipline which Christianity imposes on man's nature. Saxon Eldred typifies the love of life, of wine, of "slow moons and certain things"; his farm has become, by vow and charity, a haven of the poor and a storehouse of earth's good things. Danish Harold is the same type of man, but one whose vigor and blood have flamed into a destructive sensualism. Gaelic Colan is a mystic whose gods must be harnessed by the new God from Rome; but Danish Elf is the poet whose gods are free, and who spread their beautiful barrenness everywhere. Marcus is the lover of order for its own sake, of force and process subjected to a constructive asceticism; whereas "Ogier of the stone and sling" loves destruction for its own sake, and expresses the nihilist mystique in clear-etched lines which reveal the depths Chesterton's verse could reach:

> There lives one moment for a man
>   When the door at his shoulder shakes,
> When the taut rope parts under the pull,
> And the barest branch is beautiful
>   One moment, while it breaks.

Guthrum rises over his warriors as Alfred towers among the thanes. The pagan leader is a "clerk," whose weary sentences have the beauty of lyrics from some Greek tragedy:

> Do we not know, have we not heard,
> The soul is like a lost bird,
>   The body a broken shell?
>
> And a man hopes, being ignorant,
>   Till in white woods apart
> He finds at last the lost bird dead;
> And a man may still lift up his head,
>   But never more his heart.

This love of life is Horatian, strong within narrow limits, but desolate when the man lifts his eyes to the horizon and the encircling dark:

> The little brooks are very sweet,
>   Like a girl's ribbons curled,
> But the great sea is bitter
>   That washes all the world.

Even Guthrum, therefore, must try to forget his philosophy in the drunkenness of war. All the Danes' joy and wisdom leads to sterility and destruction. Marcus builds as a pagan, but he slowly changes into Ogier unless Christianity intervenes, "because it is only Christian men Guard even heathen things." Creation is loved with permanence only by men who believe in the Creator. The simple love of the Danes, uncomplicated by the mysteries of faith and humility, shifts with every mood, and brings ruin with its shiftings—fire on Ely fen, molten lead on Glastonbury, Roman colonnades left like "the spectre of a street," and the great hieroglyphic Horse fading, unkempt, to an undecipherable smudge on the hills. The Christians, on the other hand, keep arch and book, sing a hymn of the crafts at the height of battle, and tend the strange white sign stamped on their native earth. Alfred sees God as a laborer who fills the vines and tends the fields, and Marcus calls him "God that is a craftsman good."[14]

"LIKE A GOOD CHILD AT PLAY"

Alfred becomes the central Christian warrior by undergoing defeat, by "hardening his heart with hope" when there is no earthly hope. Only then is the vision given to him:

> In the river island of Athelney
>   With the river running past
> In colours of such simple creed
> All things sprang at him, sun and weed,

> Till the grass grew to be grass indeed,
>
> And the tree was a tree at last.

He is granted that carelessness about the world which alone reveals the world. The pagan must cling to the tree finally—making of it a god, a portent, an end—or destroy it in his rage. But the Christian recognizes the endangered and divine world as a picture wrought by the Artist who "saw that it was good."

Yet Alfred still asks for a pagan wisdom, for prevision and some power over destiny: will he win, or again be sent reeling? The Virgin answers that the Christian clarity of wisdom goes with an ignorance of such evil reckoning of the odds. The tree is a tree at last because it cannot be twisted into a magic instrument of power. It is a simple tool in the toy world of nature which reflects, in time, the City of God. Faith, like Christian hope, is based on a certain ignorance; it recognizes simple facts like trees. On this ignorance true knowledge can be built. Only Christianity has made men content with such knowledge, justifying the wisdom which grows from ignorance by making it correspond to the created reality which came from nothingness. The pagan does not believe in this radical creation of the world from nothing, nor in the formation of wisdom from innocence. He seeks always to know why he knows what he knows. He cannot begin at the beginning—his own beginning and the world's—because this involves a preliminary self-annihilation through humility, a humility which reenacts one's passage out of the abyss of nonexistence. But Alfred, stripped of all pretensions in defeat, accepts that state of ignorance in which man can be taught, as by one's mother:

> And he saw in a little picture,
>
> Tiny and far away,
>
> His mother sitting in Egbert's hall,

And a book she showed him, very small,
Where a sapphire Mary sat in stall
With a golden Christ at play.

This is the argument of *Orthodoxy* carried to its completion. In *Orthodoxy* Chesterton traced the folly of self-sufficient wisdom and claimed that the Church alone preserved knowledge—until we pulled the mitre from pontifical man and saw his head come off with it. But the approach was negative in that book; the pure intellect destroyed itself, and poetry was referred to as a sane counterbalance to such intellection. Here Chesterton looks at the *positive* wisdom of Christian innocence, the vision of trees as trees, the childlike hope and love which make Alfred follow a pillar not of fire but of darkness:

The men of the East may spell the stars,
And times and triumphs mark,
But the men signed of the cross of Christ
Go gaily in the dark.

Christianity saves even heathen things, but this "pragmatic" value of the Faith is only made possible by a deepest state of complete innocence which does not seek to use or to reject the world. The figure of the White Horse on the hill is a sacrament meant to reveal Alfred's love of his native earth in all its autonomy. But he does not fight, ultimately, to save the White Horse, or his kingdom, or the churches. He fights as Joan of Arc did, gravely and in ignorance of the reasons for which heaven bade her go forth, ready for victory or defeat, to defend that strange thing, scrawled on the earth of Europe, which we call France. Alfred is ready to lose all or win all with the same cheerfulness of faith, knowing that his home is here and yet not here.

The specifically Christian "detachment" and mysticism are ar-

ticulated with precision in this attitude of Alfred. Christian asceticism does not arise from the simple opposition of matter to spirit,
of time to eternity, of this life to some other. This cannot be the
Christian's mind on these issues, for God not only made this
world, His being supports and pervades and continues to activate
it. He is in Orm and in Guthrum. He "labors" to

> Build this pavilion of the pines,
> And herd the fowls and fill the vines,
> And labour and pass and leave no signs
> Save mercy and mystery.

Yet God constructs no lasting city here; it is a world of mystery
and adventure, where His champions must go gaily in the dark,
prepared to see their wisdom and planning collapse as ludicrously
as the Council's did in *Thursday*. Around Alfred gather all these reflections on existence as something immeasurably valuable, yet
something won by a carelessness and self-forgetfulness which only
real faith in God has ever given men.

Of course, Alfred's vision at Athelney is only the beginning of
the revelation, in and through him, of this Christian mysticism.
The poem builds to a higher vision at its climax, the center of calm
light in which a child plays—an odd, idyllic interlude placed dramatically in a setting of war and slaughter. It is this white light
which fires the motley colors of battle and heroism and victory.
Every line of the poem leads to that vision or follows from it. Alfred
expresses a new facet of it in each episode. In his call to the warriors
he repeats the Virgin's summons to the wise ignorance of faith:

> I call the muster of Wessex men
> From grassy hamlet or ditch or den,
> To break and be broken, God knows when,
> But I have seen for whom.

In the Danish camp he scorns the pagan desires, shouting his joy at defeat against their weariness of triumph. In the forest he takes as his ensign of royalty a blow from a peasant woman; and when humility lights him through and through, laughter follows:

> The giant laughter of Christian men
>   That roars through a thousand tales,
> Where greed is an ape and pride is an ass,
> And Jack's away with his master's lass,
> And the miser is banged with all his brass,
>   The farmer with all his flails.
>
> Tales that tumble and tales that trick,
>   Yet end not all in scorning—
> Of kings and clowns in a merry plight,
> And the clock gone wrong and the world gone right
> That the mummers sing upon Christmas night
>   And Christmas Day in the morning.

Laughter is very near that childlike innocence which the Virgin brought to Alfred, as we see in the laughing Madonna and Child of mediaeval art. Chesterton has fitted a separate "discovery" of his youth—laughter as a medium of knowledge and sanity—into the total Christian reality.

Before the battle, the pagan Harold delivers the ritual epic boast, but Colan makes real in this context St. Paul's "boast in the Lord":

> Oh, truly we be broken hearts;
>   For that cause, it is said,
> We light our candles to that Lord
>   That broke Himself for bread.[15]

When Colan flings his sword at Harold, Alfred sees this act as a parable of the whole campaign's meaning. Christian men are given victory because they surrender it, they are given the world as a gift only when they recognize that it is *God*'s gift and possession: "Man shall not taste of victory Till he throws his sword away":

> For this is the manner of Christian men,
> Whether of steel or priestly pen,
> That they cast their hearts out of their ken
> To get their heart's desire.

Then the champions fight according to their character—Eldred straightforwardly, by mere mass; Marcus in order, stemming the retreat when superstition begins to dissolve the Wessex line; Colan fighting, by some unworldly energy, longer than the others, only to fall like them at last:

> As to the Haut King came at morn
> Dead Roland on a doubtful horn,
> Seemed unto Alfred lightly borne
> The last cry of the Gael.

These thanes are not only dead; they have been forgotten. They fought as Christians, but without the crystalline innocence of Alfred. "The spirit of the child" which Christ recommended is seen playing on the shore, along the line which God laid to sunder earth and sea. The child builds a tower, and the sea destroys it, and the child builds it up again. So does Alfred fight, "gravely, As a good child at play." Again defeated, his brave allies dead, he continues to obey the Virgin's call to battle with as simple trust as if the day had been his:

Came ruin and the rain that burns,
Returning as a wheel returns,
And crouching in the furze and ferns
    He began his life once more.

Then comes the last hopeless charge, the vision of Mary over the field, the impossible victory, the baptism of Guthrum, the peace of Wessex instituted under Alfred. But in time the sea washes in on the tower again, and Alfred in his age must buckle on armor and fight, calmly as the child rebuilds in sand.[16] Alfred now disappears from the poem; only echoes and dusty visions return from his campaign. We are left watching the grass grow around the Horse, news returning only at intervals of the grey horse that carries Alfred in his new battles. So the king disappears into the smoke and dust of history which had been stirred up in the first few lines of the poem. The bright vision breaks up and fades, and the White Horse is seen only through a blur of green.

PART THREE (1913–1921)

Vigil

9.

THE FOUR LOYALTIES

The year 1912 marked the high point of Chesterton's popularity. Father Brown had just appeared, and *The Ballad of the White Horse*. He was writing his study of the Victorian Age and his first play. His home in Beaconsfield was new to him and his London ties still strong. With Shaw and Barrie and Baring and Cecil he light-heartedly performed in mock trials, debates, movies, masquerades, all those prewar high jinks which, in retrospect, seemed so unreal.

The chapters in the second section of this book suggest something of Chesterton's versatility during the first twelve years of his popularity, and they could be multiplied almost indefinitely to cover his work as lecturer, illustrator, or conversationalist. It is unfortunate that Chesterton never had a masculine Boswell from those tavern days. One aspect, it may be noticed, I have not mentioned, an aspect of great importance. There is no chapter here entitled "Journalism." This is not only because Chesterton was always a journalist, no matter what he was writing, just as he was always a jester (two things he made almost synonymous in his role of commentator). It is certainly true that his journalism constitutes a separate problem. He did not write for the newspapers in order to reach the stage (like Shaw), or the library shelves (like Dickens); journalism was his entire career, and he refused ever to identify his work by another name. His choice was undoubtedly sound, for the jester's is no longer an accepted office in society, and the prestige and irresponsibility of the press, its continuous appearance and discontinuity of subject matter, make it plastic to the intentions of a conscious jester. But the trade has its own perils, and Chesterton suffered from all of them. He lost his position in the enemy's journals when his last article appeared, at the beginning of 1913, in *The Daily News.* His subsequent association with the Socialist *Daily Herald* was obviously doomed, and his connection with his brother's paper did not offer the challenge of opposition, the chance for repartee, which brings out the jester's talent. The only lasting rostrum open to him was purchased at the cost of the jester's immunity; in 1905 he began writing "Our Notebook" for *The Illustrated London News,* on the condition that he *avoid the subjects of politics and religion!* Of course, he stretched this tether as far as it would go in the thirty-one years he wrote the column; but weights were put on the jongleur's dancing limbs, and the effect was almost crippling. The page to be filled was long (fifteen hundred words), and Chesterton was led to a use of foolery that was not as functional as it is in his best writing. The tripartite rhythm of his real work was thus destroyed: he prolonged the first stage of surprise at oddities as long as he possibly could; he took the bite out of the dialectic argumentation which follows on such surprise; and he rarely reached the point of vision and release which gave license to his ambitious rhetoric. Unfortunately, the convenient length of these weekly columns, and their generalized subject matter, made them the principal source of his collections of essays, even for the posthumous ones. There can be no question but that these essays, collected in twelve volumes, are an inferior (though widely read) part of Chesterton's output. They served their purpose, keeping him before the public, guaranteeing a platform for his other work.

Unfortunately, nothing but journalism remained during the dry stretch that followed his first period of spontaneous creativity. During the war and its aftermath many things combined with illness and overwork to make Chesterton's spirits flag—the one thing which destroys a jester's ability to perform. Learned men, literary craftsmen, rarely lose their specific talent; but the creator of vision needs the medium of that vision, and an intellectual buoyancy could alone sustain the difficult play of symbol and ideas which Chesterton had undertaken. There is, as he often said, an asceticism in levity, far more in the lifting and poise of the mind than in physical acrobatics.

A TIME OF TRIAL

It would be wrong, however, to make the decade or so which followed on the year 1912 a time of mere weariness and relapse. Chesterton's attention did not simply fail; it was diverted to personal problems which were not less demanding because negative in character. He could do little in these matters but sustain a vigil.

There were four major claims made upon his loyalty in these years, each of them a continuing demand.

The first claim was his brother's, in the scandal of the Marconi shares. Cecil had found the tracks, only partially effaced, of a government transaction made firm in the breezy way of the powerful: Lloyd George (then Chancellor of the Exchequer), Rufus Isaacs (the Attorney General), and Henry Isaacs invested heavily in shares of the American Marconi Company (Godfrey Isaacs, director) just before the English Marconi received a government contract for Empirewide service. Cecil determined to force the truth out of that vast machinery which can rarely be so arraigned; he deliberately courted a libel suit in order to use his trial as an investigation of the matter. Wealth, prestige, and skill were mobilized against Cecil, so effectively that it seemed, in the last stages of the trial, as if he would go to jail; but he retreated on several issues and escaped with a fine.

Chesterton devotes an entire chapter of his *Autobiography* to this trial, and that space does not exaggerate the proportions which it assumed in his life. It was his only encounter with the iron ambition of financiers and politicians; it tempered all he later wrote about politicians, libel laws, English courts, Jewish financiers, and much else. The articles he wrote in *The Daily Herald* during and after the trial (they were published five years later as *The Utopia of Usurers*) have a new bite: often as he had exaggerated, never before this had he shown an exaggerated personal bitterness.

The first claim had been on Chesterton's family affection; the second was on something rooted almost as deeply in him—patriotism. The war was a shock to him, though he had acquired Belloc's distrust of Prussia as a barbarian force (a distrust that appears in the songs of Elf and Ogier in *The White Horse*). He saw the moral issues which mere disgust with the fighting was to obscure; and despite his hatred of international finance, he refused to admit discussion on that level as the real issue. His own duty was clear to him, as we can see from a letter he wrote (but did not send) to Shaw, in which he pleads with great embarrassment and delicacy that Shaw give up the role of mere "awkward questioner" at a time when men were staking their lives on a moral commitment of the entire nation. It was time for the court fool to become Taillefer.

Then, just as the war ended, Cecil—who had volunteered for duty—died in France. Gilbert had been editing *The New Witness* since his brother enlisted, and he felt bound to continue the journal and uphold the ideals for which Cecil had risked imprisonment. This third burden of these years he carried for the rest of his life. It was an unfortunate decision. Chesterton had neither the shrewdness nor the pugnacity to accomplish the practical reforms Cecil aimed at, and he could not lead or control those who had joined in the assault on the party system's corruption. Even when, with the years, the paper's name and program were substantially altered, its followers remained a strange collection with little understanding of their nominal leader, matched only by his own inability to take their measure.

Chesterton's health was never good, and in 1914 it collapsed under the accelerating labors and misfortunes of these years. For three months he hovered near death, wandering often in the dim world of coma and forgetfulness. Because of his previous hints, as well as his mumbled words and prayers during this illness, his wife told Msgr. O'Connor to be ready, when Gilbert returned to lucidity, for a quick summons. She felt he would want to enter the Catholic Church. But at his recovery, the war work and the new burden of editing Cecil's paper absorbed Chesterton's attention, delaying that decision which most strained all his former loyalties.

In the dedication to *The White Horse* Chesterton wrote:

> Therefore I bring these rhymes to you
> Who brought the cross to me.

Some take this to mean that Chesterton became an Anglican at her urging; but it was not for some time after their marriage that he submitted to the authority of the Church of England, and that briefly; by the time *The White Horse* appeared, he was well on the way to Rome. Frances did not share this motion away from England's church; her poems and recorded statements show that she inclined rather to Puritan than to Catholic views on prayer, faith, and personal religion.

Do the words in *The White Horse* mean anything, then? Or are they only a tasteless compliment to Frances? The answer is in the *Autobiography,* where Chesterton says Frances was distinguished among all those he knew in early life by her devotion to the practice of a religious discipline. His own family was vaguely pious and uncommitted; his friends were full of theories; but she took religion, finally, as a duty calling for action. Now action was always the weakest side of Chesterton. His talent and duty were to use his brain, and he could only by conscious effort give it a rest in simple ritual or performance of any kind—even the ritual of dressing himself, even the bare performance of living.[1] With his sense for the dialectic balance of opposites, he realized that he needed Frances' practical sense in religion as in all else; and undoubtedly sensed that there was much to be fulfilled in her, as well, by this complementarity. His legendary dependence on her, inevitable as it was in any case, has the air of a tribute as well as a necessary arrangement. He paid her the highest compliment—of needing her—consciously and on all occasions, with that touch of the jester's exaggerative pantomime which characterized all his continuing attitudes.

But as Rome became a challenge demanding a personal answer, and as it became obvious to Gilbert that Frances was not with him on this issue, a radical alteration in the balance of their marriage became probable. If Chesterton entered the Church without Frances, he would take a step, incur duties, and become involved in a practice, all of which went far beyond the pious observances of Frances. He was asked, in effect, to complete himself; almost as if Frances had died, and he had been compelled to live without her balancing influence.

This challenge was the fourth claim upon his affections in the "dry decade." Those who knew Gilbert and Frances considered it a miracle that he took the step without her; went to Mass without her; defended a Church not her own. Of course, personal completion only raised the dialectic to a richer plane and made possible a higher complementarity. He "went around the world" to find her again, as Chesterton himself would put it. Frances became a Catholic two years after his own baptism.

WAR BOOKS AND TRAVEL BOOKS

Two books were written in the Marconi days—*The Utopia of Usurers, The Flying Inn*—and each bears the imprint of Cecil's treatment. The first is a withering polemic, with all the violence of a personal attack. The book has the fault of all Chesterton's direct political comments; he assumed an intellectual consistency in men's actions, associations, and statements which does not in fact pattern men's real deeds. The abuses and absurdities of financiers are fitted with corresponding philosophies in this book, and Chesterton's foes are accused of holding these diabolic views. *The Flying Inn* is driven also by the bitterness of this period; it lacks the dialectic of separate but positive principles which informs the earlier tales. Lord Ivywood is a completely evil genius; the battle against him tends rather to over-simplification than to the complication and extension of life. The joy of the novel is concentrated in the songs, which were published one by one in *The New Witness;*

while the only chapter which deepens toward human issues is "The Seven Moods of Dorian," in which Chesterton's own moods of the art school are remembered.[2]

All of Chesterton's writings during and after the war were impelled by patriotism and based upon his own belief in nationalism. *The Napoleon of Notting Hill* contained Chesterton's basic argument for the nation: the fact that the works of man should be expressions of his character. Chesterton no longer believed that the vote, or any other piece of republican machinery, could guarantee this expression; he would contend, before long, that without personal ownership men cannot stamp matter with their spirit. But the war made him realize that unless the nation is sealed with a separate character it is not worth defending. That is the reason he insisted on a moral judgment in the war. Prussia did have a character, and an evil one, in its recent relations with other nations; it was unrealistic, and therefore immoral, to deny this and make the life-and-death struggle a mere economic contest. All the modern sophistries and false humility do not weaken this moral basis for war. The world is too ready to admit that both sides are equally at fault. Chesterton did not deny that England's action had been evil; he wrote a book—*The Crimes of England*—to identify the points at which England had not only gone wrong, but gone wrong in supporting Prussia. But good actions are forever impossible to men unless they can be undertaken by the evil; every good act in this fallen world is connected with repentance. The denial of a moral conflict could only make a moral solution impossible—as it did. The distinctly Prussian poison was not isolated in Germany; the other elements were not encouraged.

The Barbarism of Berlin (1914), *Letters to an Old Garibaldian* (1915), *The Crimes of England* (1915), *Lord Kitchener* (1917), *A Short History of England* (1917) were all "war propaganda," but meant to educate the propagandists. Chesterton made one of his rare boasts when he said that his ephemeral songs of war were based on eternal ideas, that he could stand by his words, written in that crisis, as few English men of letters would care to.[3]

The collapse and mere weariness of the armistice were very discouraging for Chesterton. All the moral argument for the war was overlooked; Englishmen criticized England, not Prussia, and called their cynical reaction "internationalism." Chesterton immediately began his assault on what he called "The League of Internationalists" and "The League for the Abolition of Nations."[4] He was fighting an old foe, since Wells had become the spokesman of this internationalism in England.[5] Chesterton's argument against internationalism was the same which he had marshalled against the imperialists, or, for that matter, the theosophists. The syncretic trend, in politics as well as religion, is an attempt to solve personal difficulties by eliminating personality. The internationalist says there can be no temporal peace as long as there are nations, as the Eastern mystic says there can be no eternal peace as long as there are persons; both dissolve whatever might clash into shapeless pools. In *Orthodoxy,* Chesterton opposed the Christian doctrines of creation and charity to this Eastern longing for an impersonal peace. Charity is based on otherness, on complementarity and difference. Just as man and woman and the child make the basic society stable by a dialectic of separate virtues and mutual needs, so the ideal of Europe is of a France that needs Germany, of England that needs Italy, because they are different and contribute things which can nowhere else be found.[6]

After the war, Chesterton seemed unable to resume his work as critic and jester. He had the new troubles of his brother's death, and of the journal widowed by that death, as well as his increasing anxiety for England and Europe, his continuing religious hesitation, to disturb him. His restlessness took the form of travel, and the only books in the following years were records of his trips to Ireland, Poland, Jerusalem, Rome, and America. Their theme was still that of the war—a discussion of the nations in order to emphasize their individuality. The introduction to *What I Saw In America* gives his view of travel—that one must not deny differences, nor pretend to any easy understanding which is in fact an attempt to see one's self in all one's neighbors. The nightmare poems of Chesterton's youth, in which all the faces turned toward one are one's own, reflect the ideal toward which internationalists aspire. The healthy attitude is that which makes the traveler feel absurdly out of place, ready to laugh at strange customs—so long as this recognition of differences leads to an understanding of new things. The Christian ideal is not to see oneself in everyone but to see God differently manifested in others.

Chesterton claimed that internationalism, not nationalism, causes war. The denial that Poland is Poland, that Belgium is Belgium, leads to the imperial ambitions of super-states. The refusal to see that Prussia was Prussia led, eventually, to World War II. The same argument applies to all Chesterton's discussions of the Irish problem: just as a policy of division had ignored the fact of Poland's reality, so Unionism had ignored the reality of Ireland's distinct genius.

America, because of its new strata of colonials, pioneers, and immigrants, has special difficulties in fixing its own character. Because its traditions are not deep and formative, it must insist on the political creed which was its foundation. The melting pot must not itself melt. This explains the uniformity and self-consciousness of Americans:

> Many Americans become almost impersonal in their worship of personality. Where their natural selves might differ, their ideal selves tend to be the same. . . . There is not quite enough unconsciousness to produce real individuality. There is a sort of worship of will-power in the abstract, so that people are actually thinking about how they can will, more than about what they want.[7]

The American lack of unconscious traditions leads to a worship of causes and abstractions. Popular tradition is called "anti-intellectual" by the theorists who consider America a new experiment that must never be allowed to age. Intellectual fads have always been a danger in America, and Chesterton studies Prohibition simply as one example of this theoretical frenzy.

What I Saw in America relies, for basic understanding of American history, on Cecil's brilliantly concise history of America; but Gilbert's own observations are equally acute. The historical background of the modern controversies on security legislation are given their finest treatment in his first chapter. The highly patterned protests against conformity, the modern worship of intellect and "experts," the temptation to salvationist schemes in religion and politics, are limned in clear strokes.

In *The New Jerusalem* Chesterton tried to praise the nationalism of what was not yet a nation. Perhaps the one thing which offended Chesterton most in the Jewish financiers was their loss of national pride. An unnaturally strong family loyalty, or devotion to religion, or simple ambition seemed the result of their willingness to change names and nations so readily. The Zionist Jews, for the same reason, won his admiration and convinced him that this was the Jews' one chance to regain national pride and a sense of honor. This argument, sound in places, was everywhere exaggerated by Chesterton's insistence on intellectual consistency in the major political classes.

CONTINUING RELEVANCE
OF CHESTERTON'S NATIONALISM

Even during this trying period, when propaganda and travel books were his only products, Chesterton built a sound foundation for international understanding, one that stemmed from the dialectic ethics of *Orthodoxy*. As always, Chesterton's social thought was based on the reality of the family. This is the normative society because it is the most diversified, a wild combination of opposites, where freedom and authority make for a fluid, chafing order that exasperates and ennobles man. *Heretics* traced the war on the family to a desire for sameness and unnatural equalities. This has certainly been true in history. Over-simple "Liberalism" derives from Plato's ideal and dehydrated republic, in which women are to undertake the same tasks as men, while children are brought up in vast, impersonal nurseries. Modern Liberalism has used feminism and state education to bastion its theoretical equality, and the last stage of this scheme is, in the modern vision, the reduction of all national and social differences. The ideal of "intellectuals" who have no common ground of shared truth can only be negative— one of freedom *from* war or class or prejudice, never freedom *for* any humanly fulfilling activity, in a humanly articulated community:

> Disapproving of all soldiers, of all priests, of most merchants and especially merchant-adventurers, of all kings and princes and a great many other rulers as well, feeling only irritation against squires or gentry, sneering by habit at the *bourgeoisie* or respectable middle class, having always been taught that peasants are stagnant and superstitious, and being only too ready to believe that working men are hopeless as material for the true Scientific State or Utopia of the Intellectuals—having successfully rejected and despised all these different human traditions, as falling below some one or other of their new notions of progress, they are left with a humanity which they can love in the abstract but hardly in the concrete. There is not much of humanity left when you take away all the people whom they regard as obstacles to the progress of humanity. Therefore, any outline they trace of a world without war is a curiously hard and blank outline. They can make maps or

diagrams of how to avoid death, but they cannot make pictures; that is, any pictures of people enjoying life.[8]

Those who say that our shrinking world calls for more uniformity within "the family of man" should remember that the most subtle masters of communicating with the mind lived in Hellas, where every nook and cranny hid a nation. Speech itself is articulate, based on division—the separate sounds of man. Pentecost means speaking to every man in his own tongue, not melting all nuance into noise. How ironic had someone objected to the diverse dialects of Greek-enunciating man, to claim that these men, who have spoken so intimately to the whole human race, were cutting themselves off by rejecting a basic Esperanto or Newspeak to serve for every need. In the same way, the Mommsen school of Caesar-worshipers lament the political isolation of Greek cities—that Odysseus only wanted Ithaca, and Demosthenes would not relinquish Athens to Philip.

Chesterton's nationalism was a sense of locality and individual genius like that which he praised in the Greeks, "that labyrinth of little walled nations resounding with the lament of Troy."[9] He defended the feudal emphasis on small limits, and the Southern doctrine of states' rights in America. The theorists who would reduce human richness to a system of social digits were Chesterton's real enemies. This collectivism he called the great danger of the twentieth century. Capitalism and Communism, Socialism and Liberalism all lead to the same thing insofar as they reduce men to the simple status of workers, voters, or other such thin abstractions. Chesterton's praise of personality, of patriotism and local character, of the family, of personal ownership were all attempts to oppose this inhuman proliferation of system.

PART FOUR (1922–1936)

Incarnation

10.

THE TWO FRIARS

He loved with me, said Browning, and men wept;
   He laughed with me, said Dickens, and men smiled;
He drank with me, said Chaucer, and high feast kept;
   He played with me, said Blake, a wistful child;
He rode with me, said Cobbett, on my quest;
   With me, said Stevenson, he read man's heart;
And Johnson shouted, Me he still loved best,
   And held sane judgment for the nobler part.
So much, while Peter fumbled with his keys,
   And justice for a little strove with ruth
      Clouding the difficult passage of Heaven's door;
Till other, wiser counsellors came than these:
   Take him, said Thomas, for he served the truth;
    Take him, said Francis, for he loved the poor.

—Ronald Knox[1]

Chesterton's travels after the war were the token of an unresolved restlessness. The only books he wrote during this period were the records of his trips, toward which he took an even more negligent attitude than toward his other work. Frances says that he became unbearably fidgety before his reception into the church.[2] He knew that his decision would affect many lives. Despite the fact that his long approach to Catholicism seems easy and gradual, he affirmed in *The Catholic Church and Conversion* (1927) that the difference between an admiring approach and decision is not a matter of gradation and shades, but of a passage between sundered worlds.

Belloc, as we saw, considered Chesterton's admiration for Catholicism a matter of aesthetics. Belloc had the fierce piety of Doctor Johnson and could not understand what Chesterton meant by his own "paganism." Nor can those understand Chesterton who compare him with someone like Newman, a man haunted by religion, who would have become a fanatic if he had not achieved, under pressure, the balance of some ancient faith. Chesterton, even when he became a Catholic, did not have the kind of devotion which leads to much religious "practice." His early crisis of the intellect, his ability to entertain ideas of all sorts in a sustained dialectic, led to that dangerous mental fairness which can be seen in many Frenchmen, in the best minds of antiquity, and in men like Thomas Aquinas, men whose profession is one of detached criticism.

"TO HAVE MY SINS FORGIVEN"

Chesterton seems consciously to have formulated his decision as a re-enactment of the clash between paganism and Catholicism. His broad ability to think on all levels—of myth, philosophy, and poetry—made it impossible for him to conceive any real alternative to Catholicism, in his own case, but the humanism of pagan antiquity. The real spur to conversion, for a thinking pagan, is the need to find purgation—the quest of Orestes. When asked why he entered the Church, Chesterton's invariable answer was, simply, "to have my sins forgiven." The war and its effects had brought the reality of evil back into the foreground of his mind:

> Judged by our modern tests of emancipated art or ideal economics, it is admitted that Christ understood all that is rather

crudely embodied in Socialism or the Simple Life. I purposely insist first on this optimistic, I might almost say this pantheistic or even this pagan aspect of the Christian Gospels. For it is only when we understand that Christ, considered merely as a prophet, can be and is a popular leader in the love of natural things, that we can feel that tremendous and tragic energy of his testimony to an ugly reality, the existence of unnatural things. Instead of taking a text as I have done, take a whole Gospel and read it steadily and honestly and straight through at a sitting, and you will certainly have one impression, whether of a myth or of a man. It is that the exorcist towers above the poet and even the prophet; that the story between Cana and Calvary is one long war with demons. He understood better than a hundred poets the beauty of the flowers of the battle-field; but he came out to battle. And if most of his words mean anything they do mean that there is at our very feet, like a chasm concealed among the flowers, an unfathomable evil. . . .

. . . it is here [at Sodom] that tradition has laid the tragedy of the mighty perversion of the imagination of man; the monstrous birth and death of abominable things. I say such things in no mood of spiritual pride; such things are hideous not because they are distant but because they are near to us; in all our brains, certainly in mine, were buried things as bad as any buried under that bitter sea, and if He did not come to do battle with them, even in the darkness of the brain of man, I know not why He came.[3]

This stain which nothing can drive out but Christ's gesture of exorcism is studied very thoroughly, in *St. Francis of Assisi*, as the cause of the Dark Ages. Chesterton wrote, in *Orthodoxy*, that the Church was merely a bridge across that nocturnal interlude; but now he admits an element of truth in Gibbon's insinuation that the Church led men into darkness. There is an hysteria under the serenity of the declining Empire which marks the real exhaustion of ancient civilization. The West went to the East for ideals and inspiration; the natural had been so perverted that men were willing to accept any supernatural hint or enthusiasm. This pagan hysteria is present in the early Fathers of the Church, even in the poised mind of Augustine; but these men had a vision of sanity which they opposed to all the evil dreams; and if they stood against the declining paganism, it was because that was the road to sanity. The Church did renounce pagan civilization, not from a contempt for nature but as part of a search for the new poetry of nature on which Christian mysticism could be based:

> What was the matter with the whole heathen civilization was that there was nothing for the mass of men in the way of mysticism, except that concerned with the mystery of the nameless forces of nature, such as sex and growth and death.[4]

St. Francis marks the point when the fast and vigil of the Dark Ages broke into the new Christian poetry of nature; the pagan magic had been driven out, and men could dream and dance to the pagan poetry again:

> For water itself has been washed. Fire itself has been purified as by fire. Water is no longer that water into which slaves were flung to feed the fishes. Fire is no longer that fire through which children were passed to Moloch. Flowers smell no more of the forgotten garlands gathered in the garden of Priapus; stars stand no more as signs of the far frigidity of gods as cold as those cold fires.[5]

Man's need for absolution is the theme of the best Father Brown stories, those contained in *The Secret of Father Brown*. Father

Brown's secret is that he knows he is a criminal, and can therefore sympathize with the sinner in the full sense of practically committing the sin. As he puts it, this solves the problem of time and sin by giving one his remorse beforehand.[6] The stories are given as examples of this vicarious fall and regeneration which Father Brown suffers with each criminal, and the final story of this volume, technically the best he ever wrote, hinges entirely on the world's inability to accomplish what Father Brown can: he can absolve.[7] The first volume of stories written after Chesterton's conversion—*The Incredulity of Father Brown*—were meant to show that the Church guards reason better than the rationalists can. But *The Secret of Father Brown*, which came out in 1927, goes deeper into the mystery of the Faith, and reveals a Father Brown who can say to the champions of an Eastern fakir, "I don't care for spiritual powers much myself; I've got much more sympathy with spiritual weaknesses."[8]

The sense of guilt as the reality that reaches out toward Christ is the burden of Chesterton's first Catholic poems, those in *The Queen of Seven Swords*. Here the Virgin is seen as an anti-witch, driving out the evil dreams of the pagan goddesses;[9] or a newly-refined clay, the stuff of a new race;[10] or the answer of man and woman to lust;[11] or the Black Queen of Montserrat, whose color is a type of the regions in the mind

> Where through black clouds the black sheep runs accursed,
>   And through black clouds the Shepherd follows him.

Chesterton, the famous optimist, came in this spirit to the Church:

> To thy most merciful face of night I kneel.[12]

The voyage to the feet of the Black Virgin was a return, through the guilt of the Slade period, to the childlike innocence which even childhood does not have outside the Sacramental restoration. As he reached his goal, Chesterton wrote of this return, in a letter to Msgr. Ronald Knox:

> any public comments on my religious position seem like a wind on the other side of the world; as if they were about somebody else—as indeed they are. I am not troubled about a great fat man who appears on platforms and in caricatures; even when he enjoys controversies on what I believe to be the right side. I am concerned about what has become of a little boy whose father showed him a toy theatre, and a schoolboy whom nobody ever heard of, with his brooding on doubts and dirt and day-dreams of crude conscientiousness so inconsistent as to be near to hypocrisy, and all the morbid life of the lonely mind of a person with whom I have lived. It is that story, that so often came near to ending badly, that I want to end well.[13]

Chesterton entered the Church in the summer of 1922; in the fall of 1923 his sketch of Francis of Assisi was published. The saint's natural sense of poetry was formed only at the price of the long premediaeval night, that vigil which men call the Dark Ages; and St. Francis himself had to re-live this dark night before reaching the light. His early extravagances made a fool of Francis; and his moment of vocation came when he decided to live under that worst humiliation for a proud Italian soldier, the label of a fool:

> He saw himself as an object, very small and distinct like a fly walking on a clear window pane; and it was unmistakably a fool. And as he stared at the word "fool" written in luminous letters before him, the word itself began to shine and change . . . it was so far analogous to the story of the man making a

tunnel through the earth that it did mean a man going down and down until at some mysterious moment he begins to go up and up . . . the final spiritual overturn in which humiliation becomes complete holiness.[14]

Chesterton himself had built his world on a mystical minimum, in which everything glowed with strange value against the background of nonexistence. This intellectual measurement of all things by a minimal reality was enacted in a purely moral sense by Francis, who saw the minimal claim which he had to any of life's good things. Such self-annihilation made of each good thing he encountered a new creation:

> It was by this deliberate idea of starting from zero, from the dark nothingness of his own deserts, that he did come to enjoy even earthly things as few people have enjoyed them.[15]

Chesterton sees no contradiction between the fierce asceticism and the flowering poetry of Francis' life; they could only have existed at such intensity in the dialectic with each other which the saint's life exhibits.

ST. THOMAS

The importance of asceticism in the book on Francis does not indicate that Chesterton had ceased to believe "it is only Christian men Guard even heathen things." Francis was fighting devils, not merely blood or the flesh. Christianity reverses the Platonic belief that matter is evil, and immaterial spirits good:

> The work of heaven alone was material; the making of a material world. The work of hell is entirely spiritual.[16]

Creation is a revolutionary concept, one not contained in the pagan philosophies, and on it alone can an unshakeable respect for nature be established. This makes Christendom conquer the pagan civilization even on its own terms. Chesterton's only other venture into hagiography—*St. Thomas Aquinas*—describes this Christian rescue of Nature.

The neo-Platonist tradition of the Greek fathers stressed Inspiration rather than Creation; the Incarnation was considered as a raid into the hostile camp of "the World." This theology was admittedly based on the ascetic maxims of the New Testament, for Christ spoke as a poet, because he was speaking to all men. Parable, gesture, and drama are the techniques he used. But when phrases like "the Prince of this World" are taken as precise philosophic statements of the Devil's position in reality, the mind is forced to make a Manichean surrender of creation and matter to evil origins. Against this gnostic schematization of reality the Church stood with common sense and poetry: Ambrose won Augustine for the Church when he convinced him that the scriptural rhetoric is allegorical. Here we see the fulfillment, on a higher level, of Chesterton's realization (voiced in *Orthodoxy*) that poetry saves man. The sacramental view of life—which sees the embodiment of meaning in matter—is opposed to all forms of Manicheism, and can be explained only in terms of divine creation. Christ himself rebuked men for their failure to be poets with this "sense of sacrament," when they did not search for the symbolic meaning of the loaves and fishes (John 7.26 ff).

The whole psychology and poetry of the catacombs was that of a raid against the world: but the revealed fact of Creation made it impossible for that psychological attitude to dictate the Catholic philosophy. God made the World "and saw that it was good." Christ's birth was the return of the rightful heir to his own estate. St. Augustine distrusted marriage, but he had to distrust his distrust, since "male and female He created man."

St. Thomas finally built into all the levels of a Catholic philosophy that irreducible fragment of revelation which declared that God created the world. The construction of this system had been a slow process, for it was entirely new. Creation is not a natural concept, nor an easy one to defend. None of the major philosophies of antiquity defended it: "all return to the one idea of returning."[17] Christian philosophy invades the barren cycles of return with crisis—the instant of Creation, the Incarnation, the Judgment. Of course, St. Thomas took much of the material for his structure from the elaborate but durable reasonings of Aristotle. The belief in Creation necessitates a belief in reason and the natural achievements of man. It is no wonder St. Thomas had to defend the senses and syllogisms against the neo-Platonist theories of inspiration. Chesterton makes Augustine the foe of Aquinas on the issue of sense-derived knowledge; but Augustine only survived as the major thinker of the early Church because he had defended creation against exotic distortions and perversions of mysticism. Thomas knew this conflict was at the root of Christian thinking, and Chesterton rightly makes of the Thomistic artillery a long-range assault on the Manicheans.

Manicheism is, in one form or other, the abiding temptation of the religious mind unsteadied by revelation. It is religion turned into a simple revulsion against the world. The Orient is full of this shadowy war with matter, as was antiquity; and most of the Christian heresies, from Docetism through the Flagellants and Puritans to the Christian Scientists, have as their source of energy this mystical hatred for physical reality. Against this entire drift and uneasiness stand the certitudes of St. Thomas, whose labyrinth of investigation into separate realities is only an extension of the germinal concept that "God so loved the world":

> There really was a new reason for regarding the senses, and the
> sensations of the body, and the experiences of the common

209

man, with a reverence at which great Aristotle would have stared, and no man in the ancient world could have begun to understand. The Body was no longer what it was when Plato and Porphyry and the old mystics had left it for dead. It had hung upon a gibbet. It had risen from a tomb. It was no longer possible to despise the senses, which had been the organs of something that was more than man. Plato might despise the flesh, but God had not despised it. The senses had truly become sanctified; as they are blessed one by one at a Catholic baptism. "Seeing is believing" was no longer the platitude of a mere idiot, or common individual, as in Plato's world; it was mixed up with real conditions of real belief. Those revolving mirrors that send messages to the brain of man, that light that breaks upon the brain, these had truly revealed to God himself the path to Bethany or the light on the high rock of Jerusalem. These ears that resound with common noises had reported also to the secret knowledge of God the noise of the crowd that strewed palms and the crowd that cried for Crucifixion. After the Incarnation had become the idea that is central in our civilization, it was inevitable that there should be a return to materialism, in the sense of the serious value of matter and the making of the body. When once Christ had risen, it was inevitable that Aristotle should rise again.[18]

Because St. Thomas used reason reasonably, he contradicts the rationalist at every step of the way. The long scholastic tradition obscured this fact, and the followers of Thomas overemphasized the place of logic, just as the Augustinians forgot their master's defence of nature to repeat his praise of the supernatural. Thomas used the Aristotelian logic, but he used it against logicians as well as mystics. A great part of his work is devoted to the attack on the Platonic forms, yet he is just as opposed to the Aristotelian world of mere forms and matter. Prime matter is potentiality, something less real than the form which activates it. But there is something *more* real than the forms, than the intelligible and shaping aspect of reality. Forms limit things and protect their identity; but another principle unites them, links them to the creative source of their being, and *that* principle is precisely what is left out by formal analysis. That principle not only exists, it *is* the act of existence: "There *is* an Is."[19] At this crisis of his thinking, Thomas sees the full impact of Creation on philosophy. Being is at every instant derived from God; and, though there are separate and defined realities which receive this Act, the direct influx of God's activity is what makes these things real.

CHRISTIAN EXISTENTIALISM

The neo-Thomists—Gilson, Maritain, Pegis—have all been unrestrained in their praise of Chesterton's book; for Chesterton saw, from an independent standpoint, the existential core of Thomas' thought, which these men were patiently re-establishing in the centers of technical disputation. Chesterton sees the precise balance attained in St. Thomas' use of logic to limit logic. For instance, Thomas defends a negative manner of predicating things of God: in effect, he says that we arrive at an understanding of God by denying the limited *forms* in the reality we know and considering in pure act the principle of extra-formal reality. God is like that in man which is not merely manness, or any other form. The *act* of existence which cannot be classified among the forms is that part of creation which most accurately reflects the Creator. Chesterton saw the far-reaching impact of this argument. The very limitations placed upon being indicate the extra-formal source of perfect activity:

> He is a realist in a rather curious sense of his own, which is a
> third thing, distinct from the almost contrary mediaeval and

modern meanings of the word. Even the doubts and difficulties about reality have driven him to believe in more reality rather than less. The *deceitfulness* of things which has had so sad an effect on so many sages, has almost a contrary effect on this sage. If things deceive us, it is by being more real than they seem. As ends in themselves they always deceive us; but as things tending to a greater end, they are even more real than we think them.[20]

When Aquinas says that reality is not reached, in the first place, by any logical process, he makes perception and direct knowledge of individuals an existential contact of the mind with things. To interpose, in this contact with real particulars, some abstract process of reasoning, is a hopeless effort. This is the only answer to the "critical problem"—a denial that it exists; and Chesterton had given the same answer to this problem in *Orthodoxy*, long before he became acquainted with Thomas's demonstrations that "the primary act of recognition of any reality is real."[21]

Of course, Thomas does not believe that logic is the enemy of the mind, as the simplistic existentialists try to convince themselves. Only by formal analysis of the many realities do we arrive at that which the formal analysis could not compass. Aquinas fights in two directions—against the annihilating mystics and the minimizing rationalists—because his thinking contains opposite thrusts. The famous "hierarchy" of Thomas's study of interconnected degrees of cognition—in animals, humans, angels, and God—is a reflection of this dialectic toughness in his thought:

it was this quality of a link in the chain, or a rung in the ladder, which mainly concerned the theologian, in developing his own particular theory of degrees. Above all, it is this which chiefly moves him, when he finds so fascinating the central mystery of Man. And for him the point is always that

Man is not a balloon going up into the sky, nor a mole burrowing merely in the earth; but rather a thing like a tree, whose roots are fed from the earth, while its highest branches seem to rise almost to the stars.[22]

The same existential dialectic explains the importance of analogy and many other things, in Thomistic thought. For instance, the definition of "sacred science" with which the *Summa* opens is a justification of both reason and faith, directed against those who would reduce man's knowledge to one or the other, or separate them from mutual influence and reinforcement. When Siger of Brabant accepted these "two ways" but divorced them from the mutual limitation of dialectic, Thomas met the first of the many oversimplifications which his work would suffer. Chesterton explains the sharp retort of Aquinas on this occasion as the natural reaction of a man whose work is betrayed from within. One touch of mere relativism would shatter the balance and precision of the dialectic which leads the mind to truth: "St. Thomas was willing to allow the one truth to be approached by two paths, precisely because he was sure there was only one truth."[23] For Thomas, as for Chesterton, the multiple ways of knowing meet in a clash that is *decisive,* not merely suggestive in a pragmatic and relative sense. The retort to Siger is echoed in Chesterton's answer to thinkers for whom "everything is relative to a reality that is not there"[24]: there is an

everlasting duel between Yes and No. This is the dilemma that many sceptics have darkened the universe and dissolved the mind, solely in order to escape. They are those who maintain that there is something that is both Yes and No. I do not know whether they pronounce it Yo.[25]

The simplicity of Chesterton's book should deceive no one. He does not write an exposition of Thomas's doctrine. He rather senses, with an unerring rapidity of argument, the style of Thomas's total architecture, its balance and relation of parts, its position with respect to other ideas, its answer to internal and external conflicts. He traces in the forest of arguments those major lines of thrust, and their counter-energies, which make up the strategy of Thomism. The polarities within that philosophy—of faith and reason, essence and existence, matter and form, potency and act, nature and the supernatural, argument and intuition—are here related to the external warring of the system against rationalism on one side and irrational mysticism on the other. By a consummate use of his rhetorical "play" Chesterton suspends all these forces in their proper relation and sets them against the background of ancient, mediaeval, and modern thought. The book is the fulfillment of Chesterton's career as metaphysical jester. In *Heretics* he wrote that philosophy must be defended *ab extra;* here he undertakes that kind of defence, a prophet-jester's defence of the central philosophy of the West.

If *Thomas* is the completion of *Heretics,* a defence of philosophy, *Francis* carries to a higher level the case stated in *Orthodoxy* for poetry and mysticism. And both books answer the more personal need which brought Chesterton into the communion of these saints:

> these two great men were doing the same great work; one in the study, and the other in the streets . . . these two saints saved us from Spirituality, a dreadful doom.[26]

Francis, in cleansing nature for the poets, and Thomas, in freeing reason for the philosophers, reclaimed the evil-invaded world in its Creator's name. Chesterton does not exalt these two of all the Catholic saints because of an optimistic humanism. Theirs was a cleansing and liberating process. In saving us from Spiritualism, they saved us from the evil spirits whose domination over whole periods of history was only too real to Chesterton. The fasting of Francis and the intellectual labor of Thomas are parts of one great drama of resistance. The spirits were driven out; matter and the senses and man's reason were restored to their proper place in a sane life. But it is the entire point of Chesterton's twin biographies that only one religion, as understood and practiced by saints, could have effected this rescue. Francis and Thomas resembled their Master because they were both, in their most crucial influence, exorcists.

11.

PROPERTY AND

THE PERSON

Every man who has tried to keep any good thing going, though it were a little club or paper or political protest, sounds the depths of his own soul when he hears that rolling line which can only be rendered so feebly: "For truly in my heart I know that Troy will fall."[1]

The New Witness, formed to expose corruption in the party system, originally advanced no positive scheme of government. Cecil and his wife were never "Distributists." But Gilbert had none of his brother's interest in political maneuver, and under him the paper began to encourage that wider distribution of property outlined in *The Servile State.* As the original staff and cause of the paper shifted, its financial support disappeared; publication ceased in 1923. La-

217

boriously Gilbert put together another paper; alone this time, not as part of a young party. In 1925 *G.K.'s Weekly* began its eleven-year course, and by 1926 the Distributist League was formed, with Chesterton as its figurehead.

Any group like the Distributist League is bound to accumulate cranks. Chesterton was not one to sift men and excommunicate undesirables, though he was conscious (and could not but be) of the League's magnetic influence on fanatics: "We have had some very fantastic human forms lingering about our office."[2] The ideas of Belloc, set down in 1911, were the source of Chesterton's politics, but Belloc was not interested in the squabbles of a "little party." Chesterton himself refused to say anything about economics or the practical steps to be taken toward the Distributist goal. None of the other personalities in the movement shared this diffidence regarding the role of official spokesman. There was Vincent McNabb, O.P., for instance, who wove his own clothes and refused to use a typewriter, as part of his protest against machinery: though a friend of Belloc, he thought Chesterton and Belloc too moderate in their criticism of the modern economy.

The first major doctrinal dispute in the League was caused by Arthur Penty, who thought the Distributists should wage a war against machinery as such. The obvious answer to this is Chesterton's own:

> It seems to me quite as materialistic to be damned by a machine as saved by a machine. It seems to me quite as idolatrous to blaspheme it as to worship it.[3]

But in this, as in all other disputes, Chesterton claimed to be a mere servant of the Distributists, working to furnish them with a platform, unable to speak about the niceties of economics or the elaboration of any particular scheme. His "Distributist" books are, most of them, symbolic novels. One series of essays from the paper was published as *The Outline of Sanity;* but even this was a statement of general principles which avoided the practical disputes and narrow dogmatism of the editor's fellows. Even on his own paper he spoke from a peripheral position, the jester in a court that was, unfortunately, too comic to need his comment.

THE DISTRIBUTION OF POWER

What, aside from his improbable offices of editor of the journal and President of the League, were Chesterton's opinions with regard to the political future of his country? These had obviously changed a good deal since the early days when he had canvassed for the Liberal Party and described the French Revolution as a renewal of spirit resembling that effected by the early Christians. By 1920, the Middle Ages and their guilds had taken the place of France and the Republic in Chesterton's thought.

Chesterton always called himself a democrat, but *The New Witness*'s attack on the party system convinced him that the machinery of popular suffrage is not a meaningful expression of the genius of a people.[4] He did not react from republicanism to monarchism, as Belloc was to do; he still thought Athenian democracy the ideal, though an ideal which can only be realized in political units as small as Athens (or Notting Hill).[5] By this time he realized that true national expression depends on a complicated interplay of forces supporting a continuing tradition of national character. In English history, for instance, he thought the hopes of "democracy" received their greatest setback when the barons overrode Richard II's proposed solution for the Peasant's Revolt; the triple dialectic of King, Barons, and People was destroyed when one of these forces conquered with finality the alliance of the other two.[6] On the other hand, "England was never so little of a democracy as during the short time when she was a republic."[7] Therefore, without pinning his hopes to any one *process* of government, he took the stand that a high percentage of property owners is the thing which guarantees self-expression to individuals and to the nation as a whole. The mass of men achieves self-expression and fulfillment only when its creative capacities have been nourished by freedom—not simply the ability to vote for one of two distasteful politicians, but the ability to do things within a protected area of human sovereignty.[8] Chesterton admired the Ruskin-William Morris picture of mediaeval society because it had, in theory, many such protected areas of creativity.

It is clear that Chesterton's deepest intuitions in the matter of politics had not changed. The integrity of the person, the need for real loyalty based on local ties, the dialectic which marks the primary social unit (the family)—these were still his norms. The Middle Ages at least saw the desirability of such dialectic in society; nobles, knights, merchants, peasants, abbots, kings, guilds, Pope, and parish were poised in a balance meant to distribute power, very inefficiently by modern standards but answering to Chesterton's first vision of Notting Hill:

> even my ideal, if ever I found it at last, would be what some call a compromise. Only I think it more accurate to call it a balance. For I do not think that the sun compromises with the rain when together they make a garden; or that the rose that grows there is a compromise between green and red. But I mean that even my Utopia would contain different things of different types holding on different tenures; that as in a mediaeval state there were some peasants, some monasteries, some common land, some private land, some town guilds, and so on, so in my modern state there would be some things nationalized, some machines owned corporately, some guilds sharing common profits, and so on, as well as many absolute

individual owners, where such individual owners are most possible.[9]

Mediaeval society failed even by its own standard, as all human enterprises of great scope, dependent on many reluctant human wills, must fail. But the ideal allowed for that free will. The modern cult of mechanical efficiency when it does not actually deny man's will, makes it possible that a single failure at the center may smash the whole humming machinery of society; or, under the threat of such total failure, it mobilizes society to a total discipline and uniformity. That is why Chesterton wrote:

> We do *not* propose that in a healthy society all land should be held in the same way; or that all property should be owned on the same conditions; or that all citizens should have the same relation to the city. It is our whole point that the central power needs lesser powers to balance and check it, and that these must be of many kinds: some individual, some official, and so on. Some of them will probably abuse their privileges; but we prefer the risk to that of the State or of the Trust, which abuses its omnipotence.[10]

It will be seen that Chesterton's concepts closely resemble the Jeffersonian ideal expressed in the first stage of American politics: dialectic, local sovereignty, checks and balances, protection to property. Chesterton leagued his efforts with those of the other Distributists because he saw no one else combating, even ineptly, the acceleration of impersonal systems. Nonetheless, considering the wild history of the later Distributists, and the meaning they have given to that term, it would perhaps be more accurate to call Chesterton a federalist than a Distributist, especially since he summed up his own mentality, as opposed to the Capitalist's and the Communist's, in these words:

They are both powers that believe only in combination; and have never understood or even heard that there is any dignity in division. They have never had the imagination to understand the idea in Genesis and the great myths: that Creation itself was division. The beginning of the world was the division of heaven and earth; the beginning of humanity was the division of man and woman. But these flat and platitudinous minds can never see the difference between the creative cleavage of Adam and Eve and the destructive cleavage of Cain and Abel.[11]

To the government of a single ("classless") class, and to that of warring classes, Chesterton opposed the ideal of creative dialectic.[12]

Chesterton did not think that all the complexity of modern society could be abolished, all paper ties torn up, every borough made a kingdom; he merely claimed that man's need for a decentralization of society was going to become more drastic as the twentieth century wore on. Both Capitalism and Communism have encouraged the further reduction of human activity to a single status, each human contributing one twist to a total operation. Unfortunately, almost everything which has been opposed to such centralization has simply added to it. American labor unions are as vast, powerful, and untouchable as big business ever was; and business and labor clash through a third series of proliferating cogs and wheels in Washington, making one vast machine. The answer to over-centralization is not the creation of more giant systems, but the return to local and divided sovereignty.

Chesterton, as we have seen, did not demand a "peasant society," but a society whose various parts balance and protect each other. He laid stress on the small, independent farmer because this was the element in society most weakened by modern developments, and its total disappearance would seriously reduce that human diversity which makes for freedom. The independent farmer in contact with the earth, eating his own product, is the opposite extreme of the large combine handling one part of a mechanical process, and as such he is symbolic of all the differences and degrees spanning this gap. It is difficult to say how Chesterton would have applied his principles to the modern political tangle, especially since he made so few specific applications of them in his own day, but on one question his decision would have been clear. We are told that the "farm problem" cannot be solved by encouraging small farms, for this is not "efficient," in the abstract sense given that term by modern organizers. One must support the large "efficient" farms, even when they are producing unreal crops that can never be consumed. Chesterton would have used the devices of aid and exemption to help only or principally the small farms worked by their owners.

THE SCATTERED WRITINGS
OF AN EDITOR

Chesterton wrote only four Distributist books, all of them published in the first three years of his effort to give *G.K.'s Weekly* a solid foundation: *Tales of the Long Bow* and *William Cobbett* in 1925, *The Outline of Sanity* in 1926, and *The Return of Don Quixote* in 1927. Of these, only *The Outline of Sanity* has for its subject the Distributist program itself, and in these essays Chesterton remained as uncommitted as possible to practical proposals. He says repeatedly that the major task, at the present stage of society, is negative: to check wherever possible the dehumanization and depersonalization brought upon us by the centripetal whirl of modern commerce and politics.[13] The section of the book which contains Chesterton's most direct observation of the social malady is "The Bluff of the Big Shops." Shops had personalities for Dickens, as they have in the street Adam Wayne defends with his blood. Chesterton's words have more meaning in their English setting than in any other application. The tradition of English shops; the English ambition for growing things, which makes window boxes almost as common as windows, gardens as regular as lawns; the pure English taste in eccentricity—all of these were (and are) precious qualities, and countries which do not possess them cannot be expected to understand the urgency of Chesterton's defence of such characteristics. The modern shop is impersonal, lacking even the definition which a limited range of wares gave to special merchants and tradesmen. The companion of the dazzling modern shop is the hypnotic omnipresence of advertising. The growth of "Madison Avenue," supporting such moresmoulding institutions as television, has caused a good deal of alarm in recent years, a development Chesterton expected and described.[14]

Both Belloc and Cecil had, in the early stages of their political journal, taken Cobbett as their model: his independent voice, violent yet sonorous, had celebrated life on the land and attacked modern commerce. Chesterton makes him the patron of the Distributists, emphasizing his opposition to both the Tories and the Whigs for their refusal to see the real populace, on the one side, and the real past on the other.[15] Cobbett discovered, almost as a detective finds a victim of murder, the traces in the countryside of that crime which Chesterton most resented in England's past—the theft of the monasteries.

Not all the stories in *The Tales of the Long Bow* involve the Distributist idea, but the heroes of the separate tales eventually unite in a symbolic war for English land and poetry and eccentricity.

The Return of Don Quixote appeared serially in the early issues of *G.K.'s Weekly*. The polarity of Chesterton's earliest novels here returns: at the opposite poles are Douglas Murrel, the true Tory who understands that "our people like to be ruled by gentlemen, in a general sort of way,"[16] and John Braintree, the socialist full of logic, but lacking the real sympathy with men which Murrel the poet has. These men resemble such friends of Chesterton in either camp as George Wyndham and Shaw. The man who brings the fictional characters together in a charged field of pretence and revelation is Michael Herne, the librarian-scholar who turns an amateur drama into a continuing pageantry of mediaeval life. The Seawood house is a more complete and serious version of that boarding house which "Manalive" had filled with dignity. But at a "royal trial" Herne finally expounds the mediaeval strictures against usury, and the owners of the Seawood house drive him out of their masquerade world. Murrel and Braintree go forth with him to become a kind of three-man Distributist League, Quixotes of a disappearing chivalry.

12.

THE CRITICAL FOCUS

Chesterton concentrated, in all his biographical studies, on the philosophical issues focused in a particular man's life. This method of studying ideas as embodied in real symbols was severely tested when he became a Catholic: the focusing of eternal issues is more intense in an Assisi or Aquinas than in Dickens or Browning. He had to grapple, in concrete terms, with the whole problem of Christian asceticism and of Christian philosophy when he studied these two key figures. The style and method successfully rose to the occasion; but a greater test remained—to study that focusing of history and eternity into a specific space of time which is the life of Christ. In 1925 he published *The Everlasting Man*.

Scope and range of criticism are balanced, in the jester's style, by immediate repartee in a real situation. Chesterton found an ideal target for this treatment in Wells' *Outline of History*, which exercised so strange a fascination on the English public when it appeared, serially, in the early twenties, and when it was reprinted as a single volume in 1925. Chesterton wrote in the *Times* a review of *The Outline* which contains, germinally, the entire argument of *The Everlasting Man*. Wells made of history a single rise and advance, uniformly gradated; a process self-explanatory and enclosed by reason of its internal symmetry. Chesterton moves from an attack on this philosophy of single direction and "grey gradations" to the center of crisis in history, Christ.

WELLS' "OUTLINE"

Wells made mere process, hypostatized and omnipotent, create man before his reader's eyes. We are carried through "the subtle unreasonableness of transition"[1] in "the human forebrain,"[2] which had "no scope for theology or philosophy or superstition or speculation."[3] True, these transitional foremen drew pictures, but only of "fearless, familiar things"[4] which somehow reflect, for Wells, no human reflection. Unable to think of sowing grain (but somehow driven to bury their dead), foremen spill grain at their work of digging; later, they see things growing over the grave and get the idea—or rather the "tradition"—of agriculture.[5] The following passage shows what mileage can be got from the word "tradition":

Some of the women and children would need to be continually gathering fuel to keep up the fires. It would be a tradition that had grown up. The young would imitate their elders in this task.[6]

The comparatively early place which Greece and Rome occupy on the curve of growth which Wells has charted makes him treat them as savage societies. The Hellenic glory was concentrated in a few individuals in the single city of Athens:

This interesting and artistic outbreak in Athens . . . was not a general movement; it was the movement of a small group of people exceptionally placed and gifted.[7]

Even this flash-fire culture can be reduced to the occurrence of one individual, Pericles, a tragic figure misunderstood by his barbarian contemporaries:

Athens wore his face for a time as one wears a mask, and then became restless and desired to put him aside. There was very little that was great and generous about the common Athenian.[8]

Greek tragedy derives from some dark strain of Southern, non-Aryan blood crying for "self-abasement, self-mutilation, and the like."[9] Socrates despised beautiful things and "could write nothing consecutive."[10] Only a tradition of ancestor-worship makes us "treat the rough notes of Thucydides or Plato for work they never put in order as miracles of style."[11] Yet Wells can say farewell to Greece with hope: "Mankind is growing up. . . . The hope of man rises again at last after every disaster. . . ."[12]

Rome fares no better: "subcivilized," badly in need of the

printing press, it "carries us back to the age of Shamanism and magic."[13] Its political organization was "Neanderthal" by modern standards:[14]

> the Roman imperial system was a very unsound political growth indeed. It is absurd to write of its statecraft; it had none. At its best it had a bureaucratic administration which kept the peace of the world for a time and failed altogether to secure it.[15]

To make people advance according to schedule, inch by inch all along the line, Wells plays up other civilizations while de-emphasizing that of Hellas and Rome, maintaining a world level of growth toward our own civilization (which of course *can* secure the peace of the world). This leveling is most evident in the case of Rome and Carthage, treated as parallel and entirely equal societies, "both very necessary to the world's development,"[16] in Book Five, "The Two Western Republics." Any moral foundation Rome had was destroyed by her "cowardly victory" over Carthage.[17]

A. W. Gomme, the distinguished Hellenist and Thucydides scholar, sifted the errors in this treatment of classical history; and, in 1926, Belloc convicted Wells of an abysmal ignorance of the very Darwinian sources he invoked.[18] Both men came to the same conclusion on Wells' *Outline;* which presents, in Belloc's words,

> a childishly simple scheme of regular and, above all, slow "progress." You must make Early Man last as long as possible and be as base as possible. If the facts will not fit in with that very slow process of development, which was felt (stupidly enough!) to make a Creator less necessary, so much the worse for the facts.[19]

Or, as Gomme puts it:

> Men only differ, in Mr. Wells' view, according to the period
> in which they lived, according as they are near or far from the
> twentieth century . . . it is one of Mr. Wells' curious theories
> that morality advances parallel with thought and the material
> side of civilization. . . . Mr. Wells divides the development of
> life into five periods: (1) Discontinuous consciousness (rep-
> tiles); (2) a *tradition* of experience (mammals); (3) verbal *tra-*
> *dition* (earliest man); (4) invention of writing; (5) printing. As
> though there was as much difference in the intellectual life of
> the world between the last two of these periods as between the
> fourth and the third, or the third and the second.[20]

Wells melted all of history's events into an irreversible river of
improvement. Man follows some inverse law of gravity, and
merely *rises*. Chesterton—with his sense of paradox, logic, and dialectic in the world of ideas—responded with his most complete
study of complexity in the real happenings of history. "The story
of man" is not mere rise, but a riddle. Man, on his thousands of
levels of reality, is paradox incarnate; his contradictions only re-
solved by that corresponding and literal embodiment of mystery
which is the Incarnation. Chesterton's book is constructed on three
major levels, like the *a fortiori* parables of Christ:

> There is perhaps nothing so perfect in all language or litera-
> ture as the use of these three degrees in the parable of the lilies
> of the field; in which he seems first to take one small flower in
> his hand and note its simplicity and even its impotence; then
> suddenly expands it in flamboyant colours into all the palaces
> and pavilions full of a great name in national legend and na-
> tional glory; and then, by yet a third overturn, shrivels it to

nothing once more with a gesture as if flinging it away ". . . and if God so clothes the grass that today is and tomorrow is cast into the oven—how much more. . . ." It is like the building of a good Babel tower by white magic in a moment and in the movement of a hand; a tower heaved suddenly up to heaven on the top of which can be seen afar off, higher than we had fancied possible, the figure of a man; lifted by three infinities above all other things, on a starry ladder of light logic and swift imagination . . . this use of the comparative in several degrees has about it a quality which seems to me to hint of much higher things than the modern teaching of pastoral or communal ethics. There is nothing that really indicates a subtle and in the true sense a superior mind so much as this power of comparing a lower thing with a higher and yet that higher with a higher still; of thinking on three planes at once.[21]

The three planes which Chesterton treats are those of the animal, of man, and of the Everlasting Man—three things sundered by chasms which no rhetoric of transition or dilution can efface.

The "fearless, familiar" lines of an artist, traced centuries ago on stone, are, in their deepest significance, as wonderful an achievement—and indeed the same achievement—as the Parthenon (or, in deference to Mr. Wells, the printing press). The entrance of the human mind into the gradations of nature is like the intersection of another dimension, cutting across the processes and inter-relations of the non-human universe. The illusion of continuity which spans that break in being is conjured up by elaborate arrangements, attenuations, and—above all—lengthening. The mind that loves gradations instead of crises can forever avoid the crisis of a real explanation if it is sufficiently distracted by exploration of similarities and degrees. Accumulating time masquerades as necessity:

An event is not any more intrinsically intelligible or unintelligible because of the pace at which it moves. . . . Yet there runs through all the rationalistic treatment of history this curious and confused idea that difficulty is avoided, or even mystery eliminated, by dwelling on mere delay or on something dilatory in the processes of things.[22]

Chesterton is not attacking, nor did Belloc, the observed facts of evolution, inter-relation and development in nature; his argument applies to many areas of confusion, not only the Wellsian picture of the "human forebrain" as a kind of ramifying tentacle that can at last grapple with all things. The process Chesterton describes is a fundamental strategy for avoiding the facts of separation and the challenge of thought. The mind which can see no difference between man and ape, Rome and Carthage, Christ and Buddha, black and white, drifts toward a grey sameness which lulls the intellect to a despairing slumber.

THE FIRST CRISIS—MAN

The drawings in the cave are not only of bison and pigs; like all art, they are also representations of the artist. They have "that love of the long sweeping or the long wavering line"[23] which the mind extracts from the flow of things around it. The Impressionists remind us that the line around things is not only a mental simplification but a human invention. "Nothing in that sense could be made in any other image but the image of man."[24] In the same way, man abstracts timeless concepts from the temporal flux of sensations. The mind can do all the things which Lewis Carroll presented as "nonsense" when predicated of other realities; the abstracted smile suspended in air, the self-swallowing thing, the turning of mirrors into gates—these are fables which express what is literally possible for only one thing, in only one important degree. The mind can reflect all things, even itself; it can contain, abstract, combine. It is "both the study and the student. We cannot analyse a beetle by looking through a beetle."[25] Each of the things the mind does sounds like an insane fairy tale if told of anything else in the world. This peculiarity in man leads to an endless series of correlated oddities: "alone among the animals he is shaken with the beautiful madness called laughter."[26]

Modern conceptions of primitive society are often constructed by the same illusionistic methods that lead to the manufacture of a fictional forebrain. Wells puts the thing crudely in his story of the burial scratch that becomes, eventually, a garden. But the same assumptions color most of the evolutionary views of society. The truly human content of religion and thought is introduced in the form of inhuman pressures. Reverence and ritual and sacramentalism are given new names and imagined as subhuman things which foreran themselves:

> we cannot say that religion arose out of the religious forms, because that is only another way of saying that it only arose when it existed already. . . . Nor could anyone imagine any connection between corn and dreams and an old chief with a spear, unless there was already a common feeling to include them all. But if there was such a common feeling, it could only be the religious feeling; and these things could not be the beginnings of a religious feeling that existed already.[27]

The truth is that every bit of myth and art we have—that is, everything specifically and authentically man's—is single in its expression of the mind:

> Man could already see in these things the riddles and hints and hopes that he still sees in them. He could not only

234

dream but dream about dreams. He could not only see the dead but see the shadow of death; and was possessed with that mysterious mystification that forever finds death incredible.[28]

The earliest records show man aware of the human mystery.

This mystery is qualitative and unique, not a matter of quantity and degree. The crudest hieroglyphs are an elaborate heraldry involving that complicated union of thought and whimsy which is called a pun.[29] Not far from what is for us "the dawn of history" stand things like Homer. Wells dismisses this glint on the advancing waves in one sentence:

> One of the most interesting and informative of these prehistoric compositions of the Aryans survives in the Greek *Iliad*.[30]

But neither the comparative tricks of Wells nor the real sociological differences between a heroic age and a developed (or decadent) era can hide the self-realization in Homer's lines, where time and eternity intersect. The *Iliad* does not stand at the end of a line of compositions beginning with the bird's nest and the beaver's dam. It is in another dimension, timeless by comparison with such temporal developments:

> the last man alive would do well to quote the *Iliad* and die . . . The tale of the end of Troy shall have no ending. Troy standing was a small thing that may have stood nameless for ages. But Troy falling has been caught up in a flame and suspended in an immortal instant of annihilation; and because it was destroyed with fire the fire shall never be destroyed. . . . Hellas of the hundred statues was one legend and literature; and all that labyrinth of little walled nations resounding with the lament of Troy.[31]

MAN AND MYTHOLOGY

The variety and complexity of human societies—the simultaneous, as opposed to the successive, degrees of thought and superstition and art—exist in each man. Every man is—in various degrees, developed or potential—poet and philosopher, soldier and savage, sceptic and saint. There is no simple rite or magic as a stage in one person's mind, or one society's. Against the artificial stages and parallels of comparative religion Chesterton opposes several strata of religious doubt and speculation:

> Instead of dividing religion geographically and as it were vertically, into Christian, Moslem, Brahmin, Buddhist, and so on, I would divide it psychologically and in some sense horizontally; into the strata of spiritual elements and influences that could sometimes exist in the same country, or even in the same man. Putting the Church apart for the moment, I should be disposed to divide the natural religion of the mass of mankind under such headings as these: God; the Gods; the Demons; the Philosophers.[32]

By God Chesterton means the constant ghost of monotheism that runs through all mythology. There are always gods behind the gods, $\theta\varepsilon o\grave{\iota}\ \theta\varepsilon\hat{\omega}\nu$ as Plato calls them,[33] stretching up like a living pyramid toward some central power, a power unseen, but sketched in words like "the Moira which Zeus obeys." And at certain crises of paganism's psychology that power becomes $\theta\varepsilon\acute{o}\varsigma$ simply, standing alone in mystery. Literal monotheism, in the Jews and in other tribes, is often obscured by a lively polytheism on a more superficially poetic level.[34]

This polytheism of the myths Chesterton considers under his second heading, "the gods." Too often, in the study of myths, men have invented a "science" which simply refers all things, by some evolutionary process, to a dim and largely conjectural origin in prehistory. For instance, we are calmly assured that the fact that all savages have rites connected with what is called (by analogy from one tribe's word for it) *taboo* "leaves no reasonable doubt as to the origin and ultimate relations of the idea of holiness."[35] This is like saying that the idea of kingship came from that odd nervous twitch which made men keep sticking crowns on other men. *Taboo* and *mana* show that wherever the human thing exists there is a permanent sense of the sacredness of certain objects. To call one way of manifesting this sacramental instinct the explanation and cause of the whole human trait is like saying man's mind was evolved because he kept going through a ritual of speaking words, and had therefore to become rational in order to understand himself. The fascination with symbols had led to a belief that the symbolized thing is caused by the symbol! The phallus, the totem, the dream, the funeral gift, grain—each has been made the key to the other (and to everything). "The true origin of all the myths has been discovered much too often. There are too many keys to mythology, as there are too many cryptograms in Shakespeare."[36]

The accidents of local expression, the oddities of tribal or cultural lore—these can be catalogued and made the object of an exact science. But if we are to learn what men *meant* by a symbol, we must understand their sentiment, whimsy, superstition, and awe, which can only be grasped by empathy, which is directly opposed to "scientific objectivity":

> There is very little value in talking about totems unless we have some feeling of what it really felt like to have a totem. . . . Did a man whose totem was a wolf feel like a werewolf or like a man running from a werewolf? Did he feel like Uncle Remus about Brer Wolf or like St. Francis about his brother the wolf, or like Mowgli about his brothers the

wolves? Was a totem a thing like the British lion or a thing like the British bull-dog?[37]

When once we take up a position within myth, when we truly enter this world, we find it is a world of human expression—in act (ritual), imagination (story), and insight. Chesterton treats myth under all three of these aspects—as rite, narrative, and knowledge.

As rite: The mechanical act cannot, as some "ritual theories of myth" suggest, lead to the birth of a spiritual concept. To say this is to reverse *motive* in a psychological as well as philosophical sense, as we have seen: to make crowns produce kings, and phalli produce love stories, to make the altar produce the worshiper, and grain produce the gods. The truth is not that all these things made man, but that man made them: to say there have been many gods and altars is simply to say there has been one worshiper—man. Ritual expresses a dependence that is man's only freedom, the posture of truth:

> He not only felt freer when he bent; he actually felt taller when he bowed. Henceforth anything that took away the gesture of worship would stunt and even maim him forever. Henceforth being merely secular would be a servitude and an inhibition. If man cannot pray he is gagged; if he cannot kneel he is in irons.[38]

As narrative: Through stories man interprets nature (and the supernatural) in man's terms. A child sees a small tree and calls it a "baby tree"; implicit in the phrase is the story of a family—"poppa tree, momma tree, and baby tree." Anthropologists make this seem foreign and primitive by calling it "animism." When the child's story becomes a poet's musings on "the gods," they call it anthropomorphism. But the poets are not perturbed by this condescending term. They know they are interpreting God not in terms of man's limits, but of his limitless aspects. The unfathomable mysteries in man are that part of nature most akin to the mystery of God, man's source; and God must be talked of in terms of these or of nothing within our experience. The language that results is admittedly imprecise, but there *is* a timeless, divine quality in man's thought and choice. The story, or mythos, is as natural to man as his ability to reason or to laugh:

> Nobody understands it who has not had what can only be called the ache of the artist to find some sense and some story in the beautiful things he sees; his hunger for secrets and his anger at any tower or tree escaping with its tale untold. He feels that nothing is perfect unless it is personal.[39]

In myth man asserts that the part of him which reaches out toward the gods is precisely that which is most secretly personal and particular. Myths are connected with streams and single moments, with seasons and sex, with the family; with a local habitation and a name.[40] The cart-before-horse schools find in each of these connections an explanation. Place-names are mentioned? The myth is "aetiological." Persons? Euhemeristic. The family? Freudian. A nation? The totem. A season? Marxian, connected with the economics of the harvest. The one point common to all the explanations is that they stress one inhumanly simple, uncomplicated, abstract source of all the things which myths declare to be complex, rooted, and incarnate, reluctant to mere allegorization or bloodless symbol:

> Now we do not comprehend this process in ourselves, far less in our most remote fellow-creatures. And the danger of these things being classified is that they may seem to be comprehended. A really fine work of folk-lore, like *The Golden Bough,* will leave too many readers with the idea, for instance, that this or that story of a giant's or wizard's heart in a casket or a cave only "means" some stupid and static superstition called

239

the "external soul." . . . Very deep things in our nature, some dim sense of the dependence of great things upon small, some dark suggestion that the things nearest to us stretch far beyond our power, some sacramental feeling of the magic in material substances, and many more emotions past finding out, are in an idea like that of the external soul.[41]

As knowledge: The myths are infinitely malleable to meaning because they are not explained or exhausted by any one symbol or network of symbols. But there is a partial knowledge—not abstract, but very concrete—conveyed in the myths. Man's encounter with himself is always reflected in his portrayal of something else, as we saw in the case of the bison-drawings. Myths are the sign that man is confusedly aware of things, within himself and just beyond the range of his reason, which are more profound than our easily formulated experiences and concepts. "We do not know what these things mean, simply because we do not know what we ourselves mean when we are moved by them."[42]

GOD AND THE GODS

In myth, therefore, man recognizes that things are present to him which are not conceptually grasped. This is a negative knowledge, not one of assertion. It is a form of denial that the conscious reason has exhausted the objects of reality open to knowledge; that is why it must speak by indirection, say things true by narrating things admittedly false in a literal sense. For myth is that which has no literal sense. Two Thomist philosophers—Walter Ong, S.J., and Frederick Wilhelmsen—have brilliantly discussed myth as the language of *potential* knowledge, the incompletely activated fringe of associations and personal experiences clinging to phantasms, haunting like ghosts every explicit statement:

Just as there is no total statement, so there is no total myth, no total implicitness. The total or pure myth would be a story, not without words, but one in which the words were devoid of *any* explicit meaning—each word, that is, quite undifferentiated from the others.[43]

In this *potentiality* of knowledge—by which we say more than we say, we hardly know what—Chesterton sees the final meaning of the myths, their part in the history of religion. As a *rite,* man's gesture is an act of reaching, an expression of his own need, not of that need's goal or fulfillment:

When the man makes the gesture of salutation and of sacrifice, when he pours out the libation or lifts up the sword, he knows he is doing a worthy and a virile thing. He knows he is doing one of the things for which a man was made. His imaginative experiment is therefore justified. But precisely because it began with imagination, there is to the end something of mockery in it, and especially in the object of it. This mockery, in the more intense moments of the intellect, becomes the almost intolerable irony of Greek tragedy. There seems a disproportion between the priest and the altar or between the altar and the god. The priest seems more solemn and almost more sacred than the god. All the order of the temple is solid and sane and satisfactory to certain parts of our nature; except the very centre of it, which seems stragely mutable and dubious, like a dancing flame.[44]

As *narratives* the myths never became final or authoritative in form or meaning, but kept a wavering multiplicity which produces the mazy effect of pursuit and yearning, as Keats realized in his masterly use of the myths:

They tend continually to hover over certain passionate themes of meeting and parting, of a life that ends in death or a death that is the beginning of life. . . . There was no idea that any one of them had changed the world; but rather that their recurrent death and life bore the sad and beautiful burden of the changelessness of the world.[45]

As *knowledge* the myths are expressions of the fact that we know not what we are:

Behind all these things is the fact that beauty and terror are very real things and related to a real spiritual world; and to touch them at all, even in doubt or fancy, is to stir the deep things of the soul. We all understand that and the pagans understood it. The point is that paganism did not really stir the soul except with these doubts and fancies.[46]

From all of this Chesterton reaches his conclusion on the religious significance of mythology:

In a word, mythology is a *search;* it is something that combines a recurrent desire with a recurrent doubt, mixing a most hungry sincerity in the idea of seeking for a place with a most dark and deep and mysterious levity about all the places found.[47]

The mark of all mythology is its imaginative freedom, which baffles all literal or mechanically allegorical approaches to it. Myths are determined only by a gravitation toward something man needs in order to complete himself. In this sense the pagan gods, like the Hebrew prophets, are "forerunners." As Newman put it,

Even where there is habitual rebellion against Him, or profound farspreading social depravity, still the undercurrent, or the heroic outburst, of natural virtue, as well as the yearnings of the heart after what it has not, and its presentiment of its true remedies, are to be ascribed to the Author of all good. Anticipations or reminiscences of His glory haunt the mind of the self-sufficient sage, and of the pagan devotee; His writing is upon the wall, whether of the Indian fane, or of the porticoes of Greece. He introduces Himself, He all but concurs, according to His good pleasure, and in His selected season, in the issues of unbelief, superstition, and false worship, and He changes the character of acts by His overruling operation. He condescends, though He gives no sanction, to the altars and shrines of imposture, and He makes His own fiat the substitute for its sorceries. He speaks amid the incantations of Balaam, raises Samuel's spirit in the witch's cavern, prophesies of the Messias by the tongue of the Sibyl, forces Python to recognize His ministers, and baptizes by the hand of the misbeliever. He is with the heathen dramatist in his denunciation of injustice and tyranny, and his auguries of divine vengeance upon crime. Even on the unseemly legends of popular mythology He casts His shadow, and is dimly discerned in the ode or the epic, as in troubled water or in fantastic dreams.[48]

DEMONS AND THEORIES

The potential nature of myth distinguishes it from the two remaining strata of religious thought which Chesterton enumerated. The worship of *demons* is neither imaginative nor free. It is practical, intent on results and bound by the agreement. The "Faust" is always an alchemist trying to make gold, to get things done, no matter who or what does them. "There is always in such a mentality an idea that there is a short cut to the secret of all success; something that would shock the world by this sort of shameless thoroughness."[49] The free imagination of the poet, who merely wants to see visions and dream dreams, is not stimulated but paralyzed by this kind of belief. The *philosopher,* on the other hand, activates the knowledge which poets leave potential. His is the active intelligence, abstract, constructive, simplifying. As Chesterton points out, statistics are a great temptation to man's mind, which can never avoid connecting things that come near it. This temptation is multiplied a thousandfold when the whole universe is extended under the mind's purview. Schemes and patterns grow all-inclusive for the man who wants to deal only in the clearly intelligible. This is the impatience of the intellect which has to find cryptograms in Shakespeare, which discovers in the universe monisms and dualisms of one sort or another— determinism, idealism, materialism, nihilism or automatic recurrence. And students simplify the simplifications of even the greatest philosophers.[50]

Thus philosophy, though it is not bound as demon-worship binds, is constricting in its tendency. It excludes too much to satisfy men as a religion. An isosceles triangle cannot be born of woman, as the Logos was when it fulfilled the legends. The intellect runs, if unchecked, into the *cul de sac* of rationalism; and this intellect could not be balanced by the irresponsible myths and eroticisms and diabolisms of pagan antiquity. The philosopher was exiled from the human world of personality, locality, and mystery. Plato cast a regretful eye back toward the myths, but had to prescribe mathematics as a purification of the mind which would deal in the pure intelligibilities of philosophy.

Therefore the religious strata in the human mind, though they co-existed in individuals, never intertwined or added strength to one another. Speculation and poetry and narrowly effective magic live in different worlds; gods and demons and theories come at men from different angles. A theology which is abstracted as an intellectual creed yet incarnated in particular events, which com-

bines an ethical norm and a mystic rite and an intellectual discipline, is unknown in paganism:

> A man did not stand up and say "I believe in Jupiter and Juno
> and Neptune" etc., as he stands up and says "I believe in God
> the Father Almighty" and the rest of the Apostles' Creed . . .
> though they provide him with a calendar they do not provide
> him with a creed. . . . There was no moment when they were
> all collected into an orthodox order which men would fight
> and be tortured to keep intact.[51]

CRISIS IN HISTORY

The next stage of Chesterton's argument is the demonstration that
the merely comparative approach to civilizations is as false as the
anthropological, mythological, and religious dilutions of the paradox of man. The example he takes is Wells' own parallel, the "two
Western republics." Rome's religion, which Wells calls a crude
Shamanism, is that mythology of the field and the family, the belief in the sacredness of places and persons, which Chesterton
called "the gods."[52] But the high civilization of Carthage was practical, based on the merchant expansion of a trading center, and
their religion was of just that effective type which Chesterton calls
demon-worship. Moloch was adored with the sacrifice of children;
the civilization had no roots in the earth or in the family.[53]

The trading power of Carthage was entirely one of expansion.
There could be no reduction to a static position as long as
Carthage remained Carthage. Republican Rome, so critical of
erotic Greece and the exotic Orient, now caught between the
Punic pincers of Spain and Sicily, crushed this power at its source.
There were many motives for the war, but Rome did not pretend,

like modern states, that moral repugnance had nothing to do with the extraordinary energy of this overthrow. Wells claims that "she had destroyed and looted Carthage and so had no foothold for extension into Africa."[54] But the true result of Rome's victory, as Gomme points out, is that a very high level of culture spread through Africa and around the Mediterranean from the Academy and the Forum, a culture deeply opposed to the great merchant state that had almost enveloped the West.[55]

Rome had conquered. But what was left for it to do now? In the lingering Hellenic civilization, all the strands of religious thought met, but could not combine. Myth could only multiply narratives, or intensify its mysticism of sex.[56] Philosophy could only further simplify its patterns.[57] Demonism could only repeat the shameful offerings. At the height of man's natural achievements, it became obvious that history without a source or goal is mere succession. The great achievements could only be repeated, some day when men should have forgotten that they were re-enacting a thwarted quest. The yearning of Virgil is a good type of the highest paganism's baffled melancholy. The escape this paralysis, later pagans like Wells would try to make of succession a virtue and call it "progress." But the intellect of Hellas had seen the failure of this and all other attempts at escape from the flow of time.

Another crisis interrupted this helpless flow of history—as abrupt an entry as the human mind's intersection of material things. As the mind brought timeless understanding into relation with temporal sensation, so was this an invasion of time by eternity. Christ was born.

THE LAST CRISIS—CHRIST

To that nativity came the shepherds who lived on myths, on stories which "had not been wrong in being as carnal as the Incarnation."[58] In the Magi, philosophy came to the crib; and found the Logos in flesh because it had sought for Number in the stars. Even the darker ambition that murders children came in Herod, to massacre the innocents. And hovering behind the event was the entire history of the most loyally monotheistic of ancient nations.

The same forces stood around the Cross—the civilized sceptic asking, "What is truth?" the populace asking for bread and miracles, the priests interested in results, and the Law of the lonely Jehovah. Between these two events—the nativity and the crucifixion—every act and word of Christ polarizes the previously separated strands of religious search. Christ teaches, but he also acts; his life is a story, with inner causation, choice, and crisis:

> This is where it was a fulfillment of the myths rather than of the philosophies; it is a journey with a goal and an object, like Jason going to find the Golden Fleece, or Hercules the golden apples of the Hesperides. The gold that he was seeking was death. . . . We are meant to feel that Death was the bride of Christ as Poverty was the bride of St. Francis . . . in a deeper sense it is rather to be compared to the journey of Ulysses. It was not only a romance of travel but a romance of return; and of the end of a usurpation.[59]

Chesterton's emphasis on the story, on the effective drama of Christ's life, is paralleled by a recent discussion of the dramatic nature of Christian reality in the Rev. William Lynch's *Christ and Apollo*. Christ did not sunder heaven and earth, or lead an escape from time; he *united* all things dynamically, impregnating time with eternity. The Christian is not saved by a separately summoned act of the will, by a magic moment of "acceptance" (whether intellectual or moral); not lifted out of the human condition of darkness; rather, incorporated into the drama of Christ's life, a drama worked out in history, in the moving line of earned insights and a cognitive life that is full of sensibility, of real assents, and of statements about existence which are come by legitimately through the developing dramatic rhythms of life, and not through the illegitimate and unrooted leaps of what Cardinal Newman might have called the purely notional mind.[60]

Both Chesterton and Fr. Lynch draw attention to the fact that Christ worked his miracles not to escape time but to plunge men into the choices time presses on them. Both see a supreme testimony to the redemptive validity of time in Christ's refusal to escape any detail of his agony, when the crisis of his own life came. What is more significant, Christ lived through each stage of preparation for this crisis, growing himself and bringing to growth in others all of those human realities which were to be fused, forever, in his redemptive act. This divine endorsement of the integrated human experience is expressed in the words "My time is not yet come," spoken at the beginning of Christ's public life, and in the refusal to avoid the painful processes of instruction in the disciples. No instant "gnosis" spared him the daily battle against misunderstanding, even in those nearest him. By such integration of all things in the human reality, Christ stands apart from all mere philosophers or teachers. By his own mystery, he incarnates Truth in the historical processes. As Augustine puts it, in paradoxes that resemble Chesterton's:

Man's maker was made man that the Lord of the stars might nurse at his mother's breast, that the Bread might be hungry, the Fountain thirst, the Light sleep, the Way be tired from the journey; that the Truth might be accused by false witnesses . . . the Teacher be beaten with whips, the Vine be crowned with thorns, the Foundation be hung on a tree; that

Strength might be made weak, that He who heals might be wounded, that Life might die.[61]

Augustine had felt the void separating the various levels of pagan reality; he had engaged in the neo-Platonic search for some daimonic ladder, some progression of ascending demiurges, which should climb from man's dramatic situation to the fixed place of changeless Truth. His conversion to Christianity occurred when he saw that Christ reunited the disparate worlds of paganism by bringing Truth into the dramatic flow of events, where he became the Way that itself travels, as well as the Goal that is to be reached:

> From the mountain's wooded peak to descry the homeland of the heart (*patriam pacis*), unable to find the path to take one there, vainly attempting the pathless interval, harassed and intercepted by wandering deserters of the way (now captained by the lion and the dragon)—far different, all this, from confident adherence to the Way which goes straight there.[62]

"Raised up over the earth, I will draw all things to me" (John 12.32). Christ stands at the crossroads of man's life. He creates the crossroads, for before him the different strata could not even conflict. To the philosophers he is the Logos, to the shepherds he is the Shepherd, to the demons he is an exorcist, to the monotheists he is the One God, to the poets he is one of the Persons who must exist in the highest activity of Love: to all men an absolute answer or a living blasphemy—"to the Jews a scandal and to the Greeks folly."

> It were better to rend our robes with a great cry against blasphemy, like Caiaphas in the judgment, or to lay hold of the man as a maniac possessed of devils like the kinsmen and the crowd, rather than to stand stupidly debating fine shades of pantheism

in the presence of so catastrophic a claim. There is more of the wisdom that is one with surprise in any simple person, full of the sensitiveness of simplicity, who should expect the grass to wither and the birds to drop dead out of the air, when a strolling carpenter's apprentice said calmly and almost carelessly, like one looking over his shoulder: "Before Abraham was, I am."[65]

Because Christ polarizes what had co-existed as separate worlds of longing—philosophy and poetry, myth and creed, spirit and flesh—men easily find what look like contradictions in his claims. He is a scandal to believers and folly to philosophers because he is judged by one of those incomplete things which only find completion in their opposites. And only Christ unites such opposites in incarnate paradox, for Christ among men is a paradox more absolute than the first mystery of man among the brutes.

CHRIST IN THE CHURCH

The Church continues Christ's life in time by re-enacting the crisis of the Cross. Peter was not the cleverest student of a great teacher, but a literal-minded fisherman who passed on the physical touch which consecrates and exorcises, which centers all the many human activities of history. In "The Witness of the Heretics" Chesterton shows how the Church survived all the merely temporal fads that first acted on it, and that have been taken as its cause or explanation—the mere Orientalism of Mithras, the mere asceticism of the gnostics, the mere exorcism of the Manichees, the mere ethics of the stoics, the mere organization of the Empire's millenarists. The Church remained when all of these things had perished precisely because of their attractive simplicity:

If anybody says that philosophic maxims preserved through many ages, or mythological temples frequented by many people are things of the same class and category as the Church, it is enough to answer quite simply that they are not.[64]

The Church suffers influence and alteration in time, but at its center is a living link, through Christ, with eternity: there—in the sacrifice of the Mass—thought, poetry, morality, and drama meet. Christ is still the crossroads.

The union which the Church effected was not a dilution. It united the worlds of poetry and philosophy, it leagued the natural and the supernatural against the anti-natural; and all the components were strengthened by the combination. The personal devotion to the saints is warmer than that given to the household gods; Christian philosophy is more continuous, intense, and self-correcting than any other school of thought; Christian monks and friars are history's only balanced and long-lived experiment in asceticism; Christian missionaries are a phenomenon unique in religious history.[65] The reason for this is given in "The Escape from Paganism." The Christian myth is not merely imaginative; and the Christian philosophy is not a mere abstract pattern. These two things were united in a "philosophy of stories"—the truth about real men as seen in the life of the Son of Man, who is both archetypal pattern and real actor in the order of time.[66]

In the book's last chapter, "The Five Deaths of the Faith," Chesterton points out that time did have its attritive effect on the Church. The Church aged, and certain of its members went astray; but it was always reborn. Killing it is a new task in each generation. Heretics have tried to simplify the Church's balance, to reduce the separate elements once more to their single condition. But the simplifications fail, and the complex thing rights itself. This is what Chesterton noticed in *Orthodoxy* as the dialectic, the paradox, the "flying balance" inherent in Catholicism. Here he penetrates more thoroughly the critical nature of Catholicism, which is the paradox of Christ. The "five deaths" are not five historical accidents. "The Faith is not a survival."[67] It is a continuing crisis—at once the death and the resurrection of Christ.

To Wells' outline, therefore, Chesterton opposes a philosophy of history. The "horizontal" order of mere succession is transpierced by a "vertical" stroke of Order. Because of this cross-penetration, Gibbon felt that the Church divided men's loyalties and undermined the solid foundation of human history. But history has no solid basis of its own. The Church *saved* history by bringing order and succession into contact with each other. The only order which paganism could find in history was that of inevitable return as a faint image of the immutable. The only alternative to disjunct experience was the assertion that matter and change are illusory. Poetry, according to Aristotle, is more philosophical than history because history is nothing but the patternless succession of particulars. The Jews, it is true, perceived a goal in time shaping their history into patterns of prophecy; but this was an entirely temporal and immanent purpose, the expectation of the Messiah.

In Christ, time and eternity were at last united. The significance of this union was fully explored by St. Augustine: the City of God is the eternal order of reality placed athwart the temporal flow of events. The Church is built into the eternal city as it develops in time: "You are living stones being built into God's temple."[68] The apocalyptic prophecies of the Gospel, says Augustine, can be applied to the Church at every instant, since time is ended at each instant by this contact with the City of God—this *krisis,* or judgment—though it also continues to develop toward its supreme consummation.[69] The horizontal flow of events is intersected by a vertical judgment which is an instant impregnation of history with eternity—the filling-up of time (pleroma tou chronou).[70] "It was his loving design, centered in Christ, to give history its fulfillment by resuming everything in him, all that is in heaven, all that is in earth, summed up in him."[71] This judgment is to the world of man what man's critical intellect is to the disjunct world of subhuman things. The mind transcends time and judges all things; but it must itself be judged, and the human mirror and meeting-place is only a faint image of the junction effected by Christ at the center of history.

Eternity is an instant, and can only have a dialectic relation with time—neither transcendent nor immanent, neither a combination nor an approximation. This is the meaning of the Mass, always new and always the same: in Christ, time and eternity crash, establishing that mystery of conflict and reconciliation which is the Incarnation—the Everlasting Man.

13.

THE PLAY OF REALITY

Michael Mason, in his excellent study *The Center of Hilarity,* discusses the metaphysical concept of "play," which resembles what I have called dialectic and what Chesterton called paradox. Mr. Mason finds the *in principio finis* motto embodied in Chesterton's career. Fulfillment is in one sense a journey back to origins; advance is return. This truth, which Chesterton stated in the exploration-myth that prefaces *Orthodoxy,* was borne out in the final years of his life, and became the theme of his *Autobiography*. The "white light" of his first sensations, the edges and colors of the toy theater, the creative magic of his father's drawings; the threat implied in a planchette, in a green carnation, in a philosophy like Schopenhauer's; the need to draw, to write poems, to act out meaning in the toy theater of one's brain—these things shaped Chesterton's life from beginning to end. They even *determined* it; but only as norms, for which answering realities had to be discovered if Chesterton was to reach the goal and return to his origins on a deeper level of realization—finding his real home buried beneath the appearances of home, the tree that is a tree at last.

Chesterton, perhaps more than most men, *did* keep up the search for answers to his primary instincts. He kept the edge on his appetite for edges—through the dimmer years that follow on childhood, and even through the time when a philosophy of dissolution seemed to involve all the surrounding landscape. The child's undiscriminating wonder developed into Chesterton's first existential arguments and poems; the love of edges, of stories made tense by danger and symbol, led to his feel for dialectic and paradox; the figures cut out by his father became the power of myth and poetry to re-enact the mystery of creation. Fairy tales led to Stevenson, then on to Shakespeare and the poets; from them to the myths, and finally to the story behind all stories. The self-paralysis of logic, the imagination's attraction to non-being—these were eventually deciphered as the expression of evil's war on existence. The oldest image in Chesterton's memory was of a figure bringing a key to a high prison-tower, and his last certitude was that only the keys of Peter unlock man from his self-immurement.

"IN MY BEGINNING IS MY END"

Chesterton's later years were a true rebirth. From the time of his conversion in 1922, he began to pour out again the stories in which his intellect had first played with symbols. The first post-war volume of these tales was actually begun in 1919, though not completed for several years; *The Man Who Knew Too Much*, a series of bitter attacks on political corruption, is Chesterton's attempt to write according to the program of *The New Witness*. The man who knows too much is an aristocrat familiar with the corruption that breeds in those high places held by his fellows. More typical of this later phase are the Father Brown stories, most of which were written between 1925 and 1935.

The priest who understands sin by becoming a sinner was joined, in 1929, by a poet who understands lunatics by becoming a madman. These two become evil or insane only potentially—the priest by recognizing man's limits, the poet by experiencing the perils of a voyage into one's own mind; yet this humility and sense of peril are cathartic, and cleanse the world. The priest-sinner keeps men holy when the righteous enthusiasts and liberal theologians let them perish in their own perfection. The poet-madman keeps men sane when the rationalists have led them to the brink of lunacy. In one story, "The Crime of Gabriel Gale," the poet's real secret is uncovered, the source of his sympathy with lunatics. We know now that it is another man's secret, and another example of his return to origins in the years when this was written:

> I also dreamed that I had dreamed of the whole creation. I had given myself the stars for a gift; I had handed myself the sun and moon. I had been behind and at the beginning of all things; and without me nothing was made that was made. Anybody who has been in the centre of that cosmos knows that it is to be in hell. . . . Materialists are all right; they are at least near enough to heaven to accept the earth and not imagine they made it.[1]

Four Faultless Felons (1930) varies Chesterton's theme without adding anything to it: four men become criminals to prevent crime, so that the detective has to uncover hidden virtues like secret sins.

Chesterton's poems, in his Catholic years, were the same rhymed paradoxes he had always written, but with conceits that were more in the "metaphysical" manner, as in this Donne-like figure of the three falls—Lucifer's, man's, and God's:

> For in dread of such falling and failing
> The Fallen Angels fell
> Inverted in insolence, scaling
> The hanging mountain of hell;
> But unmeasured of plummet and rod,
> Too deep for their sight to scan,
> Outrushing the fall of man
> Is the height of the fall of God.[2]

The angel climbs down, and man falls up, because God lifts the world by his descent. Christ is the hinge on which the directions of pride and humility are reversed, the aspiring plunged downward, the lowly raised aloft. Chesterton's earlier poems had a dialectic logic of symbols, but one which balanced opposites (like Alfred and the Danes) or complementary realities (like the variety of human types who fought under Alfred). The early love poems, for example, played on the dialectic of sex, which binds all of earthly society together. The later poems are more often to the Virgin, and describe the darker meeting of heaven and earth—of realities so radically different that they seem to exist in different universes. In a poem describing the Church, the nursery rhyme is used of the famous tower "East of the Sun and West of the Moon." Neither the clear archer-god nor the obscure moon reigns over it:

> The last long shot of Apollo
> Falls spent ere it strikes the tower . . .

And the dark labyrinthine charts of the wise
Point East and point West of the land where it lies.[3]

It exists in a new land beyond the Eastern mysticism and the
Western rationalism, a place where opposite horizons meet, like "a
new corner of the sky, And the other side of things."[4]

The source of new depth in these conceits is the understanding
of time and eternity as they meet in Christ. A poem on the famous
epitaph of Arthur (*rex quondam rexque futurus*) dwells, first, on the
fact that Arthur is mythically timeless as Troy is, a future king as
Hector is. But myth points to a higher realization of its elements;
the gods lead to God. The "timelessness" of art images the fact
that eternity is a single instant, that all time radiates from, and is
equidistant from, this single center:

> In the high still hollow where Time is not
> Or all times turn and exchange and borrow,
> In the glass wherein God remembers tomorrow,
> And truth looks forward to times forgot,
>
> Where God looks back on the days to be
> And heaven is yet hoping for yesterday,
> The light in which time shall be taken away
> And the soul that faces all ways is free.[5]

The fulfillment of the man and the myth is attained in Christ, the
real king suggested by the riddle, the meeting-place of time and
eternity:

> A dream shall wail through the worm-shaped horn
> "Dead is the King that never was born"
> And a trumpet of truth from the Cross reply
> "Dead is the King who shall not die."

The Queen of Seven Swords, the fine translation from Dante, the lines which describe Christ as the fulfillment of both Zeus and Prometheus, all bear witness to the new element in Chesterton's last poems, the attempt to describe a thing

That splits the shattered sunlight from a light beyond the sun.[6]

But this development, like all the others, was a return and almost a rebirth. The sense of wonder, based on the interplay of Being and beings, is raised to a theological level, and describes the tryst of time with eternity. This reaching of one's goal in one's origins is perfectly expressed in one of his most personal poems, "A Second Childhood."

POETRY AND THE PLAY
OF EXISTENCE

In 1927 Chesterton took up again the form of drama. *The Judgement of Dr. Johnson* is not as effective or significant as *Magic;* a mere exercise in the Shavian manner, it reworks the points made in *Candida.* But Shaw's men were simply weak and his Woman effortlessly strong; in Chesterton's play the men are fools, but with depths in their folly, and the woman shows her superior strength in the ability to suffer, not in the airy insouciance of Candida. Technically, the character of Dr. Johnson is handled well, providing the solution to a series of dramatic events which his presence dominates, though he is not an agent in the situation itself.

The Surprise, published posthumously (1952), was written in 1930; it ranks with Chesterton's finest creative works—with *Magic, The Man Who Was Thursday, The Wild Knight,* and *The White Horse.* A poet-puppeteer "confesses" to a wandering friar, his confession taking the form of a pantomime—a romance of freedom, love, and song acted out by his life-sized puppets. The confession is that of the artist, the man who has become God's rival. He wants his dreams to live; other life seems stale compared to the dreams that breed day and night in his brain. But this is also the confession of a man going mad—pitting his images against actual things, half suspecting that his dreams are more real than reality.

The friar prays for a way to rescue the poet from his Promethean dilemma; and the puppets spring up unbidden, new creatures in an Eden of reality. This play begins again; but things go wrong—absurd things, pathetically entangling, in accident and misunderstanding, more serious cross-purposes. The multiple and free action of several minds and wills destroys the neat simplicity of the author's plot. At the worst crisis of misunderstanding, the poet appears from behind his stage lumber and shouts: "Stop! I'm coming down."

The poet returns to the world of actual things, which must be defended because they are worth assault. The action of real men makes *him* come to life with his puppets and step outside his dreams. But this cry of his is an echo of the Creator's Word as it became incarnate. The poet only became God's rival because he is God's image, "never more so than when he is making things."

Chesterton's return to his origins made him return to literary criticism. The passages on myth in *The Everlasting Man* are a theological criticism based entirely on a sense of style in the great narratives of mankind; they approach theology, as *Orthodoxy* did philosophy, through poetry. The metaphysics of art, left implicit in his earlier work, was stated clearly in this last stage of his career. Without denying the merits of modern art in its actual experiments (for poetry can break through the worst obstacles), Chesterton attacked the modern theories of art which work from the assumption that a lack of formal scheme or pattern (*e.g.,* rhyme and regular meter) leads to freedom and subtlety of expression. The verbal recurrence and haunting melody of poetry is not ornamental, mere incrustation. The energies of music, the continuing echoes of rhyme, resemble the potential infinity of meaning in a metaphor; they deny the limits of essential reality, overriding these hard lines of reason. The flow of a single music through language echoes that river of existence which runs, immeasurably deep, through every particle of creation:

> There is at the back of all our lives an abyss of light more blinding and unfathomable than any abyss of darkness; and it is the abyss of actuality, of existence, of the fact that things truly are, and that we ourselves are incredibly and sometimes incredulously real.

> At the back of our brains, so to speak, there was a forgotten blaze or burst of astonishment at our own existence. The object of the artistic and spiritual life was to dig for this submerged sunrise of wonder.[7]

Even Chesterton's book on Rome treats the city as a large artifact with its own style. The florid buildings and statues that have proliferated out of the Renaissance are taken as the most obvious characteristic of Rome. Chesterton does not defend the statues as perfect artifacts, but as expressions of Rome's attitude toward sacrament and image. This attitude led to many scandals and corruptions, but it kept a spiritual balance through many fads more dangerous than aesthetic styles. Puritan chapels, neo-Gothic centers for aesthetes, and the featureless patterns of Islam show that no other solution to the problems of idolatry and ceremony is permanently suited to mankind as a whole. In this book also Chesterton finds that his life had been a fulfillment but also a return. He says that the Swiss guards troubled him with some unidentifiable memory, until at last he realized that his own image of Adam

Wayne was walking before him in the sunlight, guardian of a state as tiny as Notting Hill, and even more sacred.[8]

As we have seen, Chesterton re-assessed the Victorian *fin de siècle* and his own reaction to it while writing his book on Stevenson. The stab of reality that strikes at one even in the antics of a pasteboard princess is the experiential refutation of the nihilists; and Stevenson's art is the finest articulation of that experience. The aesthetics of edges is given in the two books written at this time— *Robert Louis Stevenson* and the first part of the *Autobiography*. But Chesterton saw the limits of this style—which were his own limits: the inability to leave fictional characters in the flesh.[9] This was, of course, a more serious drawback in Stevenson's art, since Chesterton wrote novels only in the loosest sense.

The concept of play, which Mr. Mason describes as central to the mediaeval view of life, is that quality which Chesterton takes as typical of Chaucer. He does not mean by this that Chaucer was merely a genial and whimsical poet, with a gift for translation and for character sketches. The sweep of his lines to the Virgin, the weight of his lines on Troilus' sorrow, are not gay chirpings. Nonetheless it is true that there is a "penumbra of playfulness round everything he ever said or sang; a halo of humour."[10] Chaucer's ability to see things from every possible angle—to write sermons, puns, pagan myths, prayers—yet all with ease and a personal music that is unmistakable—was the result of an equilibrium at many levels. The balance and antithesis of types among the Canterbury pilgrims is an example of this sanity. Out of all the discords of such company Chaucer somehow composes his music of the mind; and in the mere colors and symbols and social grades we see the heraldic, feudal, ecclesiastical balance of the mediaeval ideal. The guilds and the cities, the friar and monk and pastor, the summoner from Rome and the scholar from Oxford, the wife and the prioress, mingle in a common pilgrimage, however different their character, intellect, and ideals. A common framework of religion makes possible this crisscrossing play of differences; and above this social counterpoint plays a higher balance of humor and wisdom, Chaucer's personal variant of the dialectic that runs through the works of Dante or Aquinas. St. Thomas may be said "to have heckled himself for hundreds of pages,"[11] using logic, faith, the Fathers, the commentators in every possible combination. Dante's poem reaches, in triple rhymes, toward a climactic circling and interweaving of dance and song in heaven.[12] Driving all these forms of dialectic is that Christian balance described in *Orthodoxy* and *The Everlasting Man*.

The complexity and equilibrium in Chaucer's work is one form of the "play" which led Chesterton from the jumbled world of solipsism to the paradoxes of Christianity. Chaucer's halo of humor came from the same instinct that made Chesterton a metaphysical jester. At the beginning of his journey, Chesterton heard faint echoes of this cosmic merriment in Dickens, and described the laughter of the stars. But he did not yield to a simple urge toward optimism; if good is to be defended, evil must be expelled. He followed the music of ideas at play, as it grew louder to him through the years—the sound of that cosmic dance, in Dante and Angelico, which goes to the measure of a "primal paradox": "His delight was to be with the children of men."

IRONY AND INTELLECT

This book opened with a series of questions which, when I wrote those first pages, I hoped in some measure to answer. Now I know that is impossible. There is no response, except multiplying echoes, to artillery trained in the wrong direction. The questions must be entirely reformulated if they are to have any possible relation to reality, and be given meaningful answers.

Did Chesterton live in an unreal world of his own? Did he simply pour his own optimism into suitable receptacles, like the works of Dickens? There is no answer to such a question. The whole picture of a "Dickensian" Chesterton—a genial and vague-minded Englishman—is mistaken. Dickens went by instant likes and dislikes, with an instinct infallible so far as it went, but non-partisan and non-ideological. He hated and loved; then gave an unforgettable name and nose to the objects of his love and hate. Chesterton gave ideas symbolic masks, but the masks are always cardboard. His was the critical mind, swift in argument, almost too headlong in logic, but entirely lacking the instinctual grasp of character, the parochial and unthinking optimism of Dickens.

Chesterton's appreciation of Dickens, Cobbett, and Johnson was that of a man who can appreciate virtues he does not share. In this way he admired Belloc, who had the melancholy poetry and ambition of Johnson, Cobbett's energy and need for tangible things, as well as Dickens' thirst for friendship. Belloc could sulk with Johnson, roar insults with Cobbett, or walk on the edge of hysteria with Dickens. Chesterton does not breathe the same air that these men did.

He lived in a far different world, opened to him by his "insomnia of intelligence." Though always courteous to others, he was happiest when, at Beaconsfield, he could walk up and down "heckling himself" for hours with ideas and arguments and symbolic duels, a participant in the eternal battle and balance of ideas. His critical faculties never slept; and the endless flow of books, anecdotes, and answers which he left behind are merely a sampling of that incessant activity which continued inside his mind. In this respect he resembles Aquinas and Augustine, those prodigious controversialists.

The danger to this kind of mind is not that of artificial serenity, but of fanaticism. This mind can enclose itself in walls of argument, but not in that hazy benevolence which some attribute to Chesterton. Nihilist arguments threatened him with such intellectual immurement, but an existential and artistic critique saved him, and set up a deepening interplay of ideas and existence which was the source of all his symbolic jesting.

Once this is realized, the problems raised by the usual criticism of Chesterton do not need to be solved. They simply disappear. Chesterton's role as a jester-critic explains the use of his efforts in symbolic narrative, over-toppling rhetoric, political comment, and journalism. The witty and detached defence of existence reflects a constant awareness of evil; but on a metaphysical level. The tales of nonsense and lunacy are his lifelong response to the threat of insanity and destructive intellection. Some have thought Chesterton lived in fairyland, where Peter Pan dances, forever irresponsible. But the only never-never land open to a critical intelligence as untiring as Chesterton's is the literal never-never land of nonexistence; and against this threat of Annihilation, which is evil's true name, he fought ceaselessly all his life. Only occasionally does the serious purpose of the jester show through the glancing play of words—in his quest for absolution; in a letter to one tempted and near despair, a letter which shows the deep sympathy of experience;[13] in an abrupt confrontation with the site of Sodom;[14] in a terribly vivid belief in the Devil. These glimpses are rare, but they alone explain the energies of levity with which the jester tries to lift the world. For all his merriment, Chesterton in this century was a nemesis of intelligence in a breaking storm of madness.

It is interesting to recall that Dickens, too, was considered an empty-headed clown until recently, when suddenly he became a morbidly tragic visionary. In the changes of critical fashion, Shakespeare continually suffers oscillation between these poles of inhuman levity and diseased gloom. Men simply will not see that humor and serious human insight can, and often do, go together. Chesterton pursued the sophistries and anomalies of mere contradiction as earnestly as he upheld the paradoxes of authentic mystery. Self-deception is not in that mind which recognized paradox of all sorts, but in the world which sees only platitudes. There has always been reason to call the artificial jester a "natural" fool, even when it was considered a mark of royal courage to expose oneself to the continual scrutiny and comment of a mind made agile by playfulness and lack of "normal" ambition. The intellect which sharply limns issues is a challenge, and there may be truth in Belloc's claim that the future reception of Chesterton's work would be one norm for judging England's willingness to think.[15] For the jester is not only the corrective anti-type, but the *test* of the mind. He is Touchstone.

CHRONOLOGY OF CHESTERTON'S

MAJOR WORKS

(in the editions cited in the Notes)

1900: *Greybeards at Play,* Sheed and Ward, 1933.
     The Wild Knight (in *Collected Poems,* Dodd, Mead, 1932).

1901: *The Defendant,* J. M. Dent, 1940.

1902: *Twelve Types,* Arthur L. Humphreys, 1902.

1903: *Robert Browning,* Macmillan, 1903.

1904: *G. F. Watts,* E. P. Dutton, 1904.
     The Napoleon of Notting Hill, Devin-Adair, 1949.

1905: *The Club of Queer Trades,* Harper, 1905.
     Heretics, Devin-Adair, 1950.

1906: *Charles Dickens, A Critical Study,* Dodd, Mead, 1906.

1908: *The Man Who Was Thursday,* Dodd, Mead, 1959.
     All Things Considered, Sheed and Ward, 1956.
     Orthodoxy, Dodd, Mead, 1957.

1909: *George Bernard Shaw,* John Lane, 1909.
     Tremendous Trifles, Sheed and Ward, 1955.
     The Ball and the Cross, John Lane, 1909.

1910: *What's Wrong With the World,* Sheed and Ward, 1956.
     Alarms and Discursions, Dodd, Mead, 1911.
     William Blake, E. P. Dutton, 1910.

1911: *Appreciations and Criticisms of the Works of Charles Dickens,* E. P. Dutton,
     1911.
     The Innocence of Father Brown (in *The Father Brown Omnibus,* Dodd, Mead,
     1957).
     The Ballad of the White Horse (in *Collected Poems,* Dodd, Mead, 1932).

1912: *Manalive,* John Lane, 1913.
     A Miscellany of Men, Dodd, Mead, 1912.

1913: *The Victorian Age in Literature,* Oxford, 1913.
     Magic, Putnam, 1913.

1914: *The Flying Inn,* Sheed and Ward, 1955.
     The Wisdom of Father Brown (in *The Father Brown Omnibus,* Dodd, Mead,
     1957).
     The Barbarism of Berlin (in *The Appetite of Tyranny,* Dodd, Mead, 1915).

1915: *Letters to an Old Garibaldian* (in *The Appetite of Tyranny,* Dodd, Mead,
     1915).
     The Crimes of England, Cecil Palmer and Hayward, 1915.

1917: *A Short History of England,* Clarke, Irwin, 1951.
     Utopia of Usurers, Boni and Liveright, 1917.

1919: *Irish Impressions,* W. Collins' Sons, 1919.

1920: *The Superstition of Divorce,* Dodd, Mead, 1920.

The Uses of Diversity, Dodd, Mead, 1921.
The New Jerusalem, Dodd, Mead, 1920.

1922: *Eugenics and Other Evils,* Dodd, Mead, 1927.
What I Saw in America, Dodd, Mead, 1922.
The Man Who Knew Too Much, Cassell, 1933.

1923: *Fancies Versus Fads,* Dodd, 1923.
St. Francis of Assisi, Doubleday, 1920.

1925: *Tales of the Long Bow,* Sheed and Ward, 1956.
The Everlasting Man, Dodd, Mead, 1947.
William Cobbett, Dodd, Mead, 1926.

1926: *The Incredulity of Father Brown* (in *The Father Brown Omnibus,* Dodd, Mead, 1957).
The Outline of Sanity, Dodd, Mead, 1927.
The Queen of Seven Swords, Sheed and Ward, 1944.

1927: *The Catholic Church and Conversion,* Macmillan, 1950.
The Return of Don Quixote, Dodd, Mead, 1927.
The Secret of Father Brown (in *The Father Brown Omnibus,* 1957).
The Judgement of Dr. Johnson, Sheed and Ward, 1933.
Robert Louis Stevenson, Sheed and Ward, 1955.

1928: *Generally Speaking,* Dodd, Mead, 1929.

1929: *The Poet and the Lunatics,* Sheed and Ward, 1955.
The Thing, Sheed and Ward, 1957.
G.K.C. As M.C., Methuen, 1929.

1930: *Four Faultless Felons,* Dodd, Mead, 1930.
The Resurrection of Rome, Hodder and Stoughton, 1934.
Come To Think Of It, Dodd, Mead, 1931.

1931: *All Is Grist,* Dodd, Mead, 1932.

1932: *Chaucer,* Sheed and Ward, 1956.
Sidelights on New London and Newer York, Sheed and Ward, 1933.
Christendom in Dublin, Sheed and Ward, 1933.

1933: *All I Survey,* Dodd, Mead, 1933.
St. Thomas Aquinas, Sheed and Ward, 1933.

1934: *Avowals and Denials*, Dodd, Mead, 1935.

1935: *The Scandal of Father Brown* (in *The Father Brown Omnibus*, Dodd, Mead, 1957).
The Well and the Shallows, Sheed and Ward, 1935.
The Way of the Cross, Hodder and Stoughton, 1935.

1936: *As I Was Saying*, Dodd, Mead, 1936.
Autobiography, Sheed and Ward, 1939.

1937: *The Paradoxes of Mr. Pound*, Cassel, 1938.

1938: *The Coloured Lands*, Sheed and Ward, 1938.

1940: *The End of the Armistice*, Sheed and Ward, 1940.

1950: *The Common Man*, Sheed and Ward, 1950.

1952: *The Surprise*, Sheed and Ward, 1953.

1953: *A Handful of Authors*, Sheed and Ward, 1953.

1955: *The Glass Walking-Stick*, Sheed and Ward, 1955.

1958: *Lunacy and Letters*, Sheed and Ward, 1958.

APPENDIX:

THE MAN WHO WAS THURSDAY

Chesterton restrained himself from being Edgar Allan Poe or Franz Kafka, but something in the makeup of his personality leaned toward the nightmarish, something secret, and blind, and central.

—Borges, *Other Inquisitions*

This 1908 novel has long enjoyed a kind of underground cult among those with a special interest in fantasy. It is the story of a conspiratorial council of seven anarchists, each one named for a day of the week, with the mysterious Sunday as their president. Admirers of the tale have included J. R. R. Tolkien, C. S. Lewis, W. H. Auden, Jorge Luis Borges, and T. S. Eliot. Kingsley Amis has frequently written about it. Yet the wider reading public remains largely unaware of it.

No wonder. It is a detective story that seems to solve itself too easily, and lose its mystery. But those who stay with it, even after they think they have seen through it, are teased back and back by its ultimately unresolved nature, all the puzzles that remain after the last pages are read. It does not give up its secrets at a glance. Even Mr. Amis, despite his enthusiasm for the tale, seems to misunderstand it—as when he writes: "What I find indigestible in the closing scenes is . . . the person of the fleeing Sunday, who at one point makes off mounted on a Zoo elephant and who bombards the pursuit with messages of elephantine facetiousness."[1] He is attacking the finest clue of all. But, more than that, he lapses into the condescending attitude he came to criticize—the view that Chesterton cannot resist buffoonery, even when he is onto something bigger and more startling than a good joke (or a bad one).

But Sunday's riddles go beyond joking, good or bad; they show a cruelty in humor like the cruelty of nature itself—they are taunts thrown back at men who have been tortured. The best parts of this racy entertainment, as Borges understood, are moments of weird near-breakdown:

> As he now went up the weary and perpetual steps, he was daunted and bewildered by their almost infinite series. But it was not the hot horror of a dream or of anything that might be exaggeration or delusion. Their infinity was more like the infinity of arithmetic, something unthinkable, yet necessary to thought. Or it was like the stunning statements of astronomy about the distance of the fixed stars. He was ascending the tower of reason, a thing more hideous than unreason itself.

The book is all a chase, an evasion, and dream; a benign nightmare prolonged, page by page, beyond our waking. It has the compelling inconsequence of nightmare, its tangle of mutually chasing loves and hates, where the impossible becomes inevitable and each wish comes partnered with its own frustration. Nightmare is described in the book itself as a world of "tyrannic accidents." Auden and others have noticed Chesterton's power to evoke the despotic mood of dreams. Borges compared him to Poe in this aspect, and C. S. Lewis to Kafka. The reason we go on reading Chesterton's tale—after we have cracked its first secret (that all the conspirators are also, unbeknownst to each other, anti-conspirators)—is that a dream mood leads us on, linking all its incidents. It aims at an effect that intrigued Chesterton in his own disturbing dreams, one achieved in some of his favorite works of literature.

> Here is the pursuit of the man we cannot catch, the flight from the man we cannot see; here is the perpetual returning to the same place, here is the crazy alteration in the very objects of our desire, the substitution of one face for another face, the putting of the wrong souls in the wrong bodies, the fantastic disloyalties of the night. . . . [2]

So, even after we know that the anarchists are also cops, the dream-suspension of things in air continues—the flight from Age, through a crippling ache of snow; a slow climb up the mad tower of pure reason; the duel with a phantom who comes apart like meat being carved but will not bleed; the endless chase by anonymous somebodies who gradually become Everybody, embodying paranoia's logic. Then, after running as the quarry, the book's accumulating heroes turn and reach new stages of bewilderment as the pursuers. They knew more as the hunted than as hunters. Desperation gave them solidarity; but at a hint of victory they come apart again, each teasing at the private riddles addressed to him by Sunday. But this dominance of a nightmare mood should not blind us to the riddles addressed to us as readers. These are nicely differentiated, and cluster around two questions. Who are the conspirators? And: Who is Sunday?

I. THE CONSPIRATORS

Then thou scarest me with dreams
and terrifiest me through visions.
—Job 7.14

The first set of clues is almost too obvious—which makes men overlook further hints, to which the first set was only our introduction. The point is not only that everyone is in disguise, but that his disguise is revealing. Each man's secret is unwittingly worn like a shield instead of an emblem. The biggest clue can be overlooked because Chesterton has placed it so prominently in the title. A man can be Thursday only because other men are already Friday, Monday, etc. Granted, the Council of Days is a device that readers quickly penetrate; and most of them focus thenceforth on the identity of Sunday. But the riddle of Monday is not disposed of simply by knowing that he is Sunday's Secretary and also the hidden Detective's right-hand man. Chesterton tries to keep reminding us of this; but readers, so far as I can tell, still keep forgetting. When Dr. Bull says, toward the end, "We are six men going to ask one man what he means," Syme replies: "I think it is six men going to ask one man what they mean."

What does the Secretary, the first and most persistent of the Council, mean—with the cruel tilt of laughter as a doubt across his face? At the final banquet he will wear robes that make him more real—a pitch black garment with the struggle of first light down its expanse. He is Monday, light out of darkness, the first unstoppable questioning that is man's last boast—"And God said: Let there be light." He comes after his fellow-conspirators in the long dream-scene of chase with a black mask on, his face a pattern of light and dark echoed in all his followers. He dwells in darkness, only to fight it, and is described from the outset as tortured with thought in its most naked form. Syme wonders why, when the Secretary gets tossed from the hood of the car, darkness comes on so soon—a minor riddle, but part of a large pattern. Monday, with his complex mind, is the simplest and truest of them all in his quest for truth. He will not stop asking impertinent questions even in the unknowable Emperor's palace.

Gogol, shaggy under his load of wild tresses, but transparent and easily found out, is as simple as the waters of the Second Day. Wednesday is the Marquis, whose absinthe philosophy brightens to the green clothing of earth. Thursday is Syme, a poet, a divider of planet from planet on a plan—as Michelangelo's sculptor-God on the ceiling shoulders moons off from the sun. Friday is the Professor, who has a nihilist's ethic of bestiality, but a deeper kinship, also, with the innocence of animals. Saturday is the last day, Man, a thing almost too open and childish to wear a disguise, an optimist of reason, the tale's French revolutionary, declaring the patent rights of man as king of the creation—each man a king.

All six of the men are puzzles, but elemental puzzles, the kind that one cannot really "solve." They represent man's status as a partner in his own creation—the question of man's questioning; the open energy of Gogol; the dim recesses of the Marquis; Syme's swagger; Friday's depths of despair; and Saturday's insaner hope. When Syme grieves that the conspirators have looked only on the fleeing back of the universe, we think his talk deals only with Sunday, since he is often glimpsed from behind in the story. But later, in the garden, all things—in dancing—turn a sudden face on the Council, each tree and lamppost. Everything has a story untold, an episode wandered into, a history only half-understood. And what is true of the clues is true of the detectives, who are themselves the main clues they must read. Each of them deceived the others because he was seen from behind or partially, at an odd angle. The "back" of intellect is doubt; of subtlety, deviousness; of energy, rage. Everything in the tale, as in the world, needs deciphering, nothing more than oneself. We are all walking signs, signaling urgently to one another in a code no one has cracked. If anyone could understand himself, he would understand everything. So the last person to guess what the man called Monday means will be Monday. Sunday is not a greater mystery than the other Days, except in one respect—he is not only a clue, and a reader of clues; he also plants the clues. He may have cracked the code. That is why they go in search of him.

The tale is not an idle play with symbols. It gets its urgency and compression from the fact that it is the most successful embodiment of the seminal experience in Chesterton's life, his young mystical brush with insanity. In that sense, it is full of clues to his own mental crisis—his depression and near-suicide as an art student in the decadent nineties. At the center of Chesterton's best fiction there is always a moment of aporia, the dark seed of all its gaudy blossomings. In *Thursday* that moment comes when the chase is urged on by the masked Secretary:

> The sun on the grass was dry and hot. So in plunging into the wood they had a cool shock of shadow, as of divers who plunge into a dim pool. The inside of the wood was full of shattered sunlight and shaken shadows. They made a sort of shuddering veil, almost recalling the dizziness of a cinematograph. Even the solid figures walking with him Syme could hardly see for the patterns of sun and shade that danced upon them. Now a

man's head was lit as with a light of Rembrandt, leaving all else obliterated; now again he had strong and staring white hands with the face of a negro. The ex-Marquis had pulled the old straw hat over his eyes, and the black shade of the brim cut his face so squarely in two that it seemed to be wearing one of the black half-masks of their pursuers. The fancy tinted Syme's overwhelming sense of wonder. Was he wearing a mask? Was anyone wearing a mask? Was anyone anything? This wood of witchery, in which men's faces turned black and white by turns, in which their figures first swelled into sunlight and then faded into formless night, this mere chaos of chiaroscuro (after the clear daylight outside), seemed to Syme a perfect symbol of the world in which he had been moving for three days, this world where men took off their beards and their spectacles and their noses, and turned into other people. That tragic self-confidence which he had felt when he believed that the Marquis was a devil had strangely disappeared now that he knew that the Marquis was a friend. He felt almost inclined to ask after all these bewilderments what was a friend and what an enemy. Was there anything that was apart from what it seemed? The Marquis had taken off his nose and turned out to be a detective. Might he not just as well take off his head and turn out to be a hobgoblin? Was not everything, after all, like this bewildering woodland, this dance of dark and light? Everything only a glimpse, the glimpse always unforeseen, and always forgotten. For Gabriel Syme had found in the heart of that sun-splashed wood what many modern painters had found there. He had found the thing which the modern people call Impressionism, which is another name for that final scepticism which can find no floor to the universe.

The dragging in of impressionism here makes no sense except by its connection with the morbid experiences of Chesterton at the

Slade School during the years 1892 through 1895, when a fashionable pessimism was cultivated by the same people who were taken with fashionable "impressionism."

Much of the material for *Thursday* comes directly out of the notebooks and poems of those art-school years, almost a decade and a half behind him when he wrote the novel. An early poem on suicide lies behind Chapter 10. The account of an art-school conversation is drawn on for the lantern episode in Chapter 12. The emergence from solipsism into fellowship, described in Chapter 8, lies behind much of his poetry from this period—like "The Mirror of Madmen," from which I quote just the opening and closing stanzas:

> I dreamed a dream of heaven, white as frost,
> The splendid stillness of a living host;
> Vast choirs of upturned faces, line o'er line.
> Then my blood froze; for every face was mine.

> Then my dream snapped: and with a heart that leapt
> I saw, across the tavern where I slept,
> The sight of all my life most full of grace,
> A gin-damned drunkard's wan half-witted face.

The same experience lies behind the novel's dedicatory poem, with its tribute to the two men who meant so much to him in his personal ordeal—Stevenson of Tusitala, who also rebelled against the aesthetes of *his* art school in Paris; and Whitman of Paumanok, who praised the mere existence of multiple things in a democracy of being. Indeed, the first sketch of what would become *Thursday* was written as an exercise in Whitman pantheism. It appears in an unpublished Chesterton notebook from the early nineties:

> The week is a gigantic symbol, the symbol
> of the creation of the world:

Monday is the day of Light.
Tuesday the day of waters.
Wednesday the day of the Earth.
Thursday: the day of stars.
Friday: the day of birds.
Saturday: the day of beasts.
Sunday: the day of peace: the day for saying
        that it is good.
Perhaps the true religion is this
that the creator is not ended yet.
And that what we move towards
Is blinding, colossal, calm
The rest of God.

Chesterton opposed the chaos in himself and the life around him by considering each man's life a reenactment, day by day, of the first verses of Genesis. One of his student letters has this passage: "Today is Sunday, and Ida's birthday. Thus it commemorates two things, the creation of Ida and the creation of the world. . . . Nineteen years ago the Cosmic Factory was at work; the vast wheel of stars revolved, the archangels had a conference, and the result was another person. . . . I should imagine that sun, wind, colours, chopsticks, circulating library books, ribbons, caricatures and the grace of God were used." Chesterton took as the ground of his hope that very sense of dissolution that threatened his sanity. By the energy of existence things keep reemerging from dissolution. Creation uses chaos as its working material—just as the spirit, freed in dreams, uses the world as a set of signs, shifting their meaning in ways that terrify man while making him the master of "unsignified" matter:

If we wish to experience pure and naked feeling we can never experience it so really as in that unreal land. There the pas-

sions seem to live an outlawed and abstract existence, uncon-
nected with any facts or persons. In dreams we have revenge
without any injury, remorse without any sin, memory without any recollection, hope without any prospect. Love, indeed,
almost proves itself a divine thing by the logic of dreams; for
in a dream every material circumstance may alter, spectacles
may grow on a baby, and moustaches on a maiden aunt, and
yet the great sway of one tyrannical tenderness may never
cease. Our dream may begin with the end of the world, and
end with a picnic at Hampton Court, but the same rich and
nameless mood will be expressed by the falling stars and by
the crumbling sandwiches. In a dream daisies may glare at us
like the eyes of demons. In a dream lightning and conflagra-
tion may warm and soothe us like our own fireside. In this
subconscious world, in short, existence betrays itself; it shows
that it is full of spiritual forces which disguise themselves as
lions and lamp-posts, which can as easily disguise themselves
as butterflies and Babylonian temples. . . . Life dwells alone in
our very heart of hearts, life is one and virgin and unconjured,
and sometimes in the watches of the night speaks in its own
terrible harmony.[3]

Chesterton was drawn back, constantly, to the Book of Genesis because of its beginning in chaos. Once one has experienced that
nothingness, the emergence of any one thing into form and meaning is a triumph, the foundation for a "mystical minimum" of aesthetic thankfulness. Then, as Blake saw, each sunrise becomes a
fiery chariot's approach.

When we say that a poet praises the whole creation, we commonly mean only that he praises the whole cosmos. But this
sort of poet does really praise creation, in the sense of the act

of creating. He praises the passage or transition from nonentity to entity. . . . He not only appreciates everything but the nothing of which everything was made. In a fashion he endures and answers even the earthquake irony of the Book of Job; in some sense he is there when the foundations of the world are laid, with the morning stars singing together and the sons of God shouting for joy.[4]

The Council of Days not only praises this transition, but effects it—as God creates through his six days. Creation is not only *the* beginning, but is *always* beginning—with the Council of Days in on the battle against chaos from the outset. They overthrow their own darker side, their evil brother, as God had to wrestle the sea-god into bonds in the Book of Job. When the six Days gather in Sunday's garden, they have gone back beyond their childhood "where a tree is a tree at last"—to the primordial self they could only accomplish by a struggle that, illogically, *forms* that self. Their end is to arrive at their own beginning, in a puzzle Chesterton often returned to:

> It is at the *beginning* that things are good, and not (as the more pallid progressives say) only at the end. The primordial things—existence, energy, fruition—are good so far as they go. You cannot have evil life, though you can have notorious evil livers. Manhood and womanhood are good things, though men and women are often perfectly pestilent. You can use poppies to drug people, or birch trees to beat them, or stones to make an idol, or corn to make a corner, but it remains true that, in the abstract, before you have done anything, each of these four things is in strict truth a glory, a beneficent specialty and variety. We do praise the Lord that there are birch trees growing amongst the

rocks and poppies amongst the corn; we do praise the Lord, even if we do not believe in Him. We do admire and applaud the *project* of a world, just as if we had been called to council in the primal darkness and seen the first starry plan of the skies. We are, as a matter of fact, far more certain that this life of ours is a magnificent and amazing enterprise than we are that it will succeed.[5]

11. SUNDAY

Behold, I go forward, but he is not there;
    and backward, but I cannot perceive him:
On the left hand, where he doth work,
    but I cannot behold him:
he hideth himself on the right hand,
    that I cannot see him.
—*Job 23.8–9*

Ronald Knox described *The Man Who Was Thursday* as a kind of *Pilgrim's Progress* rewritten in the style of the *Pickwick Papers*. Like many of Knox's epigrams, that is more witty than accurate. Chesterton's own dedicatory poem might point, rather, to a blend of Whitman's philosophy and Stevenson's adventure tales. But the imagery and model are more lofty. There is surprisingly little about the New Testament in the early writings of Chesterton— but his poems and tales are drenched in the imagery of the Hebrew prophets. Borges finds the roots of his monsters in Ezekiel and Revelations. One image that haunts this novel is taken from the Mosaic revelation, and described in Chesterton's treatise on the paintings of G. F. Watts, where an averted face is suddenly dark, glimpsed over a massive shoulder or resisting back. The turned back is man's shell, the blind side of the moon, what is left when the person has gone into hiding:

> To walk behind anyone along a lane is a thing that, properly speaking, touches the oldest nerve of awe. Watts has realized this as no one in art or letters has realized it in the whole history of the world: it has made him great. There is one possible exception to his monopoly of this magnificent craze. Two thousand years before, in the dark scriptures of a nomad people, it had been said that their prophet saw the immense Creator of all things, but only saw Him from behind. I do not know whether even Watts would dare to paint that. But it reads like one of his pictures, like the most terrific of all his pictures, which he has kept veiled.[6]

Sunday is Chesterton's attempt to paint that picture.

A recent biographer of Chesterton says there are "direct references" to the Book of Job in the novel's last scene. Actually, the references are everywhere. In the opening argument between the two poets, the anarchist says that poetry must escape the predictable, the same old station on the same old railway track. But Syme answers: "The rare, strange thing is to hit the mark; the gross, obvious thing is to miss it. We feel it is epical when man with one wild arrow strikes a distant bird. Is it not also epical when man with one wild engine strikes a distant station? Chaos is dull; because in chaos the train might indeed go anywhere, to Baker Street or to Bagdad. But man is a magician, and his whole magic is in this, that he does say Victoria, and lo! it is Victoria. . . . every time a train comes in I feel that it has broken past batteries of besiegers, and that man has won a battle against chaos." Job added an essential note to Chesterton's feel for the book of Genesis—that creation is a struggle. The God of Job's thirtieth chapter is "Conqueror of chaos in a six days war," one who wrestles the sea into place, bangs doors on it and bars them. *"And said, Hitherto shalt thou come, but no further; and here shall thy proud waves be stayed"* (38.11). Even the idea of the seven days is found in Job, where the mystical number of creation is used for the sons of Job, who feast seven days in succession, *"every one his day"* (1.4). So, at the reversal, Job's friends mourn with him wordlessly for seven days in succession (2.13). And the restoration brings back the seven sons for their week-feast (42.13). *"Why, seeing times are not hidden from the Almighty, do they that know him not see his days?"* (24.1).

The anarchic poet of the first chapter is, of course, the Accuser who tests Syme, a test by which he becomes Thursday and himself. Chesterton's feel for *Job*, the favorite book of his young creative years, is vindicated by those modern scholars who find something like a police conspiracy in the very scheme of *Job*. The model for God's court, where the Accuser comes, seems to be the Persian court with its spies—"the King's Eyes"—sent out to test the loyalty of subjects. "The Satan" is thus an *agent provocateur.*[7] This situation, set up in the primitive prose tale of the prologue, is kept in mind by the poet who wrote the poetic diatribe of Job. In the translation where Handel's Jacobean Job says *"I know that my redeemer liveth,"* he is actually calling for an advocate, a defense counsel with access to the court for answering the Spy's charges— Job knows there must be one.[8] The attitude of Syme toward Sunday repeats the feelings of Job—a strange mix of defiance and confidence; the cocky hope that he could win his case, if only his adversary would deign to argue with him; if only he had written a book; if only he could read Job's own words bitten into stone. The words translated *"Though he slay me, yet will I trust in him"* actually mean "yet I will stay confident (of my right)"—as the echoing half of the couplet makes clear: *"I will maintain mine own ways before him."*[9] All these feelings mingle in the Council's reactions of fear and hope with regard to Sunday. They must force an answer from him. But their very determination implies that Sunday must have the answers. Syme speaks for them: "Yes, you are right. I am afraid of him. Therefore I swear by God that I will seek out this man whom I fear until I find him, and strike him on the mouth. If heaven were his throne and the earth his footstool, I swear I would pull him down."

But Sunday, like Job's God, only answers question with question, and riddle with riddle—which some take to mean that he does not answer at all. This leaves him open to the taunt of Robert Frost's Job: that the one who really succumbed to the tempter was God—just trying to show off. Job has for a long time been getting the better of this argument. He is the first great rebel against divinity, the highest ancestor to Milton's Lucifer. He is so cogently blasphemous in his poems that a labor of deliberate misunderstanding hid him in the epithet "patient Job"—like referring invariably to a *timorous* Achilles or the *young* King Lear. Job is patient for two chapters, and furious for a book. He pours out hymns and canticles and arguments in denunciation of God. He is not only impatient; he curses the patience of his clever bloody-fool friends when they try to restore his patience.

The source of the patient-Job nonsense is obvious. The prose parable that lies behind the book, and supplies its prologue and epilogue, told the simple tale of a man who trusted God and was rewarded. But the great poet who took up that story used it as the deceptive front and back flaps for a long palinode meant to destroy the idea that virtue is rewarded. Just to make the game more humorous, a third artist—the composer of Elihu's speeches—seems to have missed the second one's point and tried to vindicate the first one's logic.[10] It is as if someone stuck a scene into *Hamlet* trying to show that Shakespeare missed the truly deep political wisdom of Polonius. Other additions have been made to the book—the Wisdom Poem for instance.[11] But these three main strata are the relevant ones here; and the second storyteller is the truly great poet—not simply because he sees through the first one and confuses the third one, nor for merely destructive sarcasm over the simple pieties; but for his own masterstroke, the appearance of God in the whirlwind.

The thing has been beautifully prepared. Job goes on demanding a hearing, though the pious friends assure him he is a man who cannot address the king: *"Will he reprove thee, for fear of thee? Will he enter with thee into judgment?"* (22.4). But Job keeps demanding his day in court—and gets it. He wins by the stroke of his desperate gamble, the huge oath sworn in Chapter Thirty-one. This forces God's hand. It dares the lightning—which should then strike the guilty man—to prove that God is ignoring the cries of an innocent man. Job will voluntarily stand on the scaffold, to work his way backward into court. But even this is a way of betting on God—he obviously thinks he could get justice at the court, if only he gets a hearing.

That confidence is what seems misplaced to modern readers. After all, God had entered into an anti-Job conspiracy with Satan from the outset—a mismatch if there ever was one; as if heaven and hell could be leagued against a single man. But the deeper point is that God is betting on man—that he will not break. And he wins that bet. God comes to reward as well as rebuke Job. He does not side with the pious friends. He answers Job with sarcasm and admiration. The thing that truly irks God is the argument of Job's friends. He cannot abide theologians.

I think every reader is braced to see how God rebukes his own defenders. They are glad to see him reward the man who attacked him. But the one thing withheld from Job is the very thing he asked for—an answer: Why did he suffer? God replies with a series of towering irrelevancies: Why is the ostrich silly, or the horse romantic? Why, for that matter, is Leviathan large? For a moment, the man on the dungheap and the God in the whirlwind seem to become two rabbis, each trying to stump the other with ever more recondite lore. *"Knowest thou it, because thou wast then born? Or because the number of thy days is great?"* (38.21). God mocks Job back into happiness, neither confuting him nor surrendering to him. This is the measure of the poet's genius. If God simply surrendered, he would diminish the dignity of Job's high challenge. The truly withering blast would have been a reply that shows God not only as less than terrible, but as less than Job—like going out to meet Goliath, only to find Frank Morgan dithering into his Oz machine.

Yet there is still one thing worse than giving no answer. And that is to give an answer. That would turn God into a theologian, reducing Jehovah to the level of Job's friends. The author of God's speeches in the Book of Job was the first person we know of to realize that the only theology worth having is the one that forswears theodicy. The riddling rabbi in the whirlwind obviously has answers; but not any small enough to dispense. To find them we would have to go back with him to the drawing board and understand Behemoth's linkages. Or set up the sun's timetable for it. The world says, even to us, more than anything we can say in "defense" of it. Any of God's things is a secret too deep to be fathomed—though Job is rewarded for trying. Because he is the best of God's things. God shows off Behemoth to the weirdest monster of them all, the one he had bet on, the one he can show things off to and argue with—Job himself. The true conspiracy is between God and man, by a dim pact made in a dark room, when man did not even know to whom he was giving his word. Between them, these stranger-brothers to each other, these unacquainted intimate wrestlers, confound the Accuser.

Job's friends attempt to comfort him with philosophical optimism, like the intellectuals of the eighteenth century. Job tries to comfort himself with philosophical pessimism, like the intellectuals of the nineteenth century. But God comforts Job with indecipherable mystery, and for the first time Job is comforted. Eliphaz gives one answer, Job gives another answer, and the question still remains an open wound. God simply refuses to answer, and somehow the question is answered. Job flings at God one riddle, God flings back at Job a hundred riddles, and Job is at peace. He is comforted with conundrums. For the grand and enduring idea in the poem, as suggested above, is that if we are to be reconciled to this great cosmic experience, it must be as something divinely strange and divinely violent, a quest or a conspiracy or some sacred joke. The last chapters of the colossal monologue are devoted, in a style superficially queer enough, to the detailed description of two monsters. Behemoth and Leviathan may or may not be the hippopotamus and the crocodile. But whatever they are, they are evidently embodiments of the enormous absurdity of nature. They typify that cosmic trait which anyone may see in the Zoological Gardens, the folly of the Lord which is wisdom. And in connection with one of them, God is made to utter a splendid satire upon the prim and orderly piety of the vulgar optimist. *Wilt thou play with him as with a bird? Wilt thou bind him for thy maidens?* That is the main message of the Book of Job. Whatever this cosmic monster may be, a good animal or a bad animal, he is at least a wild animal and not a tame animal. It is a wild world and not a tame world.[12]

That mention of the Zoo brings us back to the comment of Kingsley Amis with which I began. Sunday, in flight, leads his angry rebellious Council through the Zoo; where these men see, in their blurred passage, weird creatures, pelicans and hornbills, whose living hieroglyphs speak to them in unknown tongues.

Syme realizes that "nature was always making quite mysterious jokes." Then they catch sight of Sunday, far ahead, on that elephant that seems undignified to Mr. Amis. Behemoth, in the Bible that Chesterton grew up with, was translated on the assumption that he was a hippopotamus. But in the Catholic Bible which his brother and other friends were using by this time, the beast is something more fitted to the story at this point: an elephant. The effrontery of this last apparition is Chesterton's slyest way of establishing that Sunday is Job's riddling God. Sunday throws private hints to each of his pursuers, because that God has private jokes with the ostrich and intimacies with the wren. *"Knowest thou the time when the wild goats of the rock bring forth? Or canst thou mark when the hinds do calve?"* (39.1). Sunday knows (and no one else) what pink means to Gogol, or goloshes to Gabriel Syme. This God, mysterious with buffoonery and riddles as well as with terror, is the ancient of days, whose name we have not learned.

But—just as important—Sunday is Lucian Gregory, the anarchic poet. The Accuser. The book is subtitled "A Nightmare." But Syme does not wake up from it, with a start, in bed. He wakes up, just at dawn, walking with the red-haired poet he met and argued with in the first chapter. The nightmare began with that argument, and Gregory has a real existence outside it as does Syme himself. The *dream* ends with the two arguing in Sunday's court. Syme's final point is worth quoting from that argument:

Why does each thing on earth war against each other thing? Why does each small thing in the world have to fight against the world itself? Why does a fly have to fight the whole universe? Why does a dandelion have to fight the whole universe? For the same reason that I had to be alone in the dreadful Council of the Days. So that each thing that obeys law may have the glory and isolation of the anarchist. So that each man fighting for order may be as brave and good a man as the dynamiter.

Syme repels as slander the charge that he has been pampered with happiness—the smug state of "godly" Job in the first of Blake's engravings. Syme is not bribed to the cause of good by all the drugs of unlabored-for enjoyment. He is not a mere policeman.

That argument breaks off—and Syme is still talking to Gregory in a suburban street. They have argued all night, and the "nightmare" is the meaning of their argument—what Chesterton *saw* as its reality (much as Blake *saw* the sun's chariot). Chesterton's pivotal moment at the Slade School occurred one night in outdoors conversation with a "diabolist," who used the very words put into the Professor's mouth in *Thursday*: "If I did that I shouldn't know the difference between right and wrong." Out of that conversation, out of the insight he achieved through the words of a conscious blasphemer, Chesterton fashioned his first ambitious poem, "The Wild Knight," where a mystic is at last granted the vision of God for which he has prayed and fasted all his life—in the person of the story's villain, Lord Orm. Several other tales were written about antagonists who were not only each other's completion, but their own private vision of the good, not otherwise obtainable. What he put pretentiously in "The Wild Knight," he put facetiously in answer to a newspaper antagonist named Rix:

Mr. Rix has pointed out that I have often maintained all things to be Divine, and implies that my psychical hypotheses are a negation of this. Of course, I entirely agree, or, rather, I passionately maintain, that there is a divinity in all things. I am prepared to carry it out to an extent to which perhaps even Mr. Rix would waver before following me. I would be delighted to go, crowned with flowers, to worship Mr. Rix himself, but that he would violently resist me; failing this, I would with equal gaiety and a sense of equal value worship Mr. Rix's umbrella. It is quite clear that in this absolute metaphysical sense all things have a common divine origin; all things are symbols; all points are equally distant from the centre. Obviously the same omnipotent wisdom which said, "Let there be Light," said "Let there be an umbrella belonging to Mr. Rix"; or (since an absolute spiritual equality among all cosmic things is the very essence of the idea), we may express the matter otherwise by saying that the omnipotent wisdom said, rather, "Let there be a Mr. Rix belonging to this umbrella." If that is his meaning, that in the last resort all things are beautiful and awful, since all things exist, I am altogether with him. But the difficulties raised by this position are entirely obvious: I know all about them because the position is one I have been defending night and day. It is evident that though all things are divine, all things are limited. And among other divine things, man himself is limited. He has not the memory, nor the imagination, nor the vigilance, nor the sheer physical health to realize the Godhead in every atom or object that passes under his hands. A person who never neglected a divine object; a man who burst into religious tears as he fastened a divine collar with an inspired collar stud and continued thus with everything he looked at, would go mad in five minutes: he would see God and die. The only things which man, a limited animal, can do in this matter, are two: first, he can believe (as an absolute thing of faith) that there is this divinity in things, whether he sees it or not; second, he can leave himself reasonably open to those sudden revelations whereby one or two of these things, a cloud, a man's face, a noise in the dark, may for some reason no one has ever been able to offer, capriciously reveal its divinity.[13]

For all the playfulness of his mode, Chesterton was seriously prepared to receive the beatific vision in the person of Mr. Rix. Just as the Knight did in Orm. Or as Syme does in Gregory. The first mystery was easily solved—that all the conspirators were also policemen. But that seemed to leave Gregory out of the scheme—and he was scheduled to become Thursday before Syme beat him out. Gregory, however, is not outside the scheme—he is as inside it, as Sunday. He remains Syme's foe at the end, and his friend—the man through whom he had his vision (the nightmare). He is also, of course, the brother of the woman Syme has just fallen in love with. But Syme would give a far higher meaning to Romeo's words (when Tybalt tries to pick a fight):

> [I] love thee better than thou canst devise,
> Till thou shalt know the reason of my love.

Sunday is the Foe who brings a revelation; and Sunday is glimpsed only in the arguments of Lucian Gregory. Lucian is "the man of light"—not only a falling star, like Lucifer; but the source of light for Syme.

This alters the impact of the book's one quote from the New Testament. When Gregory, in the dream, accuses the Days of being ignorant where pain and doubt are concerned, Syme boasts that all the Days have suffered—unless: and he looks to Sunday. The words float toward him as Sunday's face dissolves (to be replaced by its starting point, Lucian Gregory): "Can ye drink of the cup that I drink of?" That looks at first like a mere use of Job in the patristic manner—his wounds prefiguring those of Jesus. But it is out of their shared agony, Syme's and Gregory's, that this story of heroic brothers is woven, "iliad on iliad." It is Sunday as Jehovah who thunders and defies: "You will understand the sea, and I shall be still a riddle." It is Sunday as Lucian Gregory who suffers. The mystery of the Council is the secret of us all. We are all patriots and rebels, at war with one another and ourselves. And we give each other visions.

NOTES

INTRODUCTION

1. Mrs. Cecil Chesterton, *The Chestertons* (London: Chapman and Hall, Ltd., 1941).
2. *Thought*, Winter, 1955–6.
3. G. K. *Chesterton, A Critical Study* (London: Secker, 1915), esp. ch. 8, "A Kind of Decadent."
4. *Loc. cit.*, p. 575.
5. *The Dublin Review*, 1955, pp. 51–67.
6. *Ibid.*, p. 65.

7. *Post-Victorian Poetry* (London: J. M. Dent and Sons, Ltd., 1938), ch. 11, "G. K. Chesterton and His School."

8. Robert Speaight, *Letters from Hilaire Belloc* (London: Hollis and Carter, 1958), p. 265. Msgr. John O'Connor, *Father Brown on Chesterton* (London: Frederick Muller, Ltd., 1937), pp. 128, 141.

9. Cyril Clemens, *Chesterton as Seen by His Contemporaries* (Webster Groves, Missouri: Mark Twain Society, 1939), pp. 150–51: "I consider it as being without possible comparison the best book ever written on St. Thomas. Nothing short of genius can account for such an achievement. Everybody will no doubt admit that it is a 'clever' book, but the few readers who have spent twenty or thirty years in studying St. Thomas Aquinas, and who, perhaps, have themselves published two or three volumes on the subject, cannot fail to perceive that the so-called 'wit' of Chesterton has put their scholarship to shame. He has guessed all that which they had tried to demonstrate, and he has said all that which they were more or less clumsily attempting to express in academic formulas. Chesterton was one of the deepest thinkers who ever existed; he was deep because he was right; and he could not help being right; but he could not either help being modest and charitable, so he left it to those who could understand him to know that he was right, and deep; to the others, he apologized for being right, and he made up for being deep by being witty. That is all they can see of him."

10. *Paradox in Chesterton* (New York: Sheed and Ward, 1948), p. 85.

11. *Ibid.*, pp. 102, 107.

CHAPTER 1. THE CRYSTAL PALACE

1. Significantly, these are the traits Chesterton singles out when describing his family in the *Autobiography* (pp. 6, 8, 22–3).

2. "Belloc and Chesterton," *New Age*, Feb. 15, 1905.

3. *Ibid.*

4. School report of Dec., 1887. Quoted in Maisie Ward, *Gilbert Keith Chesterton* (London: Sheed and Ward, 1944), p. 28. This book henceforth referred to simply as Ward.

5. A description of himself sent to his fiancée (Ward, p. 91).

6. Another description of his own youth, quoted by C. F. G. Masterman in the *Bookman* article on Chesterton (Jan., 1903).

7. "The Wild Goose Chase" and "The Taming of the Nightmare," both from a notebook which contains a third story of the same type, "The Queen of the

Evening Star." The length of these tales is significant. The concentration of Chesterton's later style made long narrative difficult to sustain, so that most of his detective complications are unraveled in the space these leisurely tales consume.

8. *Debater,* 3.9 (references are to volume and page; the three published volumes cover the years 1891–3). In the fictitious correspondence E. C. Bentley was E. Cusack Bremmil, barrister, and Lucian Oldershaw became Lawrence Ormond. Chesterton's important contributions to this pseudonymous series are not listed in Sullivan's bibliography.

9. *Ibid.,* 3.29.

10. *Ibid.,* 2.34.

11. *Ibid.,* 3.38, 43.

12. *E.g.,* "Danton" (2.26):

> Well may dark St. Just regard me with an evil look, askance;
> I am going, he is staying, well for me and ill for France.

13. *Ibid.,* 3.87.

14. *Ibid.,* 3.23.

15. *Ibid.,* 3.21, 86, 89. Other positions which seem anomalous when Chesterton's career is remembered are his attacks on the belief in ghosts and spirits (2.2), and his scorn for journalism (3.22), for boy's romances (2.99), for novels (3.38).

16. Chesterton's whole boyhood is in the following passage from an art-school manuscript—"A History of the J. D. C."—written when he was twenty: "But before the conclusion of the series, the Chairman was practically engaged on a more serious style, in expression of the problems of the age. . . . In these works he generally assumed an advanced and revolutionary standpoint, earning for himself the title of iconoclast."

17. "Idolatry" (2.133).

18. "Worship" (3.49–50).

19. "Ave Maria" (3.94–6).

20. "Francis of Assisi" (3.78–80). See, on the same theme, "Francis Xavier," the prize poem which brought Chesterton the privileges of the top form (printed in Ward, pp. 557–8). The reference to immurement in dim convent walls is explained by the fact that Chesterton makes the wandering friar "a monk that loved the sea-birds as they wheeled about his chapel."

21. "The Song of Labour," *Speaker,* Dec. 18, 1892. Despite his love of Scott, Chesterton was no mediaevalist, as this poem's description of "the wrack of the feudal strife" demonstrates.

22. *Gilbert K. Chesterton, A Criticism* (London: John Lane Co., 1909), p. 14. This book henceforth referred to simply as Cecil.

23. *Debater,* 2.2.

24. *Ibid.,* 2.29.

25. *Ibid.,* 3. 8–9.

26. *Ibid.,* 3.72.

27. Ward, p. 324.

28. *E.g., Watts,* p. 21.

29. Ward, p. 13.

30. *Autobiography,* pp. 2, 34.

31. Cecil, pp. 28, 60.

32. *Autobiography,* p. 3.

CHAPTER 2. NOCTURNE

1. Dedication to *The Man Who Was Thursday.*

2. *The Flying Inn,* pp. 255–6. *Thursday,* pp. 187–8. *Cf.* the remarks on Impressionism in *Twelve Types* (p. 21), *Blake* (pp. 17, 18, 137), *Stevenson* (passim), *Fancies Versus Fads* (pp. 220–1), and *The Bookman,* Dec., 1895, pp. 87–8.

3. *Autobiography,* pp. 87–8.

4. *Cf.* George Moore, quoted in Holbrook Jackson's *The Eighteen Nineties* (London: Grant Richards, Ltd., 1913), ch. 20, "British Impressionists," p. 325: "I can imagine young men and women deriving an extraordinary desire of freedom from the landscapes of Monet and Sisley: Manet too. Manet, perhaps, more than anyone liberates the mind from conventions, from prejudices. He creates a spirit of revolt. . . ."

5. *Autobiography,* p. 88.

6. *Stevenson,* p. 30. *Cf. Autobiography,* pp. 31, 105.

7. *E.g., Watts,* p. 44, *Heretics,* p. 86, *Orthodoxy,* pp. 179, 195–6, *The Speaker,* Oct. 20, 1900. The creative activity of these symbols can be gauged from the fact that they abound precisely in Chesterton's best work—in *Orthodoxy,* where the blinding sunlight of mystery is contrasted with the pale lunar quality of rationalism, where the clashing colors of Christian virtues and vices are opposed to the dilution of the Aristotelian ethic; in *The White Horse,* teeming with the purple wings of evil, colored elsewhere like the mediaeval illuminations ("keyholes of heaven and hell"), and leading up to that lucidity of the shore and of childhood which is Alfred's hidden strength. But the most clear-cut case of all is *Lepanto,* where the Eastern doubters swarm into

Europe like Impressionist tints running over a clear map. These forces are "splashed with a splendid sickness, the sickness of the pearl." But a different and more simply-dyed heraldry advances out of the shadow, gleaming faintly at first, muffled like the throbbing drums, but blazing pure in the last battle—"Scarlet running over on the silver and the gold."

8. The idea of a color-language continued to intrigue him, and he often mused how a man might extend the expressiveness of signals like the railway lights (*Watts*, p. 45, *Twelve Types*, p. 29, *The Bookman*, Dec., 1901). He achieved this strange ambition in his first play, whose eery climax is carried entirely by the silent, distant changing of a lantern's color. Shaw was certain that art played the same normative part in Chesterton's psychological processes that music did in his own (*Ward*, p. 199); Chesterton described this normative influence of color in *The Return of Don Quixote*, pp. 107–8: "All those things that for so many people are called culture and come with education had been there for her from the beginning. Certain painted shapes, certain shining colours, were things that existed first and set a standard for all this fallen world. . . . Her nearest and dearest friend would have been amazed to know that she caught her breath at the mere memory of certain wavy bars of silver or escalloped edges of peacock green, as others do at the reminder of a lost love."

9. *Autobiography*, pp. 88–9.

10. *Orthodoxy*, p. 21. *Cf.* the American edition's preface (p. vii): "It is the purpose of the writer to attempt an explanation, not of whether the Christian faith can be believed, but of how he personally has come to believe it."

11. *Ibid.*, p. 80.

12. *Ibid.*, p. 75.

13. *Stevenson*, p. 68.

14. *Autobiography*, pp. 90, 99.

15. *Ibid.*, p. 90.

16. *E.g.*, the poem "By the Babe Unborn," which Chesterton directly identifies as the product of this threatened period (*Autobiography*, p. 95).

17. "A Crazy Tale," *The Quarto*, 1897. *Cf.* reference to this story in the letter quoted in Ward, p. 27; it underwent several prose revisions before becoming the poem "By the Babe Unborn" ("If trees were tall and grasses short, As in some *crazy tale*. . ."). A vision similar to that of the pool occurs again in *Manalive* (pp. 171ff.) and *St. Francis* (pp. 108–9); in all these cases, one rediscovers reality by *forgetting*, and meets oneself as a strange child. Perception conquers argument.

18. These lines are from the major Slade notebook, that quoted extensively in Ward. This, more carefully written than the other notebooks, is a collection

of final versions of many aphorisms scribbled elsewhere. The pages have now been numbered, and all references simply to "Notebook" indicate this volume; *e.g.,* the lines quoted are from p. 2 *verso.*

19. Maisie Ward is of the opinion that Chesterton, at the Slade School, simply denied the existence of evil (p. 49): "For some time now we shall find Gilbert dismissing belief in any positive existence of evil and treating the universe on the Whitman principle of jubilant and universal acceptance." Cecil agrees, and thinks there is nothing in *The Wild Knight* but a repetition of Whitman (p. 32). Gilbert answers this misunderstanding himself (*Autobiography,* pp. 99–100). After stating that *The Man Who Was Thursday* records his early trial and temptation to pantheistic optimism, he continues: "even in the earliest days and even for the worst reasons, I already knew too much to pretend to get rid of evil. I introduced at the end one figure who really does, with a full understanding, deny and defy the good. . . . I put that statement into that story, testifying to the extreme evil (which is merely the unpardonable sin of not wishing to be pardoned), not because I had learned it from any of a million priests I had never met, but because I had learned it from myself."

20. Cecil, p. 18.

21. Ward, p. 28. Chesterton was at the Slade School from 1892 to 1895.

22. Orm: "Evil, be thou my good." The Diabolist: "What you call evil I call good."

23. And about the Diabolist: "He had a horrible fairness of intellect that made me despair of his soul."

24. A third link can be added to the chain of reflection leading from "The Diabolist" to *The Wild Knight.* When, during his early controversy with Robert Blatchford, Chesterton was accused of a placidly optimistic pantheism, he answered in a long and important article ("The Temple of Everything," *Daily News,* March 24, 1903) which defends limit, individuality, and conflict. Many phrases in that article echo this poem—*e.g.,* we should "go, crowned with flowers, to worship all things"; a person who realized this would "see God and die"; the mentality of Orm is sketched as "that freezing and theoretic philanthropy which is the worst of modern evils"; the least object often, at the most unlikely moment, "with a great cry gives up its god." These verbal reminiscences show that the article can be taken as the authoritative commentary on the poem, a statement of its doctrine. Chesterton still had to use the poetic symbols he had invented to explain this all-important matter. His argument is that being is not found in "the All" or "the Universe"—for these are abstract concepts. Reality is not in Everything but in

anything, any actual and individual object, however absurd or ignoble it may seem. This, again, is the argument from the "mystical minimum": "it is quite clear that in this absolute metaphysical sense all things have a common divine origin . . . all points are equally distant from the centre . . . all things are beautiful, since all things exist."

As he put it in another early article, "the one great fallacy of the mystics is that mysticism, religion, and poetry have to do with the abstract . . . the abstract is the symbol of the concrete . . . God made the concrete, but man made the abstract" (*The Speaker,* May 31, 1902).

25. Notebook, p. 2 *verso* (1894), p. 35 (1895).

26. *Ibid.,* p. 33 *verso* (1895). *Cf.* pp. 27 *verso,* 30 *verso.*

27. *Ibid.,* p. 36 (italics added). *Cf.* 38 *verso.* It is interesting to see Chesterton, years later, advise a troubled young person to take up the attitude of these lines *as preservative of sanity: cf.* the important letter quoted in Ward, *Return to Chesterton* (New York: Sheed and Ward, 1952), pp. 242–3.

28. The same dream appears in later work (*Collected Poems,* pp. 329, 245), *The Napoleon of Notting Hill,* pp. 192–3).

29. Ward, p. 63.

30. Notebook, pp. 7 *verso,* 37, 40, 50. *Cf.* the poem "Laughter" in *The Queen of Seven Swords.*

31. *The Napoleon of Notting Hill,* p. 41.

CHAPTER 3. PARADOX AND NIGHTMARE

1. *Cf.* the two articles on pantomime in *The Daily News,* July 2 and 9, 1904, *e.g.*: "Of all forms of art, the one which could, I think, be most effectively used for the conveying of spiritual verities is the pantomime. For a world in which donkeys come in two is clearly very near to the wild ultimate world where donkeys are made." *Cf. Stevenson,* ch. 9, "The Philosophy of Gesture."

2. *Blake,* p. 178; cited in Kenner, p. 48.

3. *Defendant,* p. 2.

4. *Heretics,* p. 14; cited in Kenner, p. 45.

5. The earliest use of the argument which I can find is in an unpublished obituary on Gladstone. After that, his work is full of this thought. He adverts to it when discussing Belloc in the *Autobiography* (p. 114). It was the subject of an early article in *The Speaker* (March 29, 1902).

6. Kenner, p. 22.

7. He wanted his early poems which took this tack destroyed (Ward, p. 127).

8. *Autobiography*, p. 98.
9. In the story itself there are many echoes of the art school. The man called Professor de Worms uses the phrase from "The Diabolist," "If I did that I shouldn't know the difference between right and wrong" (*Thursday*, American ed., 1952, p. 154). Syme defends the fire in the lantern as Chesterton had defended the spark (p. 224). The whole fantasy is a daydream which takes place during an argument with a decadent poet—a fact not remembered by those who call this a mere nightmare of senseless imagery, relying on its subtitle. The dream takes place in the daylight, called up by an actual argument. The "last and worst" fancy of Syme is an Impressionist picture; there is color-symbolism (p. 109), and the use of an early notebook (one of the many stories told about "Eric Peterson") in Syme's early argument with the policeman.
10. Chesterton was subject to dreams, and fascinated by them; some of the verses of *The White Horse* came to him in a dream (Ward, p. 164). *Cf.* "The Taming of the Nightmare" in *The Coloured Lands*, "A Midsummer Night's Dream" in *The Common Man*, "The Meaning of Dreams" in *Lunacy and Letters*. On his own dreams, *cf. Illustrated London News*, March 10, 1905.
11. *The Man Who Was Thursday*, p. 110.
12. *Ibid.*, p. 140.
13. *Ibid.*, pp. 143–4.
14. *Ibid.*, pp. 169–70.
15. *Ibid.*, p. 188.
16. *Ibid.*, p. 276.
17. "Introduction" to a 1907 edition of "Job," reprinted in *G.K.C. As M.C.* and *Selected Essays*. This seems to me his most important essay, written on the book that most profoundly influenced him all his life. Composed just before *The Man Who Was Thursday*, it could almost stand as a commentary on the novel.
18. *Autobiography*, p. 98.
19. Cecil, p. 217.
20. *Father Brown on Chesterton*, p. 119.
21. *Autobiography*, p. 298.
22. This contradiction runs through all the book; on the same page (141) we read "his largest talents lay towards myth and allegory" and, only a few words away, "he would have found his true fulfilment as a great philosopher."
23. *Ibid.*, p. 107.
24. Margaret Clarke documents (*loc. cit.*) Chesterton's acquaintance with and admiration for Aristophanes. I found his name high on a list of "prophets" drawn up by Chesterton at St. Paul's.

25. C. S. Lewis compared Chesterton and Kafka in these terms (*Time and Tide,*
Nov. 9, 1946): "while both give a powerful picture of the loneliness and bewilderment which each one of us encounters in his (apparently single-
handed) struggle with the universe, Chesterton, attributing to the universe
a more complicated disguise, and admitting the exhilaration as well as the
terror of the struggle, has got in rather more; is more balanced: in that sense,
more classical, more permanent."

26. *Daily News,* Apil 15, 1905.

27. *Charles Dickens, A Critical Study,* p. 21. This book henceforth referred to as
Dickens.

28. Kenner, p. 134.

29. *Browning,* pp. 138–9.

CHAPTER 4. THE SIGNATURE OF STYLE

1. *Daily News,* 1905: April 15, "The Great Shawkspear Mystery"; April 22,
"Sorry, I'm Shaw" (response to long letter from Shaw to *The Daily News*);
April 29, "Pessimism of Shakespeare."

2. *Twelve Types,* pp. 123–4. *Cf.* the same observation in Chesterton's introduction to *Sartor Resartus* (Cassell, 1904), pp. 5–6. On the word as *gesture* or *act,*
cf. Ill. *Lond. News,* July 30, 1912; July 5, 1930 (*All Is Grist,* pp. 38–42).

3. *Ibid.,* pp. 84 ff.

4. *Ibid.,* pp. 49 ff.

5. *Ibid.,* p. 147.

6. *Ibid.,* pp. 189 ff.

7. Cecil, pp. 61, 75 ff. West, *op. cit.,* p. 79.

8. This is the conclusion of the only complete work devoted to his criticism,
A.M.A. Bogaerts' *Chesterton and the Victorian Age* (University of Amsterdam,
1940).

9. Cecil, pp. 76–7.

10. *Daily News,* April 22, 1905.

11. When he received the commission, he had been a professional journalist for
little more than two years; he had been married for little over a year, and that
on narrow means. Before this time he had been without aim or commitment
in the matter of career.

12. He could write the conventional kind of criticism, as in his early review of a
Ruskin reader for *The Academy,* June 22, 1895.

13. *E.g., Bookman,* Dec., 1899: "That Poussin went from Villers, where he was

born, to Paris and from Paris to Rome is a fact in itself of no interest to any human being, except the inn-keepers along the road. It is made valuable to us by the inferences that may be drawn from it, and it is precisely these inferences that are crowded out. Miss Denio would have written a quite admirable book if she had cultivated the art of digression; there is no more misleading element in biography than a mean and cowardly relevancy. 'Sticking to the point' has more than a resemblance to being impaled." *Cf. Twelve Types,* pp. 1–2; *Defendant,* pp. 38–9; *Speaker,* May 26, 1900.

14. *Browning,* p. 17.

15. *Daily News,* Sept. 28, 1912.

16. *Nation,* Oct. 3, 1908.

17. The first: Browning's learning was so natural to him that he was "ignorant of the ignorance of the world" (p. 13). But we all know ignorance, none better than the wise. To know is an exertion, it has always an element of hopelessness in it which makes those who most avidly seek learning soon reach that Socratic consciousness of ignorance which is almost destructive. The second: Browning was so convinced of his vision, and so familiar with it, that he thought it needed no clarification (pp. 35–9, 67–8). If this were so, Browning would be no artist at all. Besides, Browning's "obscurity" was deliberate, and elaborated with great finesse—a thing carefully wrought, not an incidental fault forgotten in the haste or heat of communication. Chesterton's fine description of the obscurity proper to most poetry (pp. 57–8) is also mistaken: Browning presents, characteristically, not this misty distance but a tangled and thorny foreground.

18. But Chesterton applies this too indiscriminately. A "praise of refuse" certainly informs the first scene of "The Ring and the Book"; but when Chesterton tries to make this the theme of "Childe Roland to the Dark Tower Came," he misses the point. Refuse, in that poem, is not loved as a minimal sacrament of being; it is feared as a threat to Roland's deepest self. Browning's love of detail reached a stage which was familiar to Dürer also as he worked out each mole and tuft of things: the sinister energy of things, the sheer hypnosis of detail, grows wild and irrational, reaching to pluck out the brain with pure physicality. Browning several times described how patterns assailed him in this way. Here he forces his hero to ride through such a thronging nightmare—like Dürer's knight—looking desperately for a tower, even an enemy tower, where battle and blood and honor are possible, instead of absorption through mere growth or mere rotting.

19. Chesterton's confusion disappeared after this book. *Cf. The Victorian Age,*

p. 173, where he calls Browning's quaint complexities the "result rather of the gay artist in him than the deep thinker."

20. *Cf.* the echoing of phrases from *The Wild Knight* and *Thursday* on pp. 186–7.

21. *Ibid.*, pp. 169–74.

22. This is the real answer to Santayana's description of Browning as a barbarian. Chesterton responds to this description with the statement that all poetry is "primal," and touches the weak point of Santayana's entire book; but (as Cecil noted) this has nothing to do with the discussion of particular traits in Browning.

23. Ward, pp. 53–4. *Cf. Browning*, p. 112, *Bookman*, June, 1900 for other early references to Watts.

24. *Watts*, pp. 43–5.

25. *Ibid.*, pp. 57–62.

26. This appeared in America as *Charles Dickens, A Critical Study* (1906) and—with Chesterton's *Britannica* article on Dickens and a foreword by Alexander Woollcott—as *Charles Dickens, The Last of the Great Men* (1942). My citations are from the 1906 edition.

27. Eliot, *Selected Essays 1917–1932* (New York: Harcourt, Brace, and Co., 1932), p. 374: "there is probably no better critic of Dickens living than Mr. Chesterton." Trilling, *A Gathering of Fugitives* (Boston: Beacon Press, 1956), p. 41: "Chesterton, a far greater critic than his present reputation might suggest . . ." Orwell, *Dickens, Dali, and Others* (New York: Reynal and Hitchcock, 1946), pp. 1 ff.

28. Cecil, pp. 93–4.

29. *Dickens*, p. 132. *Cf. The Victorian Age*, p. 81: "he had no plan of reform; or, when he had, it was startlingly petty and parochial."

30. *Appreciations and Criticisms of Charles Dickens*, pp. 45 ff. Orwell insists also that Dickens' politics were "moral" not "ideological" (*loc. cit.*, p. 5). Edmund Wilson puts it as bluntly as Chesterton had: "Fundamentally, he was not interested in politics." *The Wound and the Bow* (Boston: Houghton Mifflin, 1941), p. 25.

31. *Dickens*, pp. 247–8.

32. *Ibid.*, p. 247.

33. The chapter is misleading even in this connection: Johnson's circle needed no lessons in high spirits or ambitious ideals, and the Revolution was hardly marked by a sense of humor.

34. *Dickens*, pp. 185–9. The chapter on Dickens' characters is not devoted to individual studies, but to the concept of "democracy" as a sense of the equal vividness of existence in all men.

35. Chesterton states the objections to Dickens' irresponsible farcicality with a

rigor unequaled by Dickens' foes, in the passage ending (p. 255) with these words: "Dickens nowhere makes the reader feel that Pumblechook has any kind of fundamental human dignity at all. It is nowhere suggested that Pumblechook will some day die. He is felt rather as one of the idle and evil fairies, who are innocuous and yet malignant, and who live forever because they never really live at all. This dehumanized vitality, this fantasy, this irresponsibility of creation, does in some sense truly belong to Dickens."

36. *Ibid.*, pp. 269–71.

37. *Ibid.*, pp. 187–91, 252–3.

38. *Ibid.*, p. 48. *Cf.* pp. 60, 169, 217.

39. *Ibid.*, p. 74. *Cf.* p. 170: "his atmospheres are more important than his stories."

40. *Ibid.*, p. 169.

41. It is the failing of a very fine analysis of Dickens' artistic growth—Edmund Wilson's, in *The Wound and the Bow*—that he gives the impression that Dickens' work was great because of the morbid, hysterical visions that haunted his imagination, and not by reason of the heroic forces of life which opposed the threatening shadows. There is more joy in the filth of Tom-All-Alone's alley than in most authors' ballrooms. Mr. Wilson regrets the introduction of "Dickens characters" into the later novels; but it is precisely the fierce attacks on Chadband and Mrs. Jellyby, on the Barnacles and the Circumlocution Office, which save Dickens from the mere sociology and grey uniformity of later novels.

42. *Ibid.*, p. 89.

43. *Ibid.*, pp. 298–9.

44. *Ibid.*, p. 21.

45. *Appreciations*, pp. 14–16.

46. *Dickens*, p. 17. Once more the example Chesterton uses is from the Book of Job: the rhinoceros "justifies" life by reflecting God's unjustifiable excess of creative joy.

47. The production of the book does not help overcome this disjointed quality. Chesterton, besides writing a long introduction to this collection, added new paragraphs to several of the introductions. These new paragraphs are not printed in their proper place, but simply put together in the front of the book.

48. *Appreciations*, p. 115.

49. *E.g.*, *Speaker*, March 23, 1901. *Cf. Appreciations*, pp. 114–16.

50. *Appreciations*, pp. 50, 62.

51. *Ibid.*, pp. 149–50.

52. *Ibid.*, p. 35.
53. *Ibid.*, pp. 260–9.
54. *Ibid.*, p. 169.
55. *Ibid.*, pp. 66–70.
56. *Ibid.*, pp. 41–2.
57. *Ibid.*, pp. 92–5.
58. *Ibid.*, pp. 106–8.
59. *Ibid.*, pp. 141–2.
60. *Ibid.*, pp. 227–8.
61. *Ibid.*, p. 7.
62. *Ibid.*, p. 8.
63. *Ibid.*, p. 203.
64. *Debater*, 2.70. True to the solemnity of his early years, he expressed greater admiration for Scott and Thackeray than for Dickens (*Debater*, 2.95, 113).
65. *The Trial of John Jasper* (Chapman and Hall, 1914).
66. *Dickens*, pp. 82–3. *Appreciations*, pp. 3, 26.
67. *Dickens*, p. 83.
68. *Ibid.*, pp. 94–9.
69. *Appreciations*, pp. 51–2. *Cf. Bookman*, Dec., 1899: "To say that Velásquez was unconscious of all this that we are reading in his pictures, is simply to say that it came out of his inmost soul. Probably the only thing in us which is really potent in art or morals is this self of which we are unconscious. Probably it is only when a trait or conception has become invisible to ourselves that it becomes vivid to the world."
70. *Victorian Age*, p. 41.
71. *Ibid.*, p. 96.
72. Chesterton's appreciation of Beardsley's style is very discerning. He calls it a painting of masks that *reveal* man. This is a passage which applies to much of modern art; that of Toulouse-Lautrec, for instance, of Degas, of Rouault.
73. Cecil, pp. 39–40.
74. Wilde, for instance, is called "an Irish swashbuckler—a fighter. Some of the Roman Emperors might have had the same luxuriousness and yet the same courage" (p. 225). *Cf.* (in *Shaw*, p. 28): "He preached his softness with hard decision; he praised pleasure in the words most calculated to give pain." Elizabeth Sewell, who bases so much of her article on Chesterton's attitude toward Wilde, neglects this aspect of his criticism, objective as are all his analyses of style.
75. *Victorian Age*, p. 40. Anyone acquainted with Chesterton's own habits will not be surprised that he makes his own sentence wait a while, in this analy-

sis, then snap shut on the last word. Chesterton was a brilliant parodist, and some of his finest criticism is parody meant to uncover strength instead of weakness. He even "translates" things in and out of an author's style to show the style's potentialities; as in *Browning*, pp. 147–57, *Daily News*, Nov. 13, 1909, March 25, 1911, *New Weekly*, Aug. 1, 1914. This appreciative mimicry is perfectly suited to his literary *persona* of metaphysical jester.

76. *Victorian Age*, pp. 126–7.

77. *Heretics*, p. 99.

78. *Victorian Age*, pp. 192–5.

79. Swinburne's own style, according to Chesterton (pp. 187–8), has some of the hardness that ennobles FitzGerald's. Swinburne was a master of wit and point and satire, not merely a vague singer whose sense was diffused in a wash of sound. His wit is so subtle that many do not see it; most of his poems were more or less conscious satire on other forms—the Bible, the romantic ballad, the mediaeval hymn.

CHAPTER 5. A GRAMMAR OF LUNACY

1. *The Speaker*, Jan. 19, 1901.

2. *Twelve Types*, p. 125; *Daily News*, Feb. 25, 1905; *Ill. Lond. News*, Oct. 28, 1905 (reprinted in *The Glass Walking-Stick* as "The Heraldic Lion").

3. *Daily News*, July 11, 1903. The *Commonwealth* series was called "The Dogmas of Free Thought," and it ran from July through December of 1903. For *Clarion* articles and answers, see Sullivan's bibliography, #510. The *Daily News* for these years has many echoes of the fray. See, for instance, in 1903, the columns for May 9, Nov. 14, Dec. 12. The debate echoed on, into *Heretics* and *Orthodoxy*, and into articles like "The Irresponsible Gospel" (*Young Man*, April 14, 1906) and "Are We Responsible For Our Actions?" (*London Opinion*, June 9, 1906). Cf. *Autobiography*, pp. 178–82.

4. Ward, p. 172. If one reads in conjunction a series of references like that which follows, it will be clear that Chesterton's early work was written on the assumption that Christ was not divine: *Twelve Types*, pp. 49, 71, 152, 156 ff., 165–6. His early habit of absolute comparison between Christ, Whitman, St. Francis and others reinforces this conclusion. Reviewing a life of Christ in *The Speaker* for Dec. 8, 1900, he urged men not to dispute over Christ's "origin and nature": "there are some people who require no letters of introduction." The same review belittles the "utterly fanciful opposition between paganism and Christianity" in their highest manifestations.

5. Quoted in Cecil, p. 111.

6. Ward, p. 176.

7. *Autobiography*, pp. 181–2.

8. *Heretics*, p. 157.

9. *Ibid.*, p. 155.

10. *Ibid.*, p. 32.

11. *Orthodoxy*, p. 15.

12. *Ibid.*, p. 60.

13. *Ibid*, p. 116.

14. *Ibid.*, p. 263.

15. Newman had a great influence on Chesterton at this period; so that, in the American edition of *Orthodoxy*, he compared his intention to Newman's in the *Apologia*. Cecil, a great admirer of Newman and a convert to Catholicism, must often have used arguments from his pages. *Cf. Speaker*, Sept. 24, 1904 (reprinted in *A Handful of Authors* as "The Style of Newman"); *Daily News*, Sept. 22, 1909; *Victorian Age*, pp. 39 ff.

16. In *Orthodoxy* Chesterton still uses his critical sense of style to assess reality. He contrasts paganism, Buddhism and Christianity, in passages that resemble Malraux, on the basis of their iconography. It is typical that some of his greatest passages of literary criticism occur in this volume—the description of poetry as a creative *knowledge*, and of metaphor as an assertion of existence through the blurring of essential distinctions (pp. 27–9, 89 ff.).

17. *Daily News*, Oct. 28, 1911.

CHAPTER 6. THE DEFENCE OF NOTTING HILL

1. *Autobiography*, pp. 118, 121.

2. *Ibid.*, pp. 126–7, 174

3. Cecil, p. 18, also p. 60.

4. *Daily News*, Aug. 24, 1912: "I am of that sort that is very difficult to dig out of its past; and even if you, Liberal Party, lost your last claim to the title, I should still always be enough of a conservative to call myself a Liberal."

5. *Cf. Collected Poems*, pp. 323–4, "To Them That Mourn."

6. *Daily News*, Feb. 17, 1905.

7. *Autobiography*, p. 280.

8. The dismal "Election Echo" dated 1906 in the *Collected Poems* (p. 159) actually appeared in 1900.

9. *Orthodoxy*, p. 82.

10. *Shaw,* p. 59.

11. In the *Autobiography* (p. 282) Chesterton claimed that his line "Cocoa is a cad and coward" was not a deliberate reference to Cadbury; but the play on his name, the familiarity of the phrase "Cocoa Press," and Shaw's jeers at Chesterton for being the personal property of George Cadbury (Ward, p. 256), make this statement less than candid.

12. *Orthodoxy,* p. 203.

13. *Ibid.,* p. 233.

14. *Shaw,* p. 66.

15. *Collected Poems,* p. 352, "The Wild Knight."

16. *Ibid.,* p. 3, "The Monster."

17. Introduction to a 1909 edition of Carlyle's *Past and Present* (Oxford University Press), pp. v–vi.

18. *Daily News,* Dec. 7, 1907.

19. *Cf. Pall Mall Magazine,* 1902, "Victor Hugo" (reprinted in *A Handful of Authors*): "If there be one thing more than another which is true of genuine democracy, it is that genuine democracy is opposed to the rule of the mob. For genuine democracy is based fundamentally on the existence of the citizen, and the best definition of a mob is a body of a thousand men in which there is no citizen. Hugo stood for the fact that democracy isolated the citizen fully as much as the ancient religions isolated the soul. . . . Therefore his sublimest figure, his type of humanity, was not either a king or a republican, but a man on a desert island."

20. *Collected Poems,* p. 62, "A Wedding in War-time." *Cf. What I Saw in America,* p. 243: "It may be that in the first twilight of time man and woman walked about as one quadruped. But if they did, I am sure it was a quadruped that reared and bucked and kicked up its heels. Then the flaming sword of some angel divided them, and they fell in love with each other."

21. Loeb edition of *The Republic,* I. lx–lxi.

22. Ward, *Return to Chesterton,* p. 51.

23. *The Paternoster,* edited by Belloc and Arthur Hungerford Pollen, aimed against the "morbid, tired, unhappy" air of the century's last years.

24. *Autobiography,* pp. 304–5. The part of "The Rebel" from which Chesterton quotes:

> When we find them, where they stand
> A mile of men on either hand,
> I mean to charge them right away

And force the flanks of their array,
And press them inward from the plains
And drive them clamouring down the lanes,
And gallop and harry and have them down,
And carry the gates and hold the town.

Marcus says:

Guthrum sits strong on either bank
And you must press his lines
Inwards, and eastward drive him down;
I doubt if you shall take the crown
Till you have taken London town.

25. *New Age,* Feb. 8, 1905.
26. Ward, p. 400.
27. *Cf.* Introduction, note 8.
28. *Autobiography,* p. 297: "vanity or mock modesty, which healthy people always use as jokes." *Cf. Shaw,* p. 233.
29. *Shaw,* p. 162.
30. *New Age,* Feb. 8, 1905.
31. *Shaw,* p. 45.
32. *Ibid.,* p. 227.

CHAPTER 7. PATTERN IN PANTOMIME

1. Notebook, p. 49 *v. Cf.* pp. 31, 37 *v.*
2. "Bookman Booklet" on Stevenson (1903), p. 27.
3. *The Judgement of Doctor Johnson,* p. 49.
4. For this reason I think the emphasis is false in Ward, p. 242: "G.K.'s affection for the sincere atheist is noteworthy. . . . It was grand to have such a man as Turnbull to convert."
5. *The Ball and the Cross,* p. 206.
6. *Ibid.,* p. 19.
7. *Ibid.,* pp. 10–11.
8. *Ibid.,* p. 207.
9. *The Club of Queer Trades,* p. 28.
10. From handwritten sheets of Fisher Unwin stationery.

11. West, *op. cit.*, p. 48.

12. Chesterton praised Conan Doyle's technique in several places, but saw this essential weakness in the conception of Holmes. *Cf. Ill. Lond. News*, Jan. 15, 1927, May 30, 1926; and the *Daily News* articles reprinted as "Sherlock Holmes" in *A Handful of Authors*.

13. "The Secret Garden."

14. "The Man in the Passage."

15. "The Invisible Man," "The Queer Feet."

16. *Cf.* "How to Write a Detective Story," *G.K.'s Weekly*, Oct. 17, 1925.

17. *Ibid.*

18. Moore wrote, nonetheless, "I am not exaggerating when I say that I think of all modern plays I like it best" (Ward, p. 315).

19. *Autobiography*, pp. 77 ff.

CHAPTER 8. RHYME AND REASON

1. *Collected Poems*, pp. 307, 310–1, 317, 321–2, 329–30, 332, 363–5, 365–6.

2. *Ibid.*, pp. 312–3, 327–8.

3. *Shaw*, p. 228.

4. *Cf.* Chesterton's own distinction between nonsense and satire in *The Defendant* ("Defence of Farce"), and his criticism of Barrie for neglecting "the congruity of nonsense" (*Nation*, Nov. 18, 1911).

5. *Cf.* Ward, p. 125. In the *Autobiography*, Chesterton overlooks his first book and calls *The Wild Knight* "my introduction into literature" (p. 91).

6. *Collected Poems*, pp. 3–6, "The Monster."

7. *The Queen of Seven Swords*, p. 2.

8. *Ibid.*, p. 5, "The Return of Eve."

9. *Autobiography*, pp. 30, 31, 127.

10. Ward, p. 164.

11. *E.g.*, "Her face was like a spoken word" became "an open word." "Under the old night's starry hood" became "nodding hood." "Under clean Christian grass to lie" became "warm Westland grass." "Their eyes were sadder than the sea" became "Their souls were drifting as the sea." "Gods of an empty will" became "of a wandering will." There are no changes in rhyme; Chesterton's facility made it unnecessary for him to write for a rhyme. The metric changes are all in the direction of irregularity, to keep the ballad's loose and vigorous form. A number of false touches are eliminated, including these stanzas:

> His spear was broken in his hand
> But his belt bore a sword;
> His heart was broken in his breast
> But he cried unto Our Lord.
> He cried to Our Lady and Our Lord
> Seven times in the sun
> And the boar and the black wolf answered him
> And the tears began to run.

False naïveté of this sort does not appear in the finished poem, whose refrains and slight archaisms are perfectly modulated. Chesterton avoided the great obstacle of this form, the "ye olde" style of which even Coleridge could not thoroughly purge the "Rime," what Chesterton called "a swagger of antiquity, like the needless outrage of calling the Mariner a Marinere" (*Ill. Lond. News,* Aug. 4, 1934, reprinted in *As I Was Saying* as "About S.T.C.")

12. *Debater,* 1. 15–16 has a report on the paper, which is in one of the extant notebooks.

13. *Eye Witness,* Sept. 7, 1911.

14. Chesterton had long admired Kipling's line, "then cometh God, the master of every trade" (*Debater,* 3.57).

15. The last line is a fine example of the compression and depth in these simple stanzas. The first mystery of the Sacrament is that bread becomes God; but a further mystery links this banquet table to the sacrificial altar. Calvary and the Last Supper meet by necessity in the Mass, for the Eucharist is both Sacrament and Sacrifice. Christ must die to feed us—"break Himself for bread."

16. Here Chesterton imitates the conclusion of "The Song of Roland," which he praised in an introduction to a 1919 edition of "Roland" (reprinted in *The Common Man*): "That high note of the forlorn hope, of a host at bay and a battle against odds without end, is the note on which the great French epic ends. I know nothing more moving in poetry than that strange and unexpected end, that splendidly inconclusive conclusion. Charlemagne, the great Christian emperor, has at last established his empire in quiet, has done justice almost in the manner of the day of judgment, and sleeps as it were upon his throne with a peace almost like that of Paradise. And there appears to him the angel of God crying aloud that his arms are needed in a new and distant land, and that he must take up again the endless march of his days. And the great king tears his long white beard and cries out against his restless life. The

poem ends, as it were, with a vision and vista of wars against the barbarians; and the vision is true. For that war is never ended which defends the sanity of the world against all the stark anarchies and rending negations which rage against it for ever."

CHAPTER 9. THE FOUR LOYALTIES

1. Chesterton told another Catholic he could not even go to Confession, or examine his own conscience, without elaborating a philosophy of humility, distinguishing the Christian and pagan varieties of pride, sketching the moral history of mankind (Ward, *Return to Chesterton,* p. 298).
2. *Cf.* p. 204: "It was one of the fallacies of his literary clique to refer all natural emotions to literary names: but it might not untruly be said that he had passed out of the mood of Maeterlinck into the mood of Whitman, and out of the mood of Whiteman into the mood of Stevenson."
3. *Autobiography,* p. 255.
4. *Ill. Lond. News,* July 13, 1918; November 3, 1923.
5. *Cf. What I saw in America,* ch. 15, "Wells and the World State."
6. *Orthodoxy,* p. 183.
7. *What I Saw,* pp. 169–70.
8. *Ill. Lond. News,* Feb. 3, 1934; *cf. Ill. Lond. News,* Oct. 9, 1926.
9. *The Everlasting Man,* p. 80.

CHAPTER 10. THE TWO FRIARS

1. *London Tablet,* June 20, 1936.
2. Msgr. O'Connor, *op. cit.,* p. 129.
3. *The New Jerusalem,* pp. 192–3, 195
4. *St. Francis,* p. 40.
5. *Ibid.,* p. 51
6. *The Father Brown Omnibus,* p. 809.
7. The first thing seen in "The Chief Mourner of Marne" is the key to the whole story, which is a model of compression and the use of "clues."
8. *The Father Brown Omnibus,* p. 767.
9. "The White Witch."
10. "The Return of Eve."
11. "Laughter."

12. "The Black Virgin."

13. Quoted in Evelyn Waugh's *Monsignor Ronald Knox* (Boston: Little, Brown and Co., 1959), pp. 207–8. *Cf.* Waugh's discerning comment (p. 198): "He did not, like Ronald, seek Authority but, surprisingly in a man of such transparent innocence, Absolution."

14. *St. Francis*, pp. 106–7.

15. *Ibid.*, pp. 109–10.

16. *Saint Thomas Aquinas*, p. 125.

17. *Ibid.*, p. 135.

18. *Ibid.*, pp. 139–40.

19. *Ibid.*, p. 206.

20. *Ibid.*, pp. 224–5.

21. *Ibid.*, p. 180.

22. *Ibid.*, pp. 203–4.

23. *Ibid.*, p. 105.

24. *Ibid.*, p. 177.

25. *Ibid.*, p. 207.

26. *Ibid.*, p. 15.

CHAPTER 11. PROPERTY AND THE PERSON

1. *Chaucer*, p. 20.

2. *G.K.'s Weekly*, April 24, 1926.

3. *The Outline of Sanity*, p. 172.

4. Chesterton had three objections to the naive use of governmental *method* (suffrage) as the *goal* of government. (1) The people are supposed to "express their will" on a variety of disparate subjects, on many of which the voters have no particular intentions; but in areas wherein the candidate can win votes by offering irrelevant rewards. In this kind of voting, the deepest intentions and abiding interests of the people are obscured; perhaps, ultimately, destroyed. (2) The party system offers a pre-chosen list of issues and candidates, so that men can be elected whom no one really wants in office. (3) The vote is meant to express reality in mathematical terms; it reduces the multiple, unique, incommensurable voices of man to the false equality of simple markers; it uses this system on questions of the very moral foundation of the government as well as on trivial matters. It is part of the substitution of process for purpose. (*Cf.* "The Vote and the Votary," *Daily News*,

Feb. 6, 1909; *Cobbet*, p. 152; *The Utopia of Usurers*, p. 178; *Ill. Lond. News*, Sept. 18, 1909, July 20, 1912.)

5. *Cobbett*, p. 17.
6. *A Short History of England*, pp. 119–28; *Chaucer*, pp. 42–6, 111–12, 202–4.
7. *A Short History of England*, p. 169.
8. *What's Wrong With the World*, pp. 42–6.
9. *The Outline of Sanity*, pp. 122–3.
10. *Ibid.*, pp. 64–5.
11. *Ibid.*, p. 242.
12. By Capitalism Chesterton, with his demand for intellectual consistency, meant the classical system of Bentham and Mill, the Utilitarian reliance on the profit motive: "Now the capitalist system . . . presumes that each side is bargaining with the other, and that *neither* is thinking primarily of the public . . . the only original case for capitalism collapses entirely if we have to ask either party to go on for the good of the public" (*ibid.*, pp. 29–30).

Chapter Two of *The Outline of Sanity* was written to show that the real economic situation, even in his own day, was post-Capitalist. Belloc invented the term "the Servile State" to describe the post-Capitalistic phase which he expected (of concentrated private ownership and a legislated status for the mass of workers); though the term is often, mistakenly, applied to the state-owned welfare-economy that is fast growing around us. The point here is that Belloc believed the post-Capitalistic phase had already begun when he called the inchoate system a servile one.

13. *The Outline of Sanity*, pp. 49, 77, 88, 94, 247.
14. *Ibid.*, p. 65; *What I Saw in America*, pp. 38–42; *G.K.'s Weekly*, Aug. 18, 1928, "Publicity and the Psycho-Analyst."
15. *Cobbett*, pp. 76–90, 270.
16. *The Return of Don Quixote*, p. 261.

CHAPTER 12. THE CRITICAL FOCUS

1. Wells, *Outline*, first fortnightly edition, p. 72.
2. *Ibid.*, p. 55.
3. *Ibid.*, p. 73.
4. *Ibid.*, p. 72.
5. *Ibid.*, pp. 68–9.
6. *Ibid.*, p. 49.
7. *Ibid.*, pp. 214–15.

8. *Ibid.*, p. 212.

9. *Ibid.*, pp. 217–18.

10. *Ibid.*, p. 219.

11. *Ibid.*, p. 222.

12. *Ibid.*, p. 224. (The dots are his, an evolutionary aspect of his style throughout the book).

13. *Ibid.*, pp. 303, 285, 304.

14. *Ibid.*, p. 304.

15. *Ibid.*, p. 337.

16. *Ibid.*, p. 294.

17. *Ibid.*, pp. 297, 283, 289.

18. Belloc's sharp polemical series was published as *A Companion to "The Outline of History"* (1926). Wells, not realizing that the scattered articles were to be collected between covers, responded almost simultaneously with *Mr. Belloc Objects* (1926), a little volume of invective which made it possible for Belloc to score a complete victory with *Mr. Belloc Still Objects* (1926). Wells sent *G.K.'s Weekly* a parting quotation and insult, the latter easily ignored, the former easily dissected, both by Belloc and Chesterton (*G.K.'s Weekly*, April 2, May 7, Sept. 25, 1926; Jan. 22, 1927).

19. *A Companion to Mr. Wells's "Outline of History,"* pp. 44–5. *Cf.*, p. 10: Wells "cannot believe in creation at all because he has discovered (rather late in the day) that things grow."

20. *Mr. Wells as Historian* (Glasgow: MacLehose, Jackson and Co., 1921), pp. 34, 35, 37. It seems almost as if Mark Twain foresaw the *Outline* when he wrote in *Life on the Mississippi* (ch. 17): "In the space of one hundred and seventy-six years the Lower Mississippi has shortened itself two hundred and forty-two miles. This is an average of a trifle over one mile and a third per year. Therefore, any calm person who is not blind or idiotic, can see that in the Old Oolitic Silurian Period, just a million years ago next November, the Lower Mississippi River was upward of one million three thousand miles long, and stuck out over the Gulf of Mexico like a fishing-rod. And by the same token any person can see that seven hundred and forty-two years from now the Lower Mississippi will be only a mile and three-quarters long. . . . One gets such wholesale returns of conjecture out of such a trifling investment of fact."

21. *The Everlasting Man*, p. 244. *Cf. Orthodoxy*, pp. 271–3.

22. *The Everlasting Man*, p. 4.

23. *Ibid.*, p. 10. On cave-paintings *cf. Ill. Lond. News*, Jan. 13, 1923; Dec. 10, 1932.

24. *Ibid.*, p. 18. *Cf.* the excellent treatment of this aspect of artistic representation in *A Handful of Authors*, pp. 185–7.

25. *Lunacy and Letters*, p. 31.

26. *The Everlasting Man*, p. 19.

27. *Ibid.*, pp. 36, 34–5.

28. *Ibid.*, pp. 38–9.

29. *Ibid.*, p. 61.

30. Wells, *op. cit.*, p. 98. Gomme's note on this passage: *"One of, interesting, informing, pre-historic, composition, Aryan.* Every word is delightful" (*op. cit.*, pp. 15–16).

31. *The Everlasting Man*, pp. 79–80.

32. *Ibid.*, p. 89.

33. *Timaeus*, 41A.

34. The actual example Chesterton takes from the Andaman Islanders is one which Andrew Lang had studied. Chesterton had a lifelong respect for Lang and a wide acquaintance with his writings, as well as those of Grant Allen. *Cf.* his reviews of books by Lang in *The Speaker*, Feb. 19, Oct. 12, 1901. The Grant Allen review which is referred to in *The Everlasting Man* (p. 20) appeared in *The Speaker*, June 23, 1900. On Lang *cf.* also *Daily News*, Jan. 5, Nov. 2, 1905, *Ill. Lond. News*, July 13, 1912. On Grant Allen, *Ill. Lond. News*, May 9, 1925.

35. W. Robertson-Smith, *Lectures on the Religion of the Semites* (London: A. and C. Black, Ltd., 1923), p. 153.

36. *The Everlasting Man*, p. 111.

37. *Ibid.*, p. 58. *Cf.* p. 161.

38. *Ibid.*, p. 123.

39. *Ibid.*, p. 112. *Cf. Daily News*, Mar. 26, 1904: "There can be as good science about a turnip as about a man. . . . Of a mechanical thing we have a full knowledge. Of a living thing we have a divine ignorance; and a divine ignorance may be called the definition of romance. The Christian gospel is literally a story; that is, a thing in which one does not know what is to happen next. This thing, called Fiction, then, is the main fact of our human supremacy. If you want to know what is our human kinship with Nature, with the brutes, and with the stars, you can find cartloads of big philosophical volumes to show it you. You will find our kinship with Nature in books on geology and books on metaphysics. But if you want to find our isolation and divinity, you must pick up a penny novelette."

40. *Ibid.*, pp. 112–13. *Cf. Uses of Diversity*, pp. 215–17, *Daily News*, Dec. 28, 1912, "The Triumph of the Concrete."

41. *Ibid.*, p. 114.
42. *Ibid.*, p. 114.
43. Walter Ong, "Myth and the Cabalas," *Modern Schoolman,* vol. 27 (1950), p. 181. *Cf.*, also in *The Modern Schoolman,* Frederick C. Wilhelmsen, "The Aesthetic Act and the Act of Being" (vol. 29, 1952), "The Philosopher and the Myth" (vol. 32, 1954). *Cf.* Blackmur, *Sewanee Review,* vol. 54 (1946), p. 588: the highest kind of symbol "stands not for what has been said or stated, but for what has not been said." *Cf. Daily News,* April 22, 1905: "The aim of good prose words is to mean what they say. The aim of good poetical words is to mean what they do not say." *Stevenson,* p. 133: "anything beautiful always means more than it says; possibly means more than it means to mean."
44. *The Everlasting Man,* pp. 123–4.
45. *Ibid.*, p. 126–7.
46. *Ibid.*, p. 118.
47. *Ibid.*, p. 125.
48. John Henry Newman, *The Idea of a University,* 3.7.4.
49. *The Everlasting Man,* p. 139.
50. For the example Chesterton uses of the philosopher's isolation from the myths, the "Heretic Pharoah" Akenahten, *cf. Ill. Lond. News,* Feb. 17, 1923.
51. *The Everlasting Man,* pp. 119–20.
52. Chesterton's comparison (on p. 165) of Greek to Roman mythology is excellent: "It would seem sometimes as if the Greek polytheism branched and blossomed upwards like the boughs of a tree, while the Italian polytheism ramified downward like the roots. Perhaps it would be truer to say that the former branches lifted themselves lightly, bearing flowers; while the latter hung down, being heavy with fruit. . . . What strikes us in the Italian cults is their local and especially their domestic character. We gain the impression of divinities swarming about the house like flies; clustering and clinging like bats about the pillars or building like birds under the eaves. . . . It was the god of the corn and not of the grass, of the cattle and not the wild things of the forest; in short the cult was literally a culture; as when we speak of agriculture."
53. *Cf.* on Carthage and Moloch, *Ill. Lond. News,* Dec. 29, 1923, July 18, 1925.
54. Wells, *op. cit.,* p. 315.
55. Gomme, *op. cit.,* pp. 41–2: "*Before* the defeat of Carthage by Rome there had been age-long hostility between the Greeks of Sicily and the Carthaginians of Africa from almost the beginning of their respective settlements; *after* if the north and south of the Mediterranean took the same side in religion, in language, in custom and culture, for many centuries (interrupted only by the

invasion of the Vandals), till the Arab conquest. . . . Tunis and Algeria were among the most flourishing provinces of the Empire."

Gomme quotes approvingly Belloc's reconstruction of Africa's Roman culture in *Esto Perpetua*. As Christopher Dawson points out, "Africa was actually the creator of the Western tradition" of Christendom, supplying all but two of the great Western theologians (*A Monument to St. Augustine*, Sheed and Ward, 1930, p. 52). The importance of the *Greek* stand against Carthage in the West has been obscured because of the simultaneous struggle with Persia in the East. But Carthage was Asia very deeply advanced into Europe, and the meaning of this advance, had it been successful, would have been the same as a victory for Persia. Three centuries before Scipio, another Hamilcar, offering human sacrifice before battle, had been defeated by Pindar's patrons at Himera. Plutarch says that a condition of the treaty was the cessation of human sacrifice (*Apophthegmata*, 175); whether this story is true or not, as Gilbert Norwood says (*Pindar*, University of California, 1945, p. 241), it "provides a notable comment on Greek opinion about the meaning of the conflict." Thucydides (VI. 34, 90) makes men of fifth-century Hellas argue from the natural opposition felt between Carthage and Athens, as if it were an unquestionable fact. *Cf.* Plutarch's life of Pericles, 20.3.

56. *The Everlasting Man*, pp. 189–90.
57. *Ibid.*, pp. 191–2.
58. *Ibid.*, p. 211.
59. *Ibid.*, pp. 253–4.
60. William F. Lynch, S.J., *Christ and Apollo* (New York: Sheed and Ward, 1960), p. 53. The reference to Newman is very apposite, since Newman's realistically dramatic epistemology is a perfect expression of man's response to the total reality which is focused in Christ. It is *dramatic* because "real assent" is fashioned, perdurably, of all the realities man lives among and moves through. The basis for this realistic epistemology is stated, in the cross-cutting shorthand of Chesterton, at p. 265 of *Orthodoxy*: "a man may well be less convinced of a philosophy from four books, than from one book, one battle, one landscape, and one old friend. The very fact that the things are of different kinds increases the importance of the fact that they all point to one conclusion."
61. *Sermo* 191. There are many resemblances between the style and thought of Augustine and Chesterton. Augustine put wonder at the center of the Christian reaction, and often said that the birth of a child was a greater miracle than the raising of Lazarus. Like Chesterton he tried to arouse this wonder by linguistic acrobatics, certain that the rhetoric of paradox could best ex-

press a theology of mystery (*Ineffabilis fit infans*). The sense of paradox, dialectic, and mystery is what saved Augustine from the determinist simplifications which later schools of Grace took from his writings.

62. *Confessions*, 7.21. Augustine always thought first of Christ as the *mediator*, the bridge, the *pontifex*—the Christ of I Timothy 2.5. (*Cf. De Civ. Dei*, 9.15.)

63. *The Everlasting Man*, pp. 240–1. Chesterton seems to have thought first of Christ as *judge*. The drawings which fill his early notebooks are of an archangel-carpenter, moving through life (as Chesterton said of another figure) like an eagle walking with wings folded. The most frequent drawing is of this figure judging his own judge—the bound hands and those which wash themselves. *Cf.*, for the emphasis on violent lightning-strokes of judgment in Christ's life, *Orthodoxy*, pp. 271–2, *The New Jerusalem*, pp. 192–3, *The Everlasting Man*, pp. 226–7, *The Way of the Cross*, pp. 25–37.

64. *Ibid.*, p. 297. *Cf.* Dawson, *loc. cit.*, pp. 47–8, and Lynch, *op. cit.*, p. 158: "Philosophy can only speculate about things already done. Theology and Christ can *act*."

65. *Ibid.*, pp. 298, 314.

66. *Ibid.*, p. 307. Lynch, *op. cit.*, p. 158: "It is the universal teaching of the Church that it was itself born, not out of the Greeks, not out of the anonymous mind, not out of the chameleon imagination, but out of His blood, at a set hour, in a set place."

67. *Ibid.*, p. 314. *Cf.* pp. 297–8.

68. Augustine, *Sermo* 156.

69. *De Civ. Dei*, 20.5.

70. Galatians 4.4.

71. Ephesians 1.10 (Knox translation). This passage contains the Greek word for crisis, so that πλήρωμα τῶν καιρῶν can almost be translated as history's "critical focus." *Cf.* Jean Daniélou, *The Lord of History* (Chicago: Regnery, 1958), pp. 32–3.

CHAPTER 13. THE PLAY OF REALITY

1. *The Poet and the Lunatics*, pp. 129–30, 128.

2. *Gloria in Profundis* (Ariel Poems, no. 5, 1927).

3. *Ubi Ecclesia* (Ariel Poems, no. 21, 1929).

4. *Collected Poems*, p. 56.

5. *The Grave of Arthur* (Ariel Poems, no. 25, 1930). *Cf. Paradiso*, 29.12: "dove s'appunta ogni *ubi* ed ogni *quando*."

6. *Collected Poems,* p. 56.

7. *Chaucer,* p. 26. *Autobiography,* pp. 90–91. *Cf. Daily News,* May 17, 1906; *Twelve Types,* pp. 84 ff.

8. *The Resurrection of Rome,* pp. 300–08.

9. *Stevenson,* p. 127. *Autobiography,* p. 298.

10. *Chaucer,* pp. 16–17.

11. *Ibid.,* p. 268.

12. *Ibid.,* pp. 145–6.

13. Ward, *Return to Chesterton,* pp. 242–3.

14. *The New Jerusalem,* pp. 192–5.

15. Belloc, *On the Place of Gilbert Chesterton in English Letters* (New York: Sheed and Ward, 1940), p. 67.

APPENDIX: THE MAN WHO WAS THURSDAY

1. *Encounter,* October, 1973. *Cf. New York Times Book Review,* October 13, 1968, and Introduction to Kingsley Amis, ed., *G. K. Chesterton, Selected Stories,* Faber and Faber, 1972, pp. 15–16.

2. Essay on "A Midsummer Night's Dream," now available in W. H. Auden, *G. K. Chesterton: A Selection,* 1970, p. 95.

3. From an early (1901) essay on "Dreams," in *The Coloured Lands,* Sheed and Ward, p. 83. *Cf. Daily News,* July 9, 1904: "A world in which donkeys come in two is clearly very near to the wild ultimate world where donkeys are made."

4. *St. Francis of Assisi,* 1928. Image edition, 1957, p. 77.

5. *T. P.'s Weekly,* 1910.

6. *G. F. Watts,* Duckworth, 1904, p. 63.

7. *Cf.* Marvin H. Pope (drawing on the work of N. H. Tur-Sinai and S. D. Luzatto), *Anchor Bible 15,* pp. xxiv–xxv, 10–11. The same idea may underlie the lamps that are God's Seven Eyes at Zekeriah 4.10 (*cf.* Zek. 3.1 and Ps. 106.6).

8. *Anchor Bible,* lxxi–lxxii, 134–35.

9. *Ibid.* pp. 95–96.

10. *Ibid.* pp. xxvi–xxvii, 211, 216, 233.

11. *Ibid.* pp. xviii, xxv–xxvi, 183.

12. Chesterton, *The Speaker,* September 9, 1905.

13. *Daily News,* March 24, 1903.

INDEX

ABOUT THE AUTHOR

GARRY WILLS is an adjunct professor of history at Northwestern University. Wills received a Ph.D. in classics from Yale and has had a distinguished career as an author, with books such as *Lincoln at Gettysburg* and *Papal Sin*. He has received numerous accolades, including the 1978 National Book Critics Circle Award for Criticism (for *Inventing America*) and the 1993 Pulitzer Prize for General Nonfiction (for *Lincoln at Gettysburg*). Wills is a member of the American Academy of Arts and Sciences, and his articles appear frequently in the *New York Review of Books*.

Printed in the United States
by Baker & Taylor Publisher Services